Water Quality Policy and Management in Asia

Asia's forty-eight countries have an estimated 1.757 billion urban population and 2.4 billion people in rural areas (or approximately 60 per cent of the global population). Divided into central, eastern, southern, south-eastern and western regions, the continent is also extremely heterogeneous in terms of water quality conditions. The policies and management practices vary significantly from one country to another, and even within one country, depending on specific economic, political, social, environmental, legal and institutional factors. In order to appreciate the complexities associated with water quality policy and management, it is important to acknowledge the multiplicity of interrelated and often conflicting events, issues, actors and interests, both within and outside the water sector that impact them. This complexity, alongside institutional inability for systematic and coordinated collaboration, are potent reasons as to why, in the second decade of the 21st century, formulation and implementation of efficient water quality management policies benefitting humankind and the environment have still not been achieved.

The book was originally published as a special issue of the *International Journal of Water Resources Development*.

Cecilia Tortajada is President of the Third World Centre for Water Management, Mexico and past President of the International Water Resources Association. She is the author and editor of more than 30 books by major international publishers. Her work has been translated into Arabic, Chinese, French, German, Japanese and Spanish languages.

T0376851

Water Quality Policy and Management in Asia

Edited by
Cecilia Tortajada

Routledge
Taylor & Francis Group

LONDON AND NEW YORK

Lee Kuan Yew
School *of* Public Policy

National University of Singapore

First published 2013
by Routledge
2 Park Square, Milton Park, Abingdon, Oxfordshire OX14 4RN

Simultaneously published in the USA and Canada
by Routledge
711 Third Avenue, New York, NY 10017

First issued in paperback 2014

Routledge is an imprint of the Taylor & Francis Group, an informa business

British Library Cataloguing in Publication Data
A catalogue record for this book is available from the British Library

ISBN 13: 978-0-415-81363-1 (hbk)
ISBN 13: 978-1-138-85059-0 (pbk)

Typeset in Times New Roman
by Taylor & Francis Books

Publisher's Note
The publisher would like to make readers aware that the chapters in this book may be referred to as articles as they are identical to the articles published in the special issue. The publisher accepts responsibility for any inconsistencies that may have arisen in the course of preparing this volume for print.

Contents

Citation Information

The chapters in this book were originally published in the *International Journal of Water Resources Development*, volume 28, issue 2 (June 2012). When citing this material, please use the original page numbering for each article, as follows:

John Fawell & Choon Nam Ong
International Journal of Water Resources Development, volume 28, issue 2 (June 2012) pp. 247-264

Chapter 6
An Overview of Policies Impacting Water Quality and Governance in India
S. R. Wate
International Journal of Water Resources Development, volume 28, issue 2 (June 2012) pp. 265-280

Chapter 7
Water Quality Management in China
Dajun Shen
International Journal of Water Resources Development, volume 28, issue 2 (June 2012) pp. 281-298

Chapter 8
An Integrated Management Approach for Water Quality and Quantity: Case Studies in North China
Jun Xia
International Journal of Water Resources Development, volume 28, issue 2 (June 2012) pp. 299-312

Chapter 9
Institutional Capacity on Water Pollution Control of the Pearl River in Guangzhou, China
Yuan Yu, Dieudonné-Guy Ohandja & J. Nigel B. Bell
International Journal of Water Resources Development, volume 28, issue 2 (June 2012) pp. 313-324

Chapter 10
Soil Erosion Control and Sediment Load Reduction in the Loess Plateau: Policy Perspectives
Zhongbao Xin, Lishan Ran & X. X. Lu
International Journal of Water Resources Development, volume 28, issue 2 (June 2012) pp. 325-342

Chapter 11
Managing Urban Rivers and Water Quality in Malaysia for Sustainable Water Resources
Ngai Weng Chan
International Journal of Water Resources Development, volume 28, issue 2 (June 2012) pp. 343-354

Chapter 12
Improving Groundwater Quality Management for the Sustainable Utilization of the Bangkok Aquifer System
Mukand S. Babel, Aldrin A. Rivas, Ashim Das Gupta & Yatsuka Kataoka

International Journal of Water Resources Development, volume 28, issue 2 (June 2012) pp. 355-372

Chapter 13
Nutrient Balance Assessment in the Mekong Basin: Nitrogen and Phosphorus Dynamics in a Catchment Scale
Ina Liljeström, Matti Kummu & Olli Varis
International Journal of Water Resources Development, volume 28, issue 2 (June 2012) pp. 373-392

Foreword

The 21st century will be the Asian century. This momentum is now unstoppable. Asian economies will continue to grow rapidly. The big question in Asia is whether Asians will develop intelligent and innovative public policies to both sustain this growth and develop better societies.

This is where the Lee Kuan Yew School of Public Policy of the National University of Singapore can make a huge difference. Even though we are barely eight years old, we have been recognized as one of Asia's best schools of public policy, providing valuable graduate education, as well as research and thought leadership on many key challenges facing Asia and the world.

One huge challenge is water. Historically, in spite of its being a strategic issue, water has not been given the attention it deserves, not only in Asia, but also all over the world. In our region, water is even more relevant because of the fast economic growth our countries are witnessing, not just China and India but also many other Asian countries. In addition, we have to deal with the extremely seasonal nature of rainfall. Many governments are thus confronted with the urgent need to support the growing water-related demands of increasing populations and industrial, energy, and agricultural activities with sources of water that are rapidly becoming scarce, over-exploited, and polluted.

The issues related to water quality policy and management are numerous and complex. They have an impact on every productive sector of the Asian countries, many times beyond their borders, and also on the quality of life of the growing populations. Therefore, it is important to put in place an overall policy, management, and governance strategy that considers not only the water sector but also other sectors which have an impact on the way water resources are used, managed, and governed.

Given the complexity and difficulty of these challenges, this publication on *Water Quality Policy and Management in Asia* could not be more timely. Asian societies have progressed rapidly, ever since the Meiji Restoration in Japan, by learning best practices from each other. This is also how Singapore developed. It learnt voraciously from other countries. In the process, it has ended up developing one of the best public policy laboratories in the world, with the world recognizing that Singapore has some of the best public policies in the world in a variety of areas. This is why Matt Miller (2010) of the *Washington Post* wrote, "Singapore achieves world-class results thanks to a bold, unconventional synthesis of liberal and conservative approaches."

In the field of water, Singapore's success was globally acknowledged when the Public Utilities Board won the prestigious Stockholm Industry Water Award at the World Water Week in Stockholm in 2007. Given Singapore's unique expertise in water, the school felt that it would be a good idea to set up the Institute of Water Policy to do in-depth research on water issues and share best practices with the world.

There can be no doubt that Asia faces many challenges on the water front. One example is the River Ganges in India. It is often claimed that the main constraint on control of water pollution in developing countries is the lack of investment funds. This has certainly not been the case with the failed effort to clean up this river, for which some US$450 million was spent during the 1980s and 1990s. The river is more polluted now than ever in history, and the government of India has recently announced a US$2.33 billion project for a second attempt to clean up the Ganges, with the help of a US$1 billion loan from the World Bank. The rest of the funds are expected to come from the five affected states in India: Uttarakhand, Uttar Pradesh, Bihar, Jharkhand, and West Bengal. Only time will tell how successful this attempt will be. One thing is certain, however. If the appropriate policies, management practices, and governance considerations are not essential components of the strategy for cleaning the river, no investment funds will ever be enough to achieve this goal.

Another example is China, where water quality challenges have been growing for several decades. The government has thus decided to allocate, in its 12th five-year plan (for 2011–2015), a budget of US$1.33 billion for water quality management.

This special issue analyzes the present situation in terms of water quality in Asia in general, and in some countries and areas in particular, especially China, India, Malaysia, Indonesia, Thailand, Japan, and the Mekong region. The importance of including economic incentives in the basket of policy alternatives to motivate improvements in water quality is discussed with examples from several Asian countries. Issues like emerging contaminants and their implications for human and ecosystem health, which are mostly ignored at present, are also discussed comprehensively.

Water quality policies and their legal and institutional requirements are also discussed. In nearly all cases, it is evident that there are serious gaps in the policies, which are affecting the efficiency of their implementation. With respect to institutions, their responsibilities tend to overlap with each other, both vertically and horizontally, as a result of which implementation of any policy decision leaves much to be desired. With respect to laws and regulations, they are often in conflict with each other, and many are either too weak to make a difference, or so stringent that they are almost impossible to implement. Overall, the analyses indicate that the countries are lagging well behind what is needed to tackle the accelerating problem of water quality deterioration in nearly all the Asian countries.

Since water quality is an important factor for the economic and social development of any country, the question that needs to be asked and answered is why these issues have been mostly ignored in the past and are continuing to be neglected at present. The overall quality of the Asian water bodies, especially those within and around urban centres, is continuing to deteriorate. If the current trends continue for another decade or so, most Asian countries will face a crisis in water quality which no other generation in history has had to face.

There can be no doubt that water is an important component in ensuring sustainable economic and social development of the Asian countries. Good water polices can contribute to the food, energy, and environmental security of these countries and can alleviate poverty, especially in South Asia, where a significant percentage of the world's poor live. This is why water policy is an important aspect of study and research at the school. As the 21st century evolves towards becoming the Asian century, the countries in the region must formulate and implement good and efficient water policies in terms of both the quality and quantity of this resource.

This special issue is a serious attempt by the school to bring together leading experts from different disciplines and sectors to assess the nature and magnitude of the problems, analyze the opportunities for and constraints on managing them, and develop a comprehensive and coordinated policy framework within which they can be successfully resolved. We realize this will be a difficult and arduous process, but it is one we are determined to tackle. I thus invite everyone interested in this subject to join us in our quest for developing appropriate policy frameworks to solve this complex problem in a timely and cost-effective manner.

Please let me conclude by congratulating the editors and writers of this volume. In particular, I would like to pay special tribute to Dr Asit Biswas and Dr Cecilia Tortajada, both of whom have contributed and are contributing enormously to the Lee Kuan Yew School of Public Policy.

Kishore Mahbubani
Dean and Professor in the Practice of Public Policy,
Lee Kuan Yew School of Public Policy, Singapore

Reference

Miller, M. (2010) What we can learn from Singapore's health-care model, Washington Post, 3 March. Available at: http://www.washingtonpost.com/wp-dyn/content/article/2010/03/03/AR2010030301396.html?hpid=opinionsbox1

Introduction

Deterioration of water bodies continues to be one of the most pressing problems facing the world at present. In Asia, the problems this spawns in different sectors are so extensive and serious that they even threaten to undermine the economic growth of the region as well as the health and quality of life of its billions of people.

Asia's forty-eight countries have an estimated 1.757 billion urban population and 2.4 billion people in rural areas (or approximately 60% of the global population). Divided into central, eastern, southern, south-eastern and western regions, the continent is extremely heterogeneous and the resulting diversity reflects in the water quality conditions. The policies and management practices vary significantly not only from one country to another but also within one country, depending upon specific economic, political, social, environmental, legal and institutional factors. In order to appreciate the complexities associated with water quality policy and management, it is essential to acknowledge the multiplicity of interrelated and often conflicting events, issues, actors and interests, both within and outside the water sector that impact them. It is this complexity, as well as the institutional inability for systematic and coordinated collaboration to work with each other, that could explain why, in the second decade of the 21st century, formulation and implementation of efficient water quality management policies benefitting humankind and the environment have still not been achieved.

The economic growth of the Asian countries, especially China and India, poses significant challenges to the local and global natural environments due to the immense impact this has both within and beyond their borders. In the case of water resources, consistently high economic growth rates not only in the above two countries but across the entire region in recent years are already having major implications in terms of access, quantity and quality of this resource as well as equity, management and investment requirements. While magnitudes of the water quality problems have increased, planning, management and institutional capacities have not increased commensurately. This has made them even more challenging because policy measures still do not address these issues either adequately or systematically. In the search for implementable and cost-effective solutions, it is not only "what" that should be discussed but also "why" and "how" and their relatives priorities.

Regarding good and implementable policies and instruments for natural resources management in Asia, it is clear that they are still needed not only for the water sector but also in related sectors such as energy, agriculture and environment, so that economic, social and equitable development can be achieved on a long-term basis. The final results of the very rapid growth rates of the Asian countries could manifest in two ways: either as a gradual improvement of water quality of surface and groundwater sources, or as their continued deterioration with the resulting negative impacts. The results would be country specific, depending upon the policy decisions that are taken.

In addition, there appear to be two realities in the world at present in terms of water quality: the one the countries and their populations are facing on the ground and a very different one that seems to be the result of the game of global target setting.

In the midst of a very complex situation where billions of people at the global level face every challenge in terms of water quality, the United Nations has announced that, as of 2010, the Millennium Development Goal (MDG) in terms of drinking water has been achieved. According to this MDG, the number of people who did not have access to 'safe' drinking water between 1990 and 2015, was met in 2010, five years ahead of what had been planned.

The 2012 Update on Progress on Drinking Water and Sanitation, notes that "Over 2 billion people gained access to improved water sources from 1990 to 2010, and the proportion of the global population still using unimproved sources is estimated at only 11 per cent. This is less than half of the 24 per cent estimated for 1990. Almost 6.1 billion people, 89 per cent of the world's population, were using an improved water source in 2010. The drinking water target has thus become one of the first MDG targets to be met." (See UNICEF and World Health Organization, Progress on Drinking Water and Sanitation, 2012 Update, p. 2. Available at
http://www.who.int/water_sanitation_health/publications/2012/jmp_report/en/index.html).

Unfortunately, 'improved' source of water does not mean that water is safe and clean, and much less drinkable without any potential health hazards. According to the UN, "improved water sources include household connections, public standpipes, boreholes, protected dug wells, protected springs, and rainwater collections. Unimproved water sources are unprotected wells, unprotected springs, vendor-provided water, bottled water (unless water for other uses is available from an improved source) and tanker truck-provided water." In addition, people should have 'reasonable access' to this water, which is broadly defined as "the availability of at least 20 litres per person per day from a source within one kilometre of the user's dwelling."

Therefore, according to the UN, half of the more than 6 billion people in 2010 should have access to 20 litres of water from a source that is improved within one kilometer from their premises. With this being the goal on drinking water, one would have thought that billions of people have gained access to clean drinking water within one kilometer from their premises. The situation, however, could not be more different: the drinking water target is based on 'improved drinking water sources', not on actual access to clean drinking water. It could equally be from a polluted well or from a bucket of polluted rainwater that is unfit for drinking water: for the UN, it does not matter as long as it fits in the statistics.

In his Foreword to the document, the UN Secretary General further obfuscates the issue. While in the first paragraph he mentions "safe drinking water", in the next paragraph he refers to "improved drinking water sources" as if "improved drinking water sources" meant "safe drinking water". That statement could not be further from the truth. In many parts of the world, even after the so-called improved drinking sources of water, quality of the resource has deteriorated. For example, in many urban centres, in 1990, people used standard filtering processes before they drank the water. However, the quality of the water during the last twenty years has declined to such an extent, that filters have given way to reverse osmosis before people feel water could be rendered safe to drink. Use of reverse osmosis at homes is now quite widespread in both urban and rural areas of the developing world. In spite of this, the UN has decided to declare 'victory' when, in reality, the water quality and delivery situations in many regions have actually deteriorated.

Because of the importance and complexities of water quality issues in Asia, the Institute of Water Policy of the Lee Kuan Yew School of Public Policy, National University of Singapore, decided to focus its Third Policy Forum, July 2011, on 'Urban water quality policies and governance practices in Asia: Present status and future challenges'. The Forum was an associated event of the Singapore International Water Week (SIWW) and was co-sponsored by the International Water Resources Association (IWRA). Eminent lecturers to the Policy Forum were invited to prepare papers on different aspects of water quality policy and management in Asia. Their papers were modified on the light of the discussions, peer reviewed and extensively revised. They are included in this book. These six lecturers were Dennis Wichelns, James Nickum, S.R. Water, Ngai Weng Chan, Mukand Babel and Jun Xia. The other six papers in the book are authored by other leading experts of this region.

Overall, this publication provides a comprehensive coverage of the complexities, difficulties, constraints and challenges associated with managing water quality in this vast continent where nearly half of humankind lives. The water quality situation is already grim in this very large region. The immense related problems can only be resolved with concurrent political will, public demand and institutional ability, as well as with attempts which are determined, systematic and consistent.

Asia is now at a crossroads in terms of water quality management, and the approaches that will ultimately be taken by the individual countries will determine their water future. While much needs to be done in the coming years, the arguments, analyses and reflections presented in this book will contribute to the debate in managing Asia's water future. The status quo can no longer be considered as a solution: countries are in urgent need to implement innovative solutions that address the multiple challenges in cost-effective and implementable ways.

I am most grateful to Prof. Kishore Mahbubani, Dean of the Lee Kuan Yew School of Public Policy, Singapore, for writing the Foreword of this book. With his strong support and encouragement, the School is establishing its name as an important institution for education, research and training in Asia. I would also like to thank Ms. Shahnila Islam, Research Associate of the Institute of Water Policy for her support during the Policy Forum. Finally, I would like to express my sincere appreciation to the referees who generously reviewed all the papers and gave detailed comments on each one of them. The overall quality of the publication is significantly enhanced because of all their perceptive comments.

Cecilia Tortajada
President
Third World Centre for Water Management
Mexico

Water Quality: Assessment of the Current Situation in Asia

ALEXANDRA E. V. EVANS[*], MUNIR A. HANJRA[**], YUNLU JIANG[†],
MANZOOR QADIR[‡] & PAY DRECHSEL[*]

[*]International Water Management Institute, Colombo, Sri Lanka; [**]Charles Sturt University, Wagga Wagga, NSW, Australia and Future Directions International, Perth, Australia; [†]College of Water Conservancy and Hydropower, University of Hohai, Nanjing, China; [‡]United Nations University Institute for Water, Environment and Health, Hamilton, Canada and International Management Institute, Colombo, Sri Lanka

ABSTRACT *The uncontrolled release of sewage, industrial wastes, and agricultural run-off continue to affect Asia. Although many Asian countries are getting closer to meeting the improved sanitation targets, much of the waste remains untreated. Comprehensive databases are rarely available and national data indicate that the water quality situation is serious. However, there are many signs of hope. Water quality monitoring efforts are improving and several countries now have systems in place that could guide other nations in the region. The efforts of basin agencies, such as the Mekong River Commission, could lead the way to transboundary or even regional assessments. Many regulatory and economic options are being tested for pollution control, but institutional and social challenges remain, in particular those related to population growth and the various ways in which it is affecting water quality across the region.*

Introduction

Clean water, fresh air, and a pristine environment are becoming rare amenities across Asia. Over the past 50 years, the growing human population and intensifying industrialization and agricultural development have profoundly altered natural ecosystems and water quality, challenges which might be exacerbated by climate change in the region (Khan & Hanjra, 2009; Park *et al.*, 2010), although the overall impact of climate change on water quantity and quality will be marginal compared to socioeconomic changes, even by 2100 (Hanjra & Qureshi, 2011). In the case of the rapidly industrializing and urbanizing economies of Asia, the trajectory of social and technical change will have consequences for local, regional, and global environments (Angel & Rock, 2009). Proactive policies and strategies are emerging in many Asian countries to strengthen environmental regulation (Hanjra *et al.*, 2011); these, combined with institutional innovations, hold the promise of creating opportunities for new pathways of development and urbanization that are less polluting.

This paper provides an assessment of the water quality situation and outlook across Asia. It examines the state of water quality in the region and looks at the major sources of pollution: the domestic sector, industry, and agriculture. The paper also compares water quality monitoring and reporting in different parts of the region and discusses efforts to implement water pollution abatement strategies and social and economic incentives. Due to the enormity of the field of water quality, the focus is on inland water resources, mostly surface water, excluding in particular the arsenic discussion.

Asia in the Global Context

Since Asia and the Pacific have the highest annual water withdrawal of the world's regions, due to geographic size, population, and extensive and intensive irrigation practices, the generation of domestic and agricultural return flows is of significant scale. A particular factor is the large number of people without improved sanitation facilities, of which about 72% live in Asia (Figure 1).

Worldwide, two-thirds of the sewage from urban areas is pumped untreated into lakes, rivers, and coastal waters; in developing countries this figure climbs to 90% (ADB, 2008b; Corcoran *et al.*, 2010). Asia is no exception; as a result, 40% of the global death toll due to unsafe or inadequate supply of water, sanitation, and hygiene occurs in Asia (WHO, 2004).

At present very few people are connected to sewers, especially in Southeast and South Asia (Table 1), and where they are, the effluent is often inadequately treated because many sewers and wastewater treatment facilities are in a state of disrepair (Corcoran *et al.*, 2010).

With more than half of global irrigation taking place in Asia and a high level of agrochemical consumption, nonpoint source pollution is considered a significant threat to water quality. Another form of nonpoint source pollution derives from the pronounced topography of the region, resulting in high sediment loads, a common feature in many basins, such as the Mekong.

Asian countries are however taking strong steps to achieve the Millennium Development Goals and to address water quality issues—steps which are accompanied by increasing emphasis on the enforcement of environmental legislation. This is particularly needed

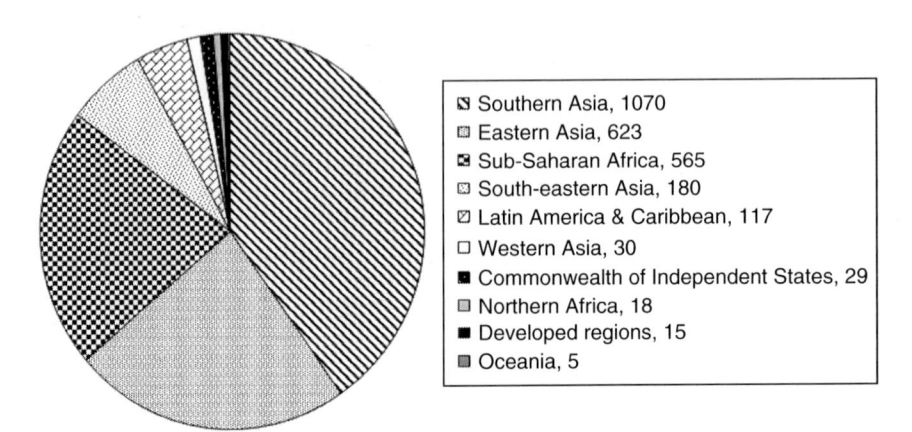

Figure 1. Regional distribution of the 2.6 billion people not using improved sanitation facilities in 2008 (millions). *Source*: WHO/UNICEF (2010).

Table 1. Development of connections to piped sewer systems in urban areas (regional averages).

	Connected urban population (%)	
Region	1988–1994	2003–2006
Eu25*, North America, Australia*		87–92
MENA	72	83
South Asia	31	31
Southeast Asia	3	3
China	38	56
Russia, Georgia, Kazakhstan, Kyrgyzstan, Uzbekistan	82	83
Latin America and the Caribbean	56	64
Sub-Saharan Africa	26	19

*Includes rural population.
Source: Authors' calculations, based on Statistics Division (2011), Eurostat (2006), JMP (N.d.), and UN (2009).

because water pollution will continue to rank among the critical issues impacting water security in Asia (ESCAP, 2011).

Sources of Pollution

Domestic Pollution

The domestic pollution problems are a factor not only of the wastewater generated but also of inadequate treatment and management measures. The volume of wastewater[1] generated annually across Asia is nearly 144 km^3, of which 37% is generated in China, 27% in South Asia, 20% in Japan, 6% in Southeast Asia, and 3% in Central Asia (FAO AQUASTAT, N.d.; Sato *et al.*, personal communication, 2011). Only an estimated 33–35% of all wastewater in Asia is treated, with the lowest treatment rates in South Asia (7%) and Southeast Asia (14%) (Table 2). Adequate treatment is generally rare.

Microbial contamination from inadequate sanitation facilities, improper wastewater disposal, and animal wastes has the greatest effect on human health (WWAP, 2009; Corcoran *et al.*, 2010). A measure of this contamination is the number of deaths per 100,000 inhabitants due to water-related diseases. In China this is less than 15 but it rises to 100–200 in certain parts of Asia, including Afghanistan, and is 30–100 across almost all of South Asia (Corcoran *et al.*, 2010).

Many of the region's rivers contain up to 3 times as much bacteria from human waste (measured in faecal coliforms) as the world average, more than 10 times the standard set in the Organization for Economic Co-operation and Development (OECD) guidelines; the reported median faecal coliform count in Asia's rivers is 50 times the World Health Organization (WHO) guidelines (ESCAP, 2000).

Inadequate wastewater management and treatment is a significant contributor to the overall water quality problem. Many of Asia's major cities do not have extensive waterborne sewer systems and rely heavily on septic tanks and latrines for waste disposal. Where sewers do exist, they often leak and contaminate the groundwater (Pak-EPA, 2005). While the focus of attention has been on megacities, a high percentage of growth will take place in urban centres with populations of 500,000 or less, creating different management issues, not least because there is likely to be less money for investment in wastewater

Table 2. Wastewater generation and treatment in Asia.

Country	Wastewater generated		Wastewater treated	
	Reporting year	Volume (km^3 yr^{-1})	Reporting year	Volume (km^3 yr^{-1})
Bangladesh	2000	0.725	–	n/a
Bhutan	2000	0.004	–	n/a
Cambodia	2000	1.184	1994	0.0002
China	2006	53.700	2004	22.100
India	1996	25.410	2004	2.555
Japan	2007	28.500	2008	14.250
Laos	2000	0.546	–	n/a
Malaysia	1995	2.690	1995	0.398
Maldives	2000	0.004	–	NA
Mongolia	2002	0.126	2002	0.083
Myanmar	2000	0.017	–	n/a
Nepal	2006	0.135	2006	0.006
Pakistan	2000	12.330	2000	0.145
Philippines	1993	0.074	1993	0.010
Republic of Korea	1996	7.947	1996	4.180
Singapore	2000	0.470	–	n/a
Sri Lanka	2000	0.950	–	n/a
Thailand	2007	2.191	2007	0.523
Viet Nam	2003	1.100	2003	0.250
Kazakhstan	1993	1.833	1993	0.274
Kyrgyzstan	2006	0.701	2006	0.148
Tajikistan	1999	0.026	1998	0.061
Turkmenistan	2000	1.181	1994	0.025
Uzbekistan	2001	2.200	2001	2.069

Source: Sato *et al.* (personal communication, 2011).
Note: – indicates that data are not available for that year

management and treatment (Biswas & Seetharam, 2008). A survey of more than 600 major cities in China found that sewage treatment took place in 43% but in cities with populations of less than 200,000 this dropped to 16% (NBSC, 2004; CAS, 2007). This situation makes untreated domestic wastewater the most important source of pollution in China in terms of volume, chemical oxygen demand (COD), and ammonia nitrogen (NH_3-N) since 1999.

Agricultural Pollution

Agriculture has been identified as the largest contributor of nonpoint source pollution of surface water and groundwater worldwide (Chhabra *et al.*, 2010). Fertilizers, which are often subsidized, are a major pollutant. The loss of reactive nitrogen from agricultural systems across Asia is a serious cause of concern, for instance in rice-producing areas across the Indo-Gangetic Plain (Figure 2) and in areas of vegetable cultivation, and has the potential to impact groundwater quality (Chowdary *et al.*, 2005).

Compared with more developed countries, the use of agricultural chemicals in many parts of Asia is still relatively limited, but with rising populations and the need to intensify agricultural production their use will grow (Biswas & Seetharam, 2008). Regional agricultural production increased some 62% from 1990 to 2002 through intensification of water and agrochemical use. The consumption of mineral fertilizers per hectare of

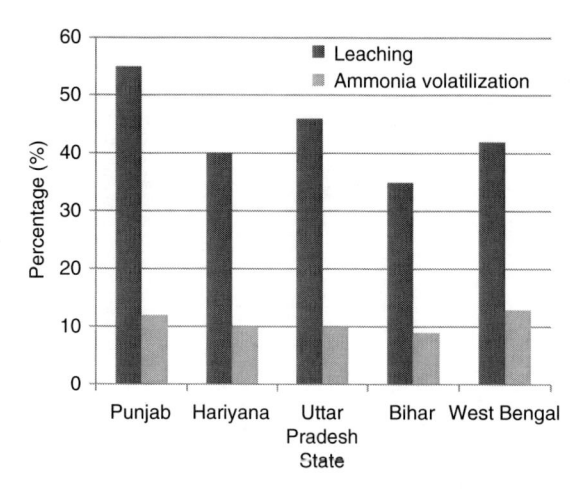

Figure 2. Estimated nitrogen loss intensity from rice crops, including kharif and rabi rice crops, in the Indo-Gangetic plains states of India. *Data source*: Chhabra *et al.* (2010).

agricultural land has increased by some 15%, in contrast to a decline in the rest of the world during 1991–2001 (Figures 3 and 4); in 2001 the region used twice as much mineral fertilizer per hectare of agricultural land as the rest of the world (ESCAP, 2005). The highest nitrate loads transported to the marine environment continue to be found in European rivers, but these levels have remained reasonably stable, while levels in major river basins in parts of Asia have increased (UNEP, 2008). Approximately 50% of the rivers in the region have exceedingly high levels of nutrients while another 25% have a moderate problem with desirable levels occasionally being exceeded (ESCAP, 1998, 2000). In some places, such as Central Asia, the excessive use of fertilizers, herbicides, pesticides, and defoliants and the resulting water quality degradation are responsible for

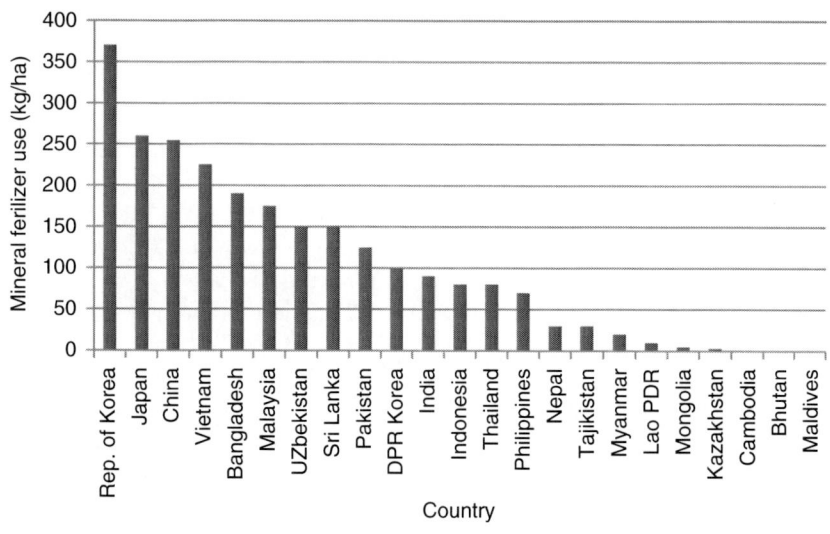

Figure 3. Mineral fertilizer use intensity, 2002. *Source*: FAOSTAT data for 2005, cited in UNESCAP (2005).

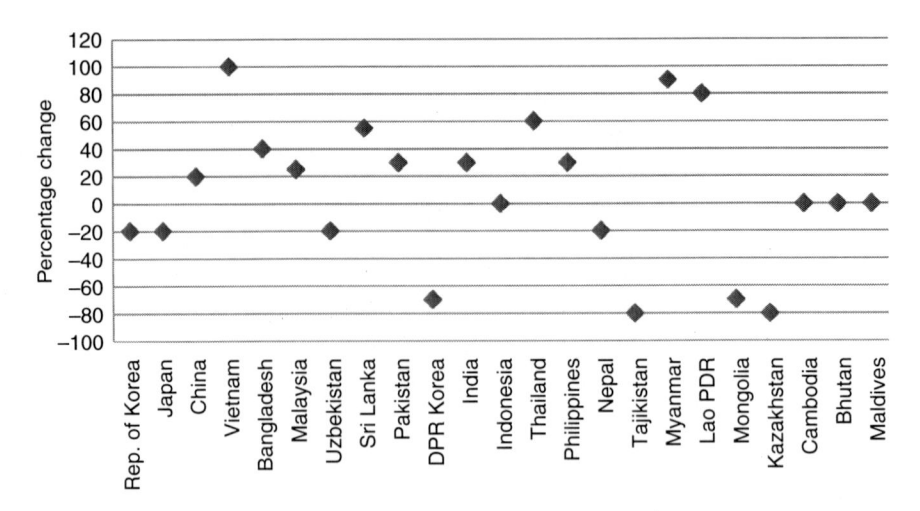

Figure 4. Percentage change in mineral fertilizer use, 1992–2002. *Source*: FAOSTAT data for 2005, cited in UNESCAP (2005).

health problems (ESCAP, 2000). Some countries are beginning to reduce fertilizer use, but others, including India, Pakistan, Sri Lanka, and Bangladesh, are increasing it (ESCAP, 2005).

Water quality data suggest that agriculture is the largest polluter of water bodies in India (MoEF, 2009). This is due to the increase in pesticide use, which grew by 750% over the second half of the 20th century, and fertilizer application, which rose from 70 kg/ha in 1991–92 to 113 kg/ha in 2006–07 (CSE, 1999; MoEF, 2009). High levels of fertilizer use have been associated with increased incidence of eutrophication in several of India's most important water bodies, such as the Hussein Sagar in Hyderabad and the Nainital in Uttar Pradesh. Levels of the chemicals HCH, DDT, endosulfan, methyl malathion, malathion, dimethoate, and ethion in excess of international recommendations have also been detected in the Ganga River (MoEF, 2009).

By contrast, the Government of Pakistan concluded that despite irrigation being by far the largest water consumer (96% of total withdrawals), the pollution caused by agriculture, particularly in relation to fertilizer use, is marginal compared to industrial and domestic sources (Pak-EPA, 2005).

Salinity in drainage water and soils is a serious issue in Pakistan, as exemplified in the large Indus Basin irrigation system (Abbas *et al.*, 2011). A study in 2004 by the Pakistan Water and Power Development Authority found that water in all drains and rivers was usable with respect to total dissolved solids (TDS) and sodium adsorption ratio (SAR) but that certain drains had high levels of residual sodium carbonate (RSC), COD and biochemical oxygen demand (BOD) (Pak-EPA, 2005). Recent data show that water quality continues to be a serious issue even in the upper Indus Basin (Table 3). In Punjab, all drains were carrying saline and sodic waters and all of them had very high values for COD and BOD (Government of Punjab, 2007). Groundwater salinity is also a problem, which restricts both agricultural and domestic use; it was estimated that 40 million residents depend on surface irrigation water for their domestic use, especially in areas where the groundwater is brackish (Government of Punjab, 2007).

Table 3. Assessment of water quality at selected sites in the upper Indus Basin, Pakistan, compared with National Environmental Quality Standards (NEQS).

Source no.	Water source	pH	EC (dS m^{-1})	SAR (mmol L^{-1})	RSC (mmol L^{-1})	TDS (mg L^{-1})	BOD (mg L^{-1})	COD (mg L^{-1})
1	Satokatla Drain	8.0	2.37	10.0	6.1	1,471	267	732
2	Water & Sanitation Authority pumps, Lahore	7.4	1.20	4.9	3.7	768	120	256
3	Hudiara Drain	7.8	1.35	7.00	2.5	850	104	255
	NEQS	*6–9*	*1.5*	*10.0*	*2.5*	*350*	*80*	*150*

Data source: Government of the Punjab (2007).

Salts in the rivers and lakes of Central Asia have emerged as a problem in the past 40 years as a result of increasing water withdrawals and return flow from agriculture, for example along the Amu Darya and Syr Darya. Residues of pesticides, herbicides, and fertilizers are also a problem (Ballance & Pant, 2003). Paradoxically, although pesticide use has declined considerably the use of small quantities of unregulated imports appear to pose a greater threat than the former high levels of controlled use because of the lack of standards and proper application, storage, and disposal of unused pesticides (ESCAP, 2005). Similar problems were observed in Sri Lanka (Howarth *et al.*, 2007).

There are also positive signs: pesticide bans have brought noticeable improvements in water quality for several rivers in China. But nutrient loads are still inadequately controlled, and increased fertilizer application and livestock waste have contributed large amounts of nutrients to downstream water bodies (Liu & Qiu, 2007; Ongley, 2004; Wang, 2006; Carr & Neary, 2008). Combined with industrial and domestic wastewater, nutrient loads from agricultural runoff are a major reason for the accelerated eutrophication of lakes in China. Total nitrogen nonpoint source contributions for Lakes Tai, Dianchi, and Chao were estimated at 59%, 33%, and 63%, respectively; and total phosphate nonpoint source contributions were 30%, 41%, and 73%, respectively (Li *et al.*, 2001). Water quality monitored in 422 agricultural districts revealed that more than half (256) did not reach the required standard (SEPA, 2010).

Industrial Pollution

Several Asian economies have gone from being largely agriculture-based to relying heavily on income from industry. The fastest-growing sectors include food and beverages; electrical equipment; cement; metals; chemicals; plastic and rubber products; and textiles, for which production has expanded in the range of 20-45%. In at least 30 Asian and Pacific countries, more than 20% of the total GDP is earned through industrial activity (ESCAP, 2005). Although environmental awareness in the industrial sector has increased, enforcement of regulations is difficult and pollution continues to rise as the region is dominated by small- and medium-scale industry. Table 4 lists industrial shares of emissions of organic water pollutants in selected countries across Asia.

Table 4. Organic water pollution resulting from industrial activities in South Asia.

Countries	Emissions of organic water pollutants (kg/day)	Industrial shares of emissions of organic water pollutants (%)							
		Primary metals	Paper and pulp	Chemical	Food and beverage	Stone, ceramics, and glass	Textiles	Wood	Other
Bangladesh	186,852	2.8	6.8	3.5	34.2	0.1	50.9	0.6	1.1
India	1,664,150	15.5	7.5	8.2	51.5	0.2	11.6	0.3	5.2
Iran	101,900	20.6	8.0	8.0	39.7	0.5	17.3	0.7	5.4
Nepal	26,550	1.5	8.1	3.9	43.3	1.2	39.3	1.7	1.0
Pakistan	114,726	14.1	5.8	7.3	39.5	0.2	30.1	0.3	2.7
Sri Lanka	55,665	1.2	8.9	7.2	42.2	0.2	38.3	0.7	1.3

Source: ESCAP (2000).

Throughout the region, industrial pollution levels, as indicated by BOD emissions per US$1,000 of GDP, are highest in some of the Central and Northeast Asian countries, namely Mongolia, Kyrgyzstan and Azerbaijan (> 10 kg BOD/US$1,000 GDP), followed by the South Asian Countries of Bangladesh and Nepal (8 kg) and Sri Lanka and Cambodia (5 kg). Other Southeast Asian countries are all below 4 kg BOD/US$1,000 GDP (ESCAP, 2005).

Within the region, the water bodies of Southeast Asia are described as the most severely polluted with heavy metals and toxic chemicals (ADB, 1997) (Table 5). A major source is mining: Asia is, for example, the largest contributor of anthropogenic atmospheric mercury. It is responsible for about half of global emissions (Li *et al.*, 2009).

In Pakistan, industrial growth is putting considerable pressure on water resources (ADB, 2008a). In North West Frontier Province, 80,000 m^3 of industrial effluent containing very high levels of pollutants is discharged every day into the River Kabul. Tanneries, food processing industries, pharmaceuticals, and textiles are all major contributors of pollutants, including high BOD levels, acids, ammonia, heavy metals, and hydrocarbons (Pak-EPA, 2005). Despite legislation, only 5% of national (compared with 91% of multinational) industries provide environmental assessments and many do not adhere to the permissible limits for pollution loads (Pak-EPA, 2005).

Industry is a relatively small water consumer in India (3% of annual water withdrawals) but its contribution to water pollution is considerable. The wastewater generated by industry has been estimated to be 55 km^3 per day, of which 68.5 million m^3 are disposed untreated into water bodies and a larger proportion has minimal treatment such as neutralization or settling. The Central and State Pollution Control Boards have identified 1,532 "grossly polluting" industries across the country (MoEF, 2009).

Table 5. Frequently reported metals in South-East Asian rivers.

Country	Number of rivers	Metals exceeding water quality standards
Malaysia	16	Mercury, lead, cadmium, zinc, copper
Thailand	10	Lead and/or mercury

Source: ESCAP (2000).

Around 70 industrial parks have been developed in Vietnam, which, in combination with the 1,000 hospitals nation-wide, produce 1 million m^3 of untreated wastewater each day. According to the Ministry of Natural Resources and Environment (MoNRE), there are about 4,000 enterprises discharging wastewater and requiring reallocation, closure, or the adoption of cleaner technologies and wastewater treatment. Surveys conducted by the Institute of Tropical Techniques and Environmental Protection (ITTEP) show that levels of contaminants in rivers in many of the cities are much higher than permissible limits. According to ITTEP, industrial parks (IPs) and export processing zones (EPZs) in the Southern Key Economic Zone discharge nearly 93 tons of waste into the Dong Nai, Thi Vai, and Saigon Rivers each day. Wastewater treatment facilities have only been introduced to 12 IPs/EPZs in Ho Chi Minh City, 3 out of 17 in Dong Nai, 2 out of 13 in Binh Duong, and none in Ba Ria-Vung Tau. An investment of over US$867 million is needed to deal with this environmental pollution (WEPA, 2011).

In Central Asia, industry contributes a large proportion of GDP, reaching 51% in Turkmenistan. Compared with agriculture, water use is low, but industry is considered the largest source of water pollution, with the most highly polluting industries being construction, mining, and petroleum refining. Fortunately, the volume of industrial waste is declining in Central Asia, from a peak of 168 million tons in 1998, of which more than half was generated in Kazakhstan and one-third in Kyrgyzstan. The mining industry has been the largest generator of industrial and toxic waste throughout the sub-region, which has more than 130 mining waste sites (ESCAP, 2005).

Water Quality Conditions, Trends, and Reporting across the Region

This section highlights the diversity not only in the conditions of water bodies across the region but also in the collection and sharing of data. India and China are two examples of countries that appear to have a relatively comprehensive monitoring and reporting system and which can reasonably well identify areas of significant water quality degradation and sources of pollution. As such, they are in a stronger position than many other countries to address water quality issues. Most other countries are very aware of the issues but still lack comprehensive data-sets.

South Asia

According to the Ministry of Water Resources (MOWR), Government of India (cited in MoEF, 2009), almost 70% of its surface water resources and a growing percentage of its groundwater reserves are contaminated. Regular water quality monitoring of 62 parameters takes place in 1,700 locations, a significant increase from the 18 locations when monitoring started in 1977. The results are published annually on the Central Pollution Control Board's (CPCB's) website (Box 1). The results for 2009 indicate that organic pollution continues to dominate. Almost 36% of the observations have BOD of more than the standard for bathing water of 3 mg/L, 19% between 3 and 6 mg/L and 17% above 6 mg/L, with 6 of the 50 rivers exceeding 100 mg/L. The desired total coliform (TC) standard for bathing water is 500 MPN/100 ml, which is exceeded in 51% of sample sites. Faecal coliform (FC) counts also exceed this figure in 30% of sites (CPCB, 2010). This represents a slight improvement since 1995. Progress has been made in wastewater

Box 1: National Water Quality Monitoring Programme of India

Under this programme, water quality data for the years 2002–2008 was analyzed and monitoring locations exceeding the water quality criteria were identified as polluted locations with respect to risk: "risk = frequency of violation of criteria × consequence (magnitude)". Polluted locations in a continuous sequence have been defined as polluted river stretches.

- Priority 1: BOD > 30 mg/L on any occasion, and all monitoring locations with BOD > 6 mg/L on all occasions. 35 stretches.
- Priority 2: BOD 20–30 mg/L on any occasion, and all monitoring locations with BOD > 6 mg/L on all occasions. 15 stretches.
- Priority 3: BOD 10–20 mg/L, and all monitoring locations exceeding BOD 6 mg/L on all occasions. 26 stretches.
- Priority 4: BOD 6–10 mg/L. 38 stretches.
- Priority 5: BOD 3–6 mg/L. 36 stretches.

Total: 150 stretches

The CPCB has taken human uses of water as the basis for identification of water quality objectives for different water bodies. The objective is to restore or maintain natural water bodies or their parts to such a quality as needed for their best uses. A Water Use Map was prepared and a Water Quality Map will be superimposed to identify water bodies in need of improvement (restoration).

Source: India Water Portal (2011).

collection; this is an important step but does not necessarily result in treatment (Figure 5) and does not translate into "clean" rivers.

Observations from 1995 to 2009 suggest only a slight decline in overall water quality in Indian rivers. In this period, rivers with BOD < 3 mg/L have increased from 57% to 64%, with a high of 68% in 2005; those with BOD > 6% have remained fairly static at 16–17%. TC contamination has actually improved slightly, with a decline from 22% to 15% of rivers with > 5000 MPN/100 mL and in increase of those with < 500. FC contamination shows a similar trend, with those with < 500 increasing from 55% to 70% (CPCB, 2010).

In Pakistan, only 1% of wastewater is treated before being discharged into rivers and drains. The first national study on the quality of water was carried out in 2003 in 21 cities, 6 rivers, and 10 reservoirs and lakes. In 17 cities, bacterial contamination was greater than 50%, and in 4 of these, 100% of the samples were unsuitable for human consumption, with coliform and *E. coli* levels greater than 16 MPN/100 ml. The inorganic contamination was also found to be very high, particularly with fluorites, iron, and sulphates. Turbidity levels ranged from 2 to 774 NTU, with TDS 46–5,318 mg/L; the National Environmental Quality Standard (NEQS) of 350 mg/L, based on a 1:10 dilution, was exceeded in 30% of samples. A second study in 2004 indicated that no appreciable improvement had been made in the conditions (Pak-EPA, 2005).

In Sri Lanka, surface water monitoring efforts remain patchy and data are not yet entered into a common database. A key issue is eutrophication due to excessive fertilizer use. Kandy Lake and Gregory Lake are examples, but many smaller irrigation reservoirs and channels were also found to contain high nutrient levels (MOFE, 2001).

China

Water quality trends in China suggest that poor water quality caused by pollution is exacerbating the existing water scarcity problem in some areas and threatening food

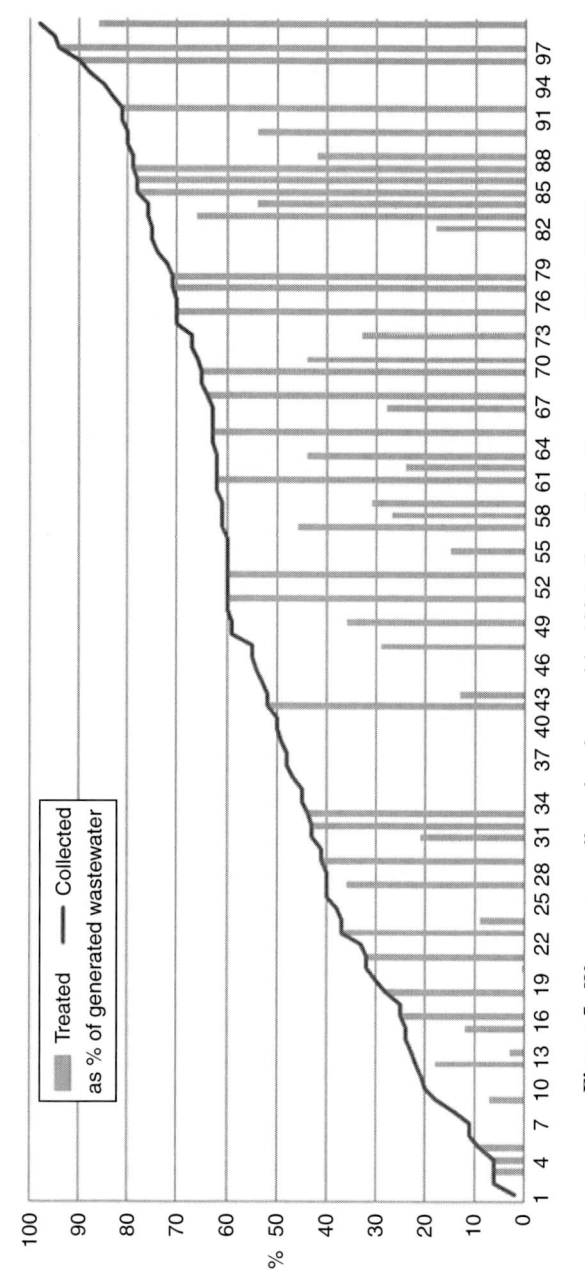

Figure 5. Wastewater collected and treated in 100 Indian cities. *Data source*: CPCB (2010).

security, economic development, and quality of life (Liu & Diamond, 2005; CAS, 2007; World Bank, 2007; Jiang, 2009).

Monitoring from 1991–2008 by the State Environmental Protection Administration (SEPA) showed that the water quality in the rivers in northern China, especially the Hai and Liao, was significantly lower than those in the south (MEP, various years; World Bank, 2001, 2006). The much smaller water flows (smaller assimilative capacity) in the rivers in northern China is an important factor, as is the relatively low population pressure in some provinces in southern China; also, industries in south China tend to be concentrated in the lower reaches of the river basins (World Bank, 2001). Water quality monitoring revealed an improvement from 1990 to 2008 in the south, in the Yangtze and Pearl Rivers, although they still contain areas of very poor water quality. A deterioration was noted in the north from 1991 to 2005 but it has steadily improved since (World Bank, 2006; Xie, 2009; MEP, various years). Currently, water in approximately 40% of the monitoring sites in the north is suitable for human consumption after treatment, as compared with 85% in the south (MEP, 2009).

Monitoring of 204 rivers in seven major river basins in 2009 found that 60% of the river sections meet the SEPA national standards for "good" (Class I, II, and III) water, meaning that they are suitable for aquaculture; 24% can be classified as "poor" (Class IV and V), only suitable for agriculture; and the remainder are highly polluted (below Class V) in terms of nitrates and BOD (Figure 6).

In 2010, among the 26 key state-controlled lakes and reservoirs, none met Class I standards and only 21% met Class II or III, while 38% were inferior to Class V. The major pollutants were nitrogen and phosphorus; more than half the lakes suffered from eutrophication.

Over the period from 2005 to 2009, water quality in the rivers has improved, with the number reaching Class I–III rising and those failing to meet Class V declining (Figure 7). Lake water quality has stayed poor (Figure 8), with the major pollutants being nitrogen (measured as total nitrogen) and phosphorus (measured as total phosphorus).

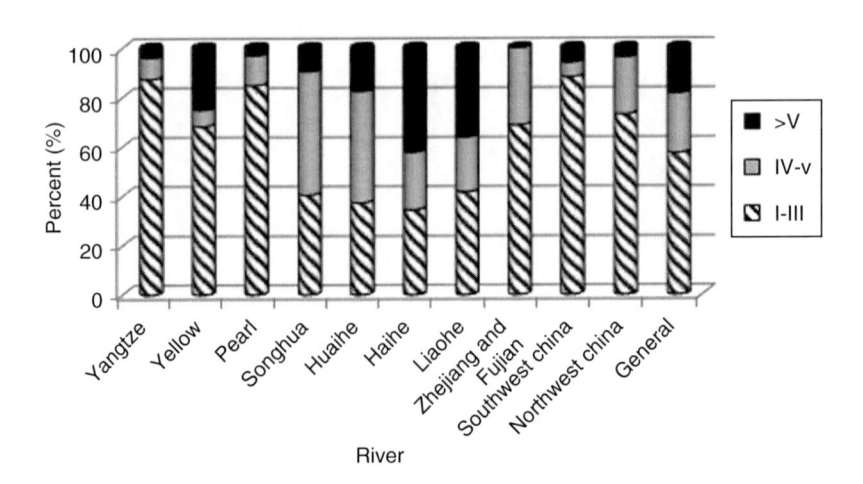

Figure 6. Water quality class percentage in seven major rivers. The eighth bar, "general", represents the water quality among the 408 sections of 203 rivers under national monitoring. *Source*: MEP (2010).

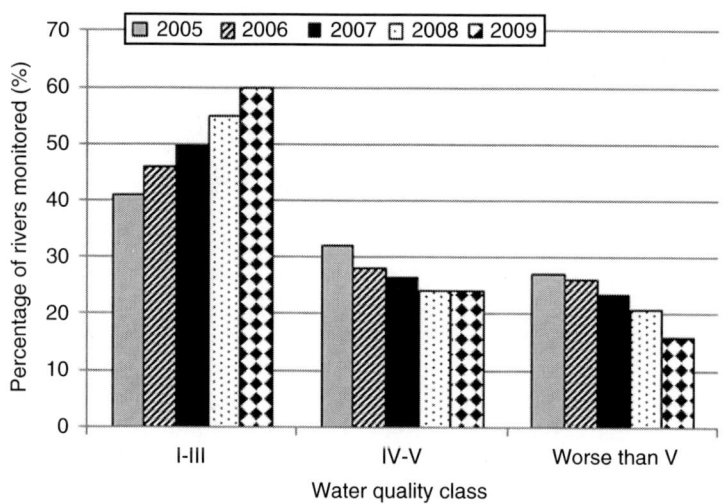

Figure 7. Trends in river water quality in China. *Data source*: MEP (2005–2009).

Southeast Asia

The results of water quality monitoring in 30 rivers in Indonesia indicate that, based on national standards, most rivers cannot be considered sources of drinking water. On the basis of BOD, only 21% of samples meet the criteria for Class 1, with most samples above 10 ppm and some as high as 100 ppm. The figures are similar for COD and dissolved oxygen (DO), and the same applies to lake water quality (WEPA, 2011).

In Malaysia, the Department of Environment (2004, 2006) recorded nearly 18,000 water pollution point sources in 2004, comprising mainly sewage treatment plants (54%), manufacturing industries (38%), animal farms (5%), and agro-based industries (3%). In 2006, monitoring of more than 1,000 locations in 146 river basins revealed that 55% of the

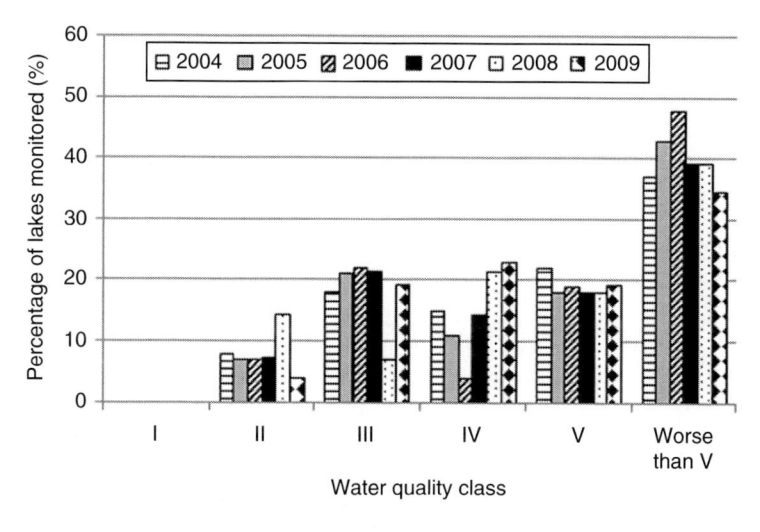

Figure 8. Trends in lake water quality in China. *Data source*: MEP (2005–2009).

basins were clean, 40% were slightly polluted, and only 5% were polluted. The major pollutants were BOD from sewage and agro-based and manufacturing industries (22 basins), nitrogen from sewage and livestock (41 basins), and suspended solids from earthworks and land-clearing activities (42 basins).

In Thailand, monitoring by the Pollution Control Department (PCD) revealed that 68% of water bodies were suitable for agriculture and general consumption ("good" and "moderate" quality) but no surface water was categorized as "very good" quality (extra-clean, suitable for aquatic animals and human consumption after normal treatment). The variation between regions was wide, with surface water bodies in the northern-central and southern regions being of particularly poor quality, while water in the eastern region was fair and that in the north-eastern region was good.

Compared with the three countries above, surface water quality monitoring is more limited or ad hoc in Laos and Vietnam. In both countries, there are many difficulties, in particular the unclear definition of responsibilities and competences among different ministries and agencies at national and provincial scales (Duc Hanh & The Dong, 2008; Komany, 2008). However, with the Mekong being of major transboundary importance, the Mekong River Commission (MRC) supported water quality monitoring across the subregion (Box 2). The results confirmed national studies which showed that water quality in upstream sections of most rivers remains good, while downstream pollution, mainly from urban areas and industries, affects water quality (Komany, 2008; Duc Hanh & The Dong, 2008). Trends indicate that the levels of two primary pollution indicators, ammonium nitrogen (NH_4-N) and BOD, vary considerably and exceed NEQS Class A (Figure 9). The problems are worst during the dry season, when the flows in the rivers are reduced.

Based on a water quality monitoring index that rates the human impact of water quality using DO, ammonium (NH_4), COD, and TP as A for no impact, B for slight impact, C for impact, and D for severe impact, it can be said that the water quality of the Mekong has declined. In 2000, 75% of samples were rated B and 25% C, but by 2008, 31% were categorized as B, 38% C, and 25% D.

Central Asia

Intensive development of irrigated farming, land drainage, and increasing water use for industrial and household needs, in Central Asia as a whole, have resulted in more

Box 2. MRC Water Quality Monitoring Programme

Under the MRC Water Quality Monitoring Programme (WQMP), around 100 sampling points on the Mekong and its tributaries have been monitored since 1985 and over 20,000 samples have been taken. There are pressures from municipalities, industries, aquaculture, and agriculture. Nitrogen losses from agriculture are around 300,000 t/year and phosphorus losses are 37,000 t/year, most of which is divided between Thailand and Vietnam. These figures are respectively 10 and 5 times those of urban areas. Although discharged waste from densely populated areas and agriculture affects some locations, in general the water quality is still good and transport of pollutants across boundaries is not yet a problem, but some "hotspots" need further attention. Results suggest that the WQMP should develop a strategy for future monitoring of toxic substances. The Environment Programme and the Water Utilization Programme are collaborating to develop water quality rules and to introduce catchment-based management.

Source: Mekong River Commission (2004, 2007).

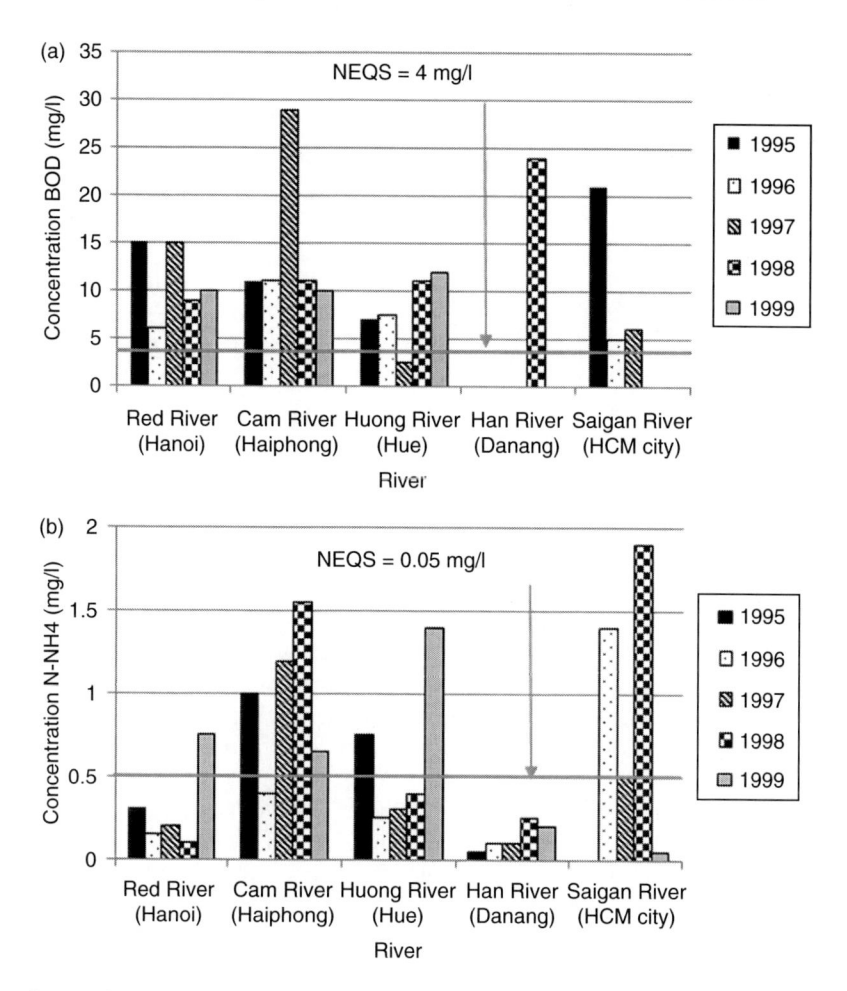

Figure 9. (a) BOD, (b) NH$_4$ levels in major Vietnamese rivers. *Source*: AIT-UNEP RRC.AP (2001), WEPA (2011).

abstractions of fresh water and discharges of polluted return flow into water bodies. The main pollution sources are agrochemicals and insufficiently treated effluents from municipal and industrial sewers. National reports also note increased contamination of groundwater due to substandard management of municipal and industrial waste sites, especially in the mining industry. On average, from 1995–2001, 8–15% of water samples failed to satisfy bacteriological requirements and 20–40% fell short of physical and chemical standards (UNECE & UNESCAP, 2004). Across the region, national experts have voiced concern over the unsatisfactory condition of the 60–70% of sewage disposal facilities that fail to provide efficient treatment or effectively ceased to exist (Ballance & Pant, 2003). The most-polluted bodies with municipal and industrial waste are the Irtyish, Nura, Syr Darya, and Ili Rivers, as well as Lake Balkhash. Salinity and chemical contamination from agricultural drainage water are also of significant concern in many parts of Central Asia, including Kazakhstan and Uzbekistan.

Trends

Even where data has been collected for several years, such as in India, China, and the Mekong, it is difficult to identify clear trends. In general it appears that water quality is declining but there are exceptions which national trends may hide. Coarser regional statistics on DO and alkalinity from 1976–2008 indicate some improvement in Asia, but the changes are not dramatic (UNEP, 2008). Nitrate levels at river mouths remained relatively steady across the region between 1990–1999 and 2000–2007, with some significant declines in parts of India. Phosphorus levels appear not to have changed much as a regional trend but have variously increased and decreased in different parts of India. Nitrogen and phosphorus levels have increased across Central Asia (UNEP, 2008).

The clear trends of population growth, urbanization, and industrialization, without evident large-scale concomitant introduction of mitigating measures, does however imply that water quality degradation has been taking place and will continue.

Managing Water Quality

Monitoring

Demographic changes, industrialization, and increased use of agrochemicals have serious implications for water quality across Asia. Managing these challenges requires an appropriate monitoring programme, which so far only exists as a patchwork across the region. Most countries have legislation that controls water quality and the emission of pollutants to water bodies, based on concentrations of specific pollutants and dilution requirements. However, as Biswas and Seetharam (2008) note in their comprehensive report for the Asian Development Bank: "A major issue in preparing the Asian Water Development Outlook has been the paucity of data on all aspects of water-related issues.... Even when data were available, their reliability was often unknown. The problem was further compounded by the presence of either inconsistent national datasets or different data from various national sources on the same parameters, and/or significant differences in many cases between national and international datasets." This statement can be reinforced from the water quality sector, where monitoring is facing the challenge of a broad range of indicators describing physical, chemical, and microbial water health. The multitude of national and international guidelines for the evaluation of water quality makes it unsurprising that basin-wide agreements are only slowly crystallizing, although the concept of indexing water quality with a numerical value across physical, chemical and biological parameters could standardize transboundary assessments (Lumb *et al.*, 2011).

Significant progress is however reported at the national level, for example from India, China, Pakistan (Box 3), and Southeast Asia, which points at important developments in the sector (ESCAP, 2000).

Policies and Strategies

Proactive policies for water quality improvement are emerging across Asia, although many are in their infancy and a unified framework has yet to evolve. Several countries are implementing large-scale and ambitious programmes aimed at rehabilitating degraded water resources. These programmes and plans are typically given legislative or statutory

Box 3: Surface Water Quality Monitoring Action Plan, Punjab, Pakistan

In Pakistan, the Surface Water Quality Monitoring Action Plan focuses on rivers, headworks, canals, drains, and critical areas. Monitoring includes:

- Rivers: 25 sites for agricultural and 2 sites for drinking water quality
- Canals: 101 sites for agricultural water quality
- Canals: 20 sites for drinking water quality
- Canals: 56 sites for agricultural use and hotspots for NEQS.

The samples are analyzed for Ca, Mg, Na, K, carbonates (CO_3^{2-}), bicarbonates (HCO_3^-), chlorides (Cl^-), sulphates (SO_4^{2-}), RSC, pH, electrical conductivity (EC), SAR, Cu, Pb, Zn, and Ni.

In general, the first sampling point at each river is near the boundary of the province where the river enters Pakistan, and the next sampling points are before and after the entry point of a main drain into the river. All the rivers and headworks are monitored bi-monthly. Monitoring is bi-annual for the drinking water quality checks and the hotspots for NEQS. A database using GIS is used to reflect the quality of the river system.

Source: Government of the Punjab (2007).

authority, such as that provided by Thailand's National Water Quality Act, the Philippines' Water Quality Code, India's Environment Protection Act, China's Water Law, or the Republic of Korea's Water Quality Preservation Act (ESCAP, 1999, 2000). Clean-up campaigns for rivers, canals, lakes, and other water bodies have become widespread throughout the region (Table 6).

The enforcement of water quality is particularly difficult in emerging economies, where institutional capacities do not keep pace with rapid industrialization (Kathuria & Sterner, 2006) and economic instruments, like taxation and removal of fertilizer subsidies, clash with other development goals. Moreover, monitoring is costly and voluntary compliance is poor (Table 7).

A number of countries in the region have strengthened local administration through the devolution of functions and responsibilities. The Philippines implemented the Local Government Code of 1991, under which local governments were given increased autonomy, more responsibilities for provision of services, and greater access to financial resources. As a result, Metro Manila's local government has substantially increased its development activities. In the Republic of Korea, too, the management of pollutant-discharging industries and the regulation of waste collection have been entrusted to local government (ESCAP, 2000).

Table 6. Selection of waterway rehabilitation projects.

Country	Rivers
Bangladesh	Buriganga
PR China	Huihe, Haihe, Liaohe
India	Ganges
Indonesia	Various
Malaysia	Sungai Merliwan, Klang
The Philippines	Pasig
Thailand	Chao Phraya and Bangkok waterways
Singapore	Singapore and Kallang

Source: ESCAP (1999, 2000).

Table 7. Status of pollution control and defaulters in highly polluting industries under the Program of Industrial Pollution Control in India.

State/Union territory	Number of units identified	Units with adequate facilities to comply with standards, Dec. 1995	Units with adequate facilities to comply with standards, Dec. 2000	Defaulters, Aug. 1997	Closed since	Acquired requisite treatment/ disposal facilities	Defaulters, Dec. 2000
Andhra Pradesh	173	32	1	60	17	37	6
Assam	15	5	1	7	5	0	2
Bihar	62	11	2	14	4	10	0
Goa	6	0	0	0	0	0	0
Gujarat	177	8	0	17	3	14	0
Haryana	43	7	0	21	8	12	1
Himachal Pradesh	9	0	0	0	0	0	0
Jamu and Kashmir	8	4	0	0	0	0	0
Karnataka	85	21	0	20	2	17	1
Kerala	28	4	0	36	4	32	0
Madhya Pradesh	78	21	5	2	1	0	1
Maharash- tra	335	28	5	6	3	3	0
Orissa	23	10	4	9	1	4	4
Punjab	45	11	0	18	1	16	1
Rajasthan	49	2	0	0	0	0	0
Tamil Nadu	119	8	0	366	118	248	0
Uttar Pradesh	224	40	3	241	59	176	6
West Ben- gal	58	27	3	30	23	23	0
Delhi	5	3	0				
Pondi- cherry	6	4	0	4	4	4	0
Other states/UT	3	6	0				
Total	1,551	252	24	851	233	596	22

Based on CPCB Annual Reports 1994–1995 and 2000–2001, as cited in Goldar and Banerjee (2004).

There are a wide variety of economic instruments to support sustainable environmental management, including user charges and effluent charges (ADB, 2008b). It is widely believed that introducing the polluter-pays principle is crucial to success. A charge levied by volume is the most effective method for domestic sewerage and industry, by insisting on on-site treatment to levels comparable to domestic waste before discharge into the sewerage system. However, in many Asian cities, conventional sewerage systems were never installed in a comprehensive way and to build them retroactively is both expensive and disruptive (ADB, 2008b). Payment for environmental services might offer a solution where agricultural nonpoint source pollution affects downstream users. While the downstream urban areas, at an advanced stage of economic development as in China, demand clean water, the upstream towns and poor villages will still continue to prioritize economic development by enhancing their agricultural production. The inherent tension between upstream and downstream areas will raise serious equity and social justice issues because the poor polluters have legitimate rights to development, which will limit the application of command-and-control measures or pollution taxes (Jiang *et al.*, 2011).

Conclusions

Although there is not yet a comprehensive, up-to-date or comparable database on water quality in Asia, national data derived from systematic monitoring and project-based assessments imply that the situation remains serious but with many positive developments and signs of hope.

There is certainly a great diversity in water pollution issues across the region and it is difficult to find a particular problem only in a certain sub-region (for an attempt, see ESCAP, 2000). The most immediate challenge for governments is that of domestic sanitation because of the health risk. Although many Asian countries are making major strides towards achieving the Millennium Development Goals, collection and treatment are still minimal.

On the positive side, water quality monitoring efforts are on the increase and there are several countries with systems in place that could guide other nations in the region. The efforts of strong basin agencies such as the MRC in facilitating monitoring across political boundaries could lead the way.

Many regulatory and economic options exist to address the problems but progress is constrained by challenges that range from low institutional capacities, social pressure, and political will, to inadequate financial resources (Jiang *et al.*, 2011; Carr & Neary, 2008). If instruments are not put in place, pollution of water bodies will continue to rank among the critical issues impacting water security. More than half of the population of the region is expected to live in towns and cities by 2030 (ESCAP, 2011). The challenges of population growth, urbanization, wastewater management, and the need to feed Asia will continue to affect water quality in the years to come. Asian countries will need to make concerted efforts to address these threats.

Note

1. The definition given by the FAO is the quantity of water that has been polluted by adding waste. The origin can be domestic or industrial wastewater routed to the wastewater treatment plant. It does not include agricultural drainage water.

References

Abbas, A., Khan, S., Hussain, N., Hanjra, M. A. & Akbar, S. (2011) Characterizing soil salinity in irrigated agriculture using a remote sensing approach, *Physics and Chemistry of the Earth, Parts A/B/C*, DOI: 10.1016/j.pce.2010.12.004.

AIT-UNEP RRC.AP (Regional Resource Centre for Asia and the Pacific) (2001) Surface water, *State of the Environment in Vietnam 2001*, Available at: http://www.rrcap.unep.org/pub/soe/vietnam/issues/pressure/inland_water.htm#Surface%20water1 (accessed 6 February 2012).

Angel, D. & Rock, M. T. (2009) Environmental rationalities and the development state in East Asia: prospects for a sustainability transition, *Technological Forecasting and Social Change*, 76, pp. 229–240.

Asian Development Bank [ADB] (1997) *Emerging Asia: Changes and Challenges* (Mandaluyong City, Philippines: Asian Development Bank).

Asian Development Bank [ADB] (2008a) *Islamic Republic of Pakistan Country Environment Analysis* (Mandaluyong City, Philippines: Asian Development Bank).

Asian Development Bank [ADB] (2008b) *Managing Asian cities: Sustainable and Inclusive Urban Solutions* (Mandaluyong City, Philippines: Asian Development Bank).

Ballance, R. & Pant, B. D. (2003) Environment Statistics in Central Asia: Progress and Prospects. ERD Working Paper Series, No. 36 (Economics and Research Department, Asian Development Bank). Available at: http://www.adb.org/Documents/ERD/Working_Papers/wp036.pdf

Biswas, A. K. & Seetharam, K. E. (2008) Achieving water security for Asia, *International Journal of Water Resources Development*, 24(1), pp. 145–176.

Carr, G. M. & Neary, J. P. (2008) *Water Quality for Ecosystem and Human Health*, 2nd ed., United Nations Environment Programme Global Environment Monitoring System (GEMS)/Water Programme. Available at: http://www.unep.org/gemswater/Portals/24154/publications/pdfs/water_quality_human_health.pdf

Centre for Science and Environment [CSE] (1999) Perpetual thirst: faucets of the problem, *Down to Earth*, 7(19), February 28.

Chhabra, A., Manjunath, K. R. & Panigrahy, S. (2010) Non-point source pollution in Indian agriculture: estimation of nitrogen losses from rice crop using remote sensing and GIS, *International Journal of Applied Earth Observation and Geoinformation*, 12, pp. 190–200.

Chinese Academy of Science [CAS] (2007) *China Sustainable Development Strategy Report 2007: Water Governance and Innovation* (Beijing: Scientific Press).

Chowdary, V. M., Rao, N. H. & Sarma, P. B. S. (2005) Decision support framework for assessment of non-point-source pollution of groundwater in large irrigation projects, *Agricultural Water Management*, 75, pp. 194–225.

Central Pollution Control Board [CPCB] (2010) *Status of Water Quality in India: 2009*, Monitoring of Indian Aquatic Resources Series: MINARS 2009-10 (Ministry of Environment and Forests, Government of India).

Corcoran, E., Nellemann, C., Baker, E., Bos, R. D. & Osborn, H. S. (Eds) (2010) *Sick Water? The Central Role of Wastewater Management in Sustainable Development: A Rapid Response Assessment* (United Nations Environment Programme, UN-Habitat, GRID-Arendal).

Department of Environment (2004) *Malaysia Environment Quality Report 2004* (Department of Environment, Ministry of Natural Resources and Environment, Government of Malaysia).

Department of Environment (2006) *Malaysia Environment Quality Report 2006* (Department of Environment, Ministry of Natural Resources and Environment, Government of Malaysia).

Duc Hanh, H. & The Dong, N. (2008) The current state of river basins in Vietnam: pollution and solution, Paper presented at *3rd WEPA International Forum*, 23–24 October 2008, Putrajaya, Malaysia. Available at http://www.wepa-db.net/activities_200810forum.htm

Economic and Social Commission for Asia and the Pacific [ESCAP] (1999) *ESCAP Population Data Sheet, Population and Development Indicators for Asia and the Pacific, 1999* (Bangkok: United Nations ESCAP).

Economic and Social Commission for Asia and the Pacific [ESCAP] (2000) *State of the Environment in Asia and the Pacific* (Bangkok: United Nations ESCAP).

Economic and Social Commission for Asia and the Pacific [ESCAP] (2005) *State of the Environment in Asia and the Pacific* (Bangkok: United Nations ESCAP).

Economic and Social Commission for Asia and the Pacific [ESCAP] (2011) *Statistical Yearbook for Asia and the Pacific 2011* (Bangkok: United Nations ESCAP), Available at http://www.unescap.org/stat/data/syb2011/II-Environment/Water-availability-and-use.asp (accessed 6 March 2012).

Eurostat (2006) *News release, 21 March: 90% of EU25 population connected to waste water collection systems* (Luxembourg: Eurostat Press Office), Available at http://epp.eurostat.ec.europa.eu/cache/ITY_PUBLIC/8-21032006-AP/EN/8-21032006-AP-EN.PDF (accessed 6 March 2012).

Food and Agriculture Organization of the United Nations [FAO] (2003) *Selected Indicators for Food and Agricultural Development in Asia and the Pacific 1992–2002* (Bangkok: FAO Regional Office for Asia and the Pacific).

FAO AQUASTAT (N.d.) FAO's information system on water and agriculture (Food and Agriculture Organization of the United Nations), Available at http://www.fao.org/nr/water/aquastat/main/index.stm (accessed 7 June 2011).

FAOSTAT (N.d.) Time-series and cross sectional data relating to food and agriculture for some 200 countries (Food and Agriculture Organization of the United Nations), Available at http://faostat.fao.org (accessed 15 November 2005).

Goldar, B. & Banerjee, N. (2004) Impact of informal regulation of pollution on water quality in rivers in India, *Journal of Environmental Management*, 73, pp. 117–130.

Government of Punjab (2007) *Surface Water Quality Monitoring Plan (Revised), September 2007* (Lahore, Pakistan: Irrigation and Power Department, Government of the Punjab).

Hanjra, M. A., Blackwell, J., Carr, G., Zhang, F. & Jackson, T. M. (2011) Wastewater irrigation and environmental health: implications for water governance and public policy, *International Journal of Hygiene and Environmental Health*, DOI: 10.1016/j.ijheh.2011.10.003.

Hanjra, M. A. & Qureshi, M. E. (2010) Global water crisis and future food security in an era of climate change, *Food Policy*, 35(5), pp. 365–377, DOI: 10.1016/j.foodpol.2010.05.006.

Howarth, S., Ismael, A. E., Tharme, R., Abeysekera, T., Clemett, A., Lashin, I., Jinapala, K., Mei, M., Meilhac, C., Murphy, S. E., Someratne, P. G., Terry, G., Turner, S. & Thomas, C. M. (2007) *Diffuse Agricultural Pollution: Impacts and Options for Mitigation. Final Report*, Department for International Development Knowledge and Research Services Contract R8337, unpublished report.

India Water Portal (2011) *Polluted River Stretches in India: Criteria and Status – A Report by Central Pollution Control Board*, Available at http://www.indiawaterportal.org/node/20590 (accessed 5 March 2012).

Jiang, Y. (2009) China's water scarcity, *Journal of Environmental Management*, 90(11), pp. 3185–3196.

Jiang, Y., Jin, L. & Lin, T. (2011) Higher water tariffs for less river pollution: evidence from the Min River and Fuzhou City in China, *China Economic Review*, 22, pp. 183–195.

JMP (N.d.) WHO/UNICEF Joint Monitoring Programme for Water Supply and Sanitation, Available at: http://www.wssinfo.org (accessed 6 March 2012).

Kathuria, V. & Sterner, T. (2006) Monitoring and enforcement: is two-tier regulation robust? A case study of Ankleshwar, India, *Ecological Economics*, 57, pp. 477–493.

Khan, S. & Hanjra, M. A. (2009) Footprints of water and energy inputs in food production: global perspectives, *Food Policy*, 34, pp. 130–140.

Komany, S. (2008) Water quality monitoring and management in Lao PDR: the case study of Nam Ngum River basin, Paper presented at *3rd WEPA International Forum*, 23–24 October 2008, Putrajaya, Malaysia. Available at: http://www.wepa-db.net/activities_200810forum.htm

Li, G. B., Yin, C. Q. & Zhou, H. D. (2001) Three-lake water problem of China and its countermeasures and management, *Water Problem Forum*, 3, pp. 36–39, [in Chinese].

Li, P., Feng, X. B., Qiu, G. L., Shang, L. H. & Li, Z. G. (2009) Mercury pollution in Asia: a review of the contaminated sites, *Journal of Hazardous Materials*, 168, pp. 591–601.

Liu, J. & Diamond, J. (2005) China's environment in a globalizing world, *Nature*, 435, pp. 1179–1186.

Liu, W. & Qiu, R. L. (2007) Water eutrophication in China and the combating strategies, *Journal of Chemical Technology and Biotechnology*, 82, pp. 781–786.

Lumb, A., Sharma, T. C. & Bibeault, J. F. (2011) A review of genesis and evolution of water quality index (WQI) and some future directions, *Water Quality, Exposure and Health*, 3, pp. 11–24.

Mekong River Commission (2004) *Annual Technical Meeting*, Nov. 15–16, Vientiane, Lao PDR. Available at: http://www.mrcmekong.org/assets/Publications/conference/Proceedings-ATM1-EP-2004.pdf

Mekong River Commission (2007) Environment programme, *Annual Technical Meeting*, 16–17 January, Chiang Mai, Thailand. Available at: http://www.mrcmekong.org/assets/Publications/conference/Proceedings-ATM3-EP-2006.pdf

Ministry of Environment and Forest [MoEF] (2009) *State of Environment Report, India 2009* (Government of India).

Ministry of Environmental Protection [MEP] (various years) *Report on the State of the Environment in China* (Beijing: MEP), Available at: http://english.mep.gov.cn/standards_reports/soe/ (accessed 10 August 2010).

Ministry of Environmental Protection [MEP] (2009) *Report on the State of the Environment in China 2008* (Beijing: MEP).

Ministry of Environmental Protection [MEP] (2010) *Report on the State of the Environment in China 2009* (Beijing: MEP), Available at: http://english.mep.gov.cn/standards_reports/soe/soe2009/201104/t20110411_208976.htm (accessed 6 February 2012).

Ministry of Forestry and Environment [MOFE] (2001) *State of the Environment, Sri Lanka* (Battaramulla, Sri Lanka: Ministry of Forestry and Environment).

National Bureau of Statistics of China [NBSC] (2004) *China Urban Statistical Yearbook 2004* (Beijing: National Bureau of Statistics Press).

Ongley, E. D. (2004) Non-point source water pollution in China: current status and future prospects, *Water International*, 29, pp. 299–306.

Pakistan Environmental Protection Agency [Pak-EPA] (2005) State of the Environment Report. Commissioned by Pak-EPA, Ministry of Environment, Government of Pakistan. Available at: http://www.environment.gov. pk/Publications.htm%20

Park, J. H., Duan, L., Kim, B., Mitchell, M. J. & Shibata, H. (2010) Potential effects of climate change and variability on watershed biogeochemical processes and water quality in Northeast Asia, *Environment International*, 36, pp. 212–225.

State Environmental Protection Administration [SEPA] (2010) *China Environmental Bulletins 2010* (Beijing: State Environmental Protection Administration).

State Environmental Protection Administration [SEPA] (1991–2007) *China Environmental Bulletins 1990–2006* (Beijing: State Environmental Protection Administration).

Statistics Division (2011) *Environmental Indicators: Inland Water Resources* (United Nations Statistics Division), Available at: http://unstats.un.org/unsd/environment/wastewater.htm (accessed 6 March 2012).

UNECE & UNESCAP (2004) Strengthening Cooperation for Rational and Efficient Use of Water and Energy Resources in Central Asia. (New York; United Nations) Available at: http://www.unece.org/fileadmin/ DAM/env/water/damsafety/effuse_en.pdf

United Nations Environment Programme [UNEP] (2008) *Vital Water Graphics: An Overview of the State of the World's Fresh and Marine Waters*, 2nd ed (UNEP, GRID Arendal), Available at: http://www.unep.org/ dewa/vitalwater/index.html (accessed 6 March 2012).

UN (2009) *World Urbanization Prospects, the 2009 Revision* (United Nations, Department of Economic and Social Affairs, Population Division), Available at: http://esa.un.org/unpd/wup/index.htm (accessed 6 March 2012).

Wang, X. Y. (2006) Management of agricultural non-point source pollution in China: current status and challenge, *Water Science and Technology*, 53, pp. 1–9.

Water and Power Development Authority [WAPDA] (2004) *Effect of Different Environmental Pollutants on Drainage System of Pakistan: Interim Report* (Pakistan: WAPDA).

Water Environment Partnership in Asia [WEPA] (2011) *State of Water Environmental Issues: Indonesia*, Available at: http://www.wepa-db.net/policies/state/indonesia/indonesia.htm (accessed 23 November 2011).

WHO/UNICEF Joint Monitoring Programme for Water Supply and Sanitation (2010) Progress on Sanitation and Drinking-water: 2010 Update. Geneva and New York. Available at: http://www.who.int/water_sanitatio n_health/publications/9789241563956/en/index.html

WHO. 2004. Global Health Observatory Data Repository, World Health Organization. Available at: http://apps. who.int/ghodata/?vid=10012# (accessed 12 January 2012).

World Bank (2001) *China: Air, Land and Water* (Washington, DC: World Bank).

World Bank (2006) *China: Water Quality Management. Policy and Institutional Considerations* (Washington, DC: World Bank).

World Bank (2007) *Cost of Pollution in China: Economic Estimates of Physical Damages* (Washington, DC: World Bank).

World Water Assessment Programme [WWAP] (2009) *The United Nations World Water Development Report 3: Water in a Changing World* (Paris: UNESCO; London: Earthscan).

Xie, J. (2009) *Addressing China's Water Scarcity: Recommendations for Selected Water Resource Management Issues* (Washington, DC: World Bank).

Economic Incentives Can Enhance Policy Efforts to Improve Water Quality in Asia

SOUMYA BALASUBRAMANYA & DENNIS WICHELNS

International Water Management Institute, Colombo, Sri Lanka

ABSTRACT *This article describes the conceptual advantages of including economic incentives in the basket of policy alternatives available for motivating improvements in water quality. With a particular focus on Asia, we discuss the incentives available for encouraging reductions in point and nonpoint source pollutants in urban, rural, and peri-urban settings. Several countries in Asia are implementing some form of economic incentives, either directly, in the form of effluent taxes or subsidies, or in combination with regulatory measures that help to ensure water quality standards are achieved. We also describe the importance of institutional capacity and political will in support of economic incentives, and the increasing usefulness of incentive programmes as economies develop and expand. The discussion includes several examples of programmes in China and Thailand, along with observations from India, Japan, Korea, and the Philippines.*

The Challenge Is Urban, Rural and Peri-urban

Some of the most visible water quality problems in Asia involve densely populated cities. Water supply and sanitation facilities are notably inadequate in many rapidly growing urban areas, particularly in slums and other settings where residents lack formal utility services or the services are simply unable to keep pace with rapid population growth (Ooi, 2009). As a result, waste materials are discharged untreated into streams, drains, and ditches that flow through residential areas, thus creating unhealthy conditions for millions of residents. In the densely populated cities of Karachi, Lahore, and Islamabad in Pakistan, much of the municipal drinking water supply is polluted, and cannot be recommended for consumption (Azizullah *et al.*, 2011). Some residents can afford to purchase bottled water, while many are persistently exposed to health risks from drinking contaminated water.

An estimated 88% of the global incidence of diarrhoeal disease, which is the second leading cause of death in children younger than five years (after respiratory illnesses), is attributed to unsafe drinking water, inadequate sanitation, and poor hygiene (Bartram *et al.*, 2005). Partly for this reason, the mortality rate among children younger than five years of age generally is higher in urban slums than in rural settings (Patel et al., 2009). Worldwide, an estimated 2 million persons succumb to diarrhoeal diseases each year, and most of those deaths occur in developing countries (Ali *et al.*, 2009).

Yet the cities are not the only areas in Asia suffering from degraded water quality. Pollutants from both industrial and agricultural sources have impacted rural areas as well. Much of Asia remains agricultural, and millions of farmers apply fertilizer, pesticides, and other chemicals in pursuit of higher yields and larger net revenues. Most of the farmers cultivate small plots and receive little guidance regarding optimal application rates or methods for minimizing the surface runoff and deep percolation that carry undesirable constituents into streams and shallow aquifers. Even with such information, individual farmers would have little incentive to invest time and effort in reducing off-farm impacts, in the absence of a policy framework that requires or motivates those investments.

The sources of industrial pollution in rural areas have been increasing over time, with the development of non-farm rural enterprises and investments in activities that add value to agricultural production. The goal of such investments generally is to enhance rural economic development by providing employment opportunities and diversifying the portfolio of income-generating activities. In many areas, that goal might initially outweigh public concerns regarding water quality degradation, such that little effort is invested by firms or public agencies in minimizing pollutant discharges from rural factories, processing plants, and livestock operations.

Water quality is also degraded where the city meets the countryside, in those areas known by some as peri-urban and by others as the urban fringe. It is in this zone where many households earn their living in agriculture while directly serving urban markets. Millions of peri-urban households engage in crop production for sale in retail markets or for provision to urban restaurants. The prices received for fresh vegetables in such markets are sufficient to generate substantial household income, particularly in comparison with alternative opportunities (Raschid-Sally *et al.*, 2005).

In many peri-urban areas, households rely on partly treated or untreated wastewater for irrigation, as they lack access to a higher-quality source. The use of wastewater generates notable health hazards for farmers, their communities, and the consumers of fresh vegetables (Khan *et al.*, 2008; Holm *et al.*, 2009; Srinivasan & Reddy, 2009; Akbar *et al.*, 2010). Investments in wastewater treatment would ostensibly benefit millions of residents of peri-urban areas and the consumers they serve in urban markets, while also improving water quality in streams and shallow groundwater.

Yet if wastewater is treated before discharge, many poor households might lose their source of irrigation water, as commercial enterprises, wealthier households, or those with better political connections would probably secure the new source of higher-quality water. This is one conundrum of addressing water quality issues in peri-urban areas. The poor might prefer to retain their informal access to wastewater rather than having no water at all. Farmers in Chakera Village on the edge of Faisalabad City in Pakistan already have demonstrated the likelihood that such a conundrum might arise. Facing the prospect of wastewater treatment upstream, the farmers pursued a lengthy legal battle to retain access to the wastewater they had relied on for many years (Weckenbrock *et al.*, 2011).

Farm-level use of untreated wastewater for irrigation will increase in future, with increasing demands on fresh-water resources, in both rural and peri-urban areas (Scheierling *et al.*, 2011). Already in northern China, farmers apply wastewater on an estimated $40,000\,km^2$ of farmland, with potentially harmful impacts on soil and water resources (Zhang *et al.*, 2010). Worldwide, an estimated one-fourth of the 800 million farmers engaged in urban agriculture irrigate with some form of low-quality water, including untreated wastewater (Qadir *et al.*, 2010). Economic incentives, such as the development of certified, consumer-safe labelling programmes for vegetables produced by farmers who use risk-reducing methods when irrigating with wastewater, might be well received by farmers and consumers in areas where fresh vegetables are sold directly into retail markets (Wichelns *et al.*, 2011).

Point and Nonpoint Sources Require Different Approaches

Overlaying this geographic approach to water quality issues (urban, rural, and peri-urban) is the distinction between point and nonpoint sources of pollutants. Factories, processing plants, and some livestock feeding facilities are point sources, at which pollution discharges can be monitored, measured, and assessed at reasonable cost. Point sources of pollution are easier to regulate than nonpoint sources. Many environmental agencies in Asia and elsewhere have implemented successful point source reduction programmes. Many of the improvements in water quality observed in recent years are the result of those successful efforts.

The primary source of water quality degradation in many rural areas is runoff from farm fields. Fertilizers, pesticides, and other farm chemicals find their way into surface streams and aquifers in a manner that essentially precludes any affordable mapping of pollutant loads to sources. Generally it is not possible to determine how much pollution any one farmer or household generates, or to apportion responsibility for ambient concentrations or loads across an agricultural community. Thus, some of the regulatory programmes and financial incentives that are effective in reducing point source pollution are not effective in reducing pollution from nonpoint sources.

Water quality degradation in peri-urban areas involves a mix of point and nonpoint sources. The small-scale households utilizing commingled stream water and wastewater for irrigation are engaged in a nonpoint source activity, while factories and processing plants discharge effluent through pipes or other outlets that can be monitored at reasonable cost. Policy efforts to improve water quality are likely to focus first on the point sources of pollution, while leaving nonpoint source activities outside the scope of public policy attention.

The economic incentives most helpful in reducing point source pollution include effluent taxes and subsidies for investments in water treatment systems. Water pricing also is an important policy tool, given the link between water volumes used in production processes and the volumes of effluent discharged in many settings. Higher water prices can be helpful in reducing nonpoint source pollution as well, particularly in agriculture. Much of the surface runoff and deep percolation that carry pollutants into streams and groundwater can be reduced if farmers are motivated financially to improve their management of irrigation water. Per-unit taxes on polluting inputs also can be effective in reducing both point and nonpoint source pollution. Such taxes are particularly helpful in nonpoint settings, given the inherent difficulty of placing taxes on effluent.

The Challenge also Involves Livelihoods

The potential gains from improving water quality are substantial in Asia, due partly to the large numbers of individuals impacted by degraded water resources. Many of those individuals are quite poor and they depend on water for many aspects of their livelihood activities. Yet they often have inadequate access to affordable, high-quality water supplies, and they suffer disproportionately when water quality is degraded (Dasgupta, 2004).

Public efforts to motivate reductions in pollution in Asia must acknowledge the commercial, cultural, and spiritual implications of policies that influence the ways in which people interact with land and water resources. The potential for generating unintended impacts of policies pertaining to water quality is not trivial, particularly in areas where poverty reduction and economic development are equally important objectives. Choosing policies to enhance environmental quality, while not compromising efforts to achieve other important goals, or causing unintended harm, is not always a straightforward exercise (Dasgupta *et al.*, 2004).

An Array of Policy Tools are Available

Given the extent, severity, and complexity of water quality issues in many areas of Asia, and the critical importance of water resources in sustaining the livelihoods of many poor residents, public officials must consider an array of policy alternatives in their efforts to reduce pollution and improve water quality. In many areas, regulatory standards will be needed for some time, to protect health and welfare and to ensure consumers of the safety of their water supplies. It is likely, also, that many agencies will continue using command-and-control approaches to water quality management, in which firms are required to adopt selected technologies or to modify production practices in ways that the agencies deem will improve water quality. Yet, much can be gained by broadening the array of policy choices to include economic incentives that might be helpful in quickening the pace and reducing the cost of achieving water quality objectives.

The policy tools available for motivating reductions in point source pollution include regulations, input standards, effluent taxes, pollution permit trading, investment subsidies, and other forms of economic incentives. Regulations and input standards are generally placed within the category of command-and-control programmes, in which an environmental authority determines an appropriate standard or target and implements policies to ensure compliance. For example, an environmental authority might require that all effluent discharged from a point source meet a prescribed water quality standard. An authority might alternatively require all factories or firms to utilize a selected technology, with the goal of achieving an aggregate effluent load target or an ambient concentration standard in local or regional waterways.

Economic incentives can encourage reductions in point source pollution at lower aggregate cost than is possible through the use of command-and-control programmes. Environmental authorities are generally not effective in presupposing the best methods for achieving desirable water quality standards. In most cases, the aggregate cost of achieving a standard will be smaller if firms are motivated by an effluent tax to choose or develop the most appropriate technology for generating output while maintaining or improving water quality conditions (Jaffe *et al.*, 2003). Enabling firms to trade pollution allotments also provides a financial incentive for companies to develop low-cost methods of reducing pollution. Firms that can reduce effluent at an incremental cost, below the market value of a pollution allotment, can gain net revenue by reducing their emissions and selling some portion of their allotment to a willing buyer.

Motivating reductions in nonpoint source pollution is notably more challenging than encouraging reductions in point source effluent, due largely to the impossibility or prohibitive cost of measuring discharges from nonpoint sources. Given that inherent difficulty, economic instruments can take the form of incentive payments for the adoption of desirable production techniques, taxes on inputs that generate pollution, and payments for the attainment of ambient water quality standards. For example, farmers might be offered subsidies to implement soil conservation practices to reduce erosion. They might also face taxes per unit of fertilizer or pesticide. Groups of farmers might be given financial compensation in exchange for achieving a regional ambient concentration standard at a designated site within an agricultural watershed. The goal of such programmes is to impose or engender financial responsibility on the part of producers (farmers) who generate nonpoint source pollution, given that alternative efforts to enforce techniques or measure individual contributions to pollutant loads generally would not be effective.

The Evidence in Asia is Limited, but Encouraging

Several low- to middle-income countries in Asia are using economic incentives to improve water quality, most notably in urban areas. For example, the Phnom Penh Water Supply Authority and the Bangkok Metropolitan Waterworks Authority have restructured their tariff systems to include separate volumetric rates for domestic and industrial consumers (Biswas & Tortajada, 2010; Babel et al., 2010). China has implemented an Urban Water Quota Management System that aims to match the demand for water with the available supply, and to formalize the water entitlements of prefectures and individual consumers within prefectures (Fu, 2008; Jiang et al., 2008; Jin et al., 2004). Metro Manila Water Authorities have used payment guarantees to attract investments from the private sector in water infrastructure (Porciuncula, 2009).

China Has Implemented Several Incentive Programmes

Long ago, local and provincial authorities in China recognized the potential role of policies incorporating economic incentives in reducing waste discharge into waterways. In 1995, the city of Shanghai established the legal foundation for pollution permit trading with the passage of the Shanghai Regulation of Environmental Protection Law (Wang et al., 2008a). In the first case of pollution trading in China, the Minhang Tangwang Electroplating Facility was closed and its wastewater discharge permit (10 tons per day) was traded to the Shanghai Steel Facility (Wang et al., 2004). It is not clear whether pollution trading has been sustained in Shanghai since the 1990s, but water quality conditions in the city have deteriorated with continuous expansion of industrial and residential activities (Zhang et al., 2008). Perhaps the concept of permit trading could be extended to include trades involving both point and nonpoint sources, and both urban and peri-urban settings, given that many industries have been moved some distance from the city centre (Wang et al., 2008a).

Economic incentives are less common in rural areas, but China has experimented with several approaches in recent years. Policy makers are motivated by the increasing demand for fresh water in the country, the unsustainable overdraft of aquifers in northern provinces, and the degraded quality of water in many rivers and lakes (Cai, 2008). One consequence of the rapid increase in economic development in China since the late 1970s has been the establishment of many small-scale rural enterprises that discharge waste materials, with little or no treatment, into surface waters (Skinner et al., 2003). An estimated 80% of the industrial waste in China, generated largely in rural areas, is untreated, and is discharged into rivers, lakes, and the sea (Wang et al., 2008b). Ongley *et al.* (2010) describe the array of nonpoint sources of water quality degradation in China, and they suggest that substantial time might be required to develop a comprehensive approach to reducing nonpoint source pollution.

Reducing pollution from small-scale rural enterprises through regulatory measures is made difficult by the dispersed nature of production and the desire of many local governments to promote economic growth. Thus, many local governments in China are shifting their focus from regulatory measures to economic incentives that motivate farmers to assume responsibility for reducing nonpoint source pollution (Chen *et al.*, 2008; Shao, 2010). While the shift in policy focus is likely to require substantial time and effort, the intent is appropriate, given the inherent difficulty of achieving water quality improvements in nonpoint source settings when relying only on regulatory programmes. In addition, economic incentives to reduce pollution can be designed in ways that do not restrict economic development.

Much of China's rural population obtains drinking water from surface streams and lakes that are subject to pollution from agricultural, industrial, and domestic sources (Qu *et al.*, 2011). The remarkable economic growth that has occurred in rural areas since 1978 has brought about notable increases in waste generation, with consequent impacts on water quality (Cheng & Hu, 2011). Chen *et al.* (2008) suggest that domestic waste production per person is approaching the level observed in urban areas, while rural wastewater discharge per person is almost half the rate in cities. The rate of investment in rural waste collection and treatment facilities has not kept pace with the increase in waste generation, to the detriment of water quality in many areas. Qi *et al.* (1999) suggest that 80% of China's rivers reflect some degree of contamination. Also, in many rural areas shallow groundwater is polluted by wastewater discharges from industrial sources (Xie, 2009).

China implemented national water pricing regulations in 2004, with the goal of promoting wiser use of water in agriculture and other sectors (Qu *et al.*, 2011). Water tariffs in many cities now include both a water supply fee and a wastewater treatment fee. In some cities, the tariff also includes a component that reflects the environmental or scarcity value of water resources (Jiang *et al.*, 2011). Addressing scarcity values directly in the water pricing structure can be quite helpful in encouraging users to consider a wider range of incremental costs and benefits when determining how much water to divert for irrigation and other activities. The opportunity to trade water also provides an economic incentive to use water wisely, whether one is a buyer or a seller in the marketplace.

In recent years, China also has allowed the price of fertilizer to increase in response to demand and supply conditions, in part to reduce nonpoint source pollution by encouraging farmers to discontinue applying excessive amounts of fertilizer (Qu *et al.*, 2011). Wei *et al.* (2009) examine the excessive use of irrigation water and nitrogen on farms in Inner Mongolia, where nitrate leaching into groundwater is a pressing policy issue. The authors show that increases in the price of irrigation water would motivate reductions in nitrate leaching, but would also reduce farm income. They also show that if the water price increases were combined with subsidies for adopting nitrate leaching mitigation practices, the improvements in water quality could be achieved at lower cost.

China's recent experience with institutional reform and economic incentives in the irrigation sector is informative for those seeking guidance regarding similar structures for use in improving water quality. With the goal of motivating efficient use of irrigation water in northern China, the central government in the mid-1990s began encouraging local groups of farmers to form water user associations or hire contractors to manage the allocation and delivery of irrigation water. Water user associations are overseen by boards of directors elected by farmers, while contractors are paid a fixed fee for services. Some contractors are paid a flat fee per hectare of service area, while others might be compensated in part for the quality of service they provide (Huang *et al.*, 2010).

In their study of traditional, contractual, and water user association management structures, Huang *et al.* (2010) find that water user associations provide greater transparency regarding water delivery operations, invest more in canal maintenance, provide higher-quality delivery service, and collect a larger proportion of service fees than either the traditional or contractual forms of governance. In addition, Huang *et al.* (2010) found that in villages in which managers were provided a financial incentive to reduce water deliveries, water use declined by about 40%, without impacting crop yields. It is likely that water quality objectives could be added to the set of goals a water user association manager is charged with achieving each year, and that a financial incentive programme could be designed to increase the likelihood of success.

China also provides helpful examples of payment-for-environmental-services (PES) programmes, which can be designed to improve both land and water management. Perhaps the most widely known of China's PES programmes are the Sloping Land Conversion Programme (also called Grain for Green) and the Natural Forest Protection Project. In both programmes, farmers are compensated for converting their current land use to an activity that reduces soil erosion, improves watershed management, or enhances biodiversity (Bennett *et al.*, 2011; Yu *et al.*, 2011; Wang & Maclaren, 2012). In theory, the public is willing to compensate the farmers for the opportunity costs imposed by the conversion, because the public gains the benefits of the environmental services. This theory applies also to the protection of water quality.

In 2005, Fuzhou City, which is located at the downstream end of the Min River basin, crafted a PES agreement with the upstream municipalities of Nanping and Sanming for the purpose of improving water quality in the river (Jiang *et al.*, 2011). The Min River is the primary source of drinking water for Fuzhou City's 2.3 million residents, and thus they are motivated to invest in upstream activities that would improve river water quality. A survey conducted in 2003 showed that 63% of the chemical oxygen demand and nitrogen loads in the Min River could be attributed to pollution from upstream livestock production. In Nanping alone, there are 480,000 livestock farms (Jiang *et al.*, 2011). Fuzhou City, the provincial government, and other impacted municipalities agreed to provide up to CNY100 million per year in exchange for the implementation of pollution-reducing livestock production practices in Nanping and Sanming. The results of the PES programme are not yet documented, but the intent and design are consistent with the conceptual underpinnings of a potentially viable incentive programme.

Thailand also Uses Incentives to Improve Water Quality

The Royal Thai Government began promoting the use of economic instruments to improve water quality management in 1992, with the passage of the Enhancement and Conservation of National Environmental Quality Act (NEQA) (Sujaritpong & Nitivattanonon, 2009). The legislation established an Environmental Fund from which local government agencies could obtain subsidized loans for the construction of wastewater treatment plants. The goal was to promote such investments across Thailand, in the interest of improving water quality, following many years of rapid economic growth in the country (Rammont & Amin, 2010).

The NEQA gave legal status to the notion of charging for wastewater services, as agencies receiving loans from the Environmental Fund would be required to implement wastewater charges. The agencies were also expected to contribute 5% of the revenue they generated through charges to refurbish and expand the Environmental Fund (Rammont & Amin, 2010). That requirement, while conceptually appealing and economically sound, has contributed to the very limited use of the Environmental Fund by local governments, which are reluctant to impose charges on their customers (Rammont & Amin, 2010). As of 2009, of the 95 local government authorities operating wastewater treatment facilities, only 3 had implemented wastewater tariffs (Simachaya, 2009).

Of the three governments implementing wastewater charges, one chose to establish a fixed rate per business or residence, while two selected a volumetric price schedule. In Patong, the fixed rates were set at THB400 per year for houses and THB600 per room per year for hotels (Simachaya, 2009). Fixed rates are helpful in raising revenue to pay for operations and maintenance, but they do not provide incentive to reduce wastewater volumes. In Pattaya, the local government set the initial wastewater charge at THB2.5 per m^3 in 2001, with the goal of increasing the rate by THB0.25 per m^3 each year through 2020. Local officials in Saensuk included a water quality component in their volumetric charge, such that customers generating wastewater with less than 200 mg/L biochemical oxygen demand are required to pay THB2 per m^3.

In one sense, Thailand's conceptual support for wastewater charges is notable, yet implementation of payment programmes has been quite limited. Simachaya (2009) suggests that several factors have contributed to this apparent conundrum: (1) the lack of commitment on the part of the Royal Thai Government, (2) a weak sense of ownership on the part of local government agencies, (3) an apparent disconnect between customer willingness to pay and agency willingness to charge for wastewater services, (4) politicization of the tariff-setting process, (5) institutional separation of water and wastewater services, and (6) capacity limitations within local government agencies.

While the central government favours the notion of establishing wastewater charges, it has placed the burden of designing and implementing cost-recovery programmes on local government agencies. Those groups may perceive that customers are not willing to pay for wastewater service, and thus be reluctant to implement a fee structure. Yet consumers might actually be willing to pay for service, provided they understood the costs and benefits. Roomratanapun (2001) found that two-thirds of Bangkok residents generally preferred centralized wastewater treatment systems, and most were willing to pay either a flat fee or a volumetric charge for wastewater service. The estimated rates of willingness to pay were THB87 per month or THB3.28 per m^3. By coincidence, the rate proposed (thought not implemented) by the Bangkok Metropolitan Authority was BHT3.50 per m^3. Despite this apparent willingness to pay, at a rate that would provide substantial revenue, the Bangkok Metropolitan Authority has not yet enforced the collection of wastewater fees (Rammont & Amin, 2010).

Perhaps one of the most visible cases of water quality degradation in Thailand in recent years has been the impact of aquacultural operations on surface and coastal waters. The aquaculture industry grew rapidly during the late 1980s and early 1990s in Thailand, in response to increasing global demand for farmed shrimp. Many small-scale farmers converted rice paddies into shrimp ponds and began cultivating high-density stocks that required heavy inputs of feed and chemicals. The farmers discharged the wastewater from their ponds with little concern for off-site impacts, thus creating large areas of badly degraded soil and water resources (Bluffstone *et al.*, 2006).

The Thachin River basin provides a useful example of the environmental impacts of aquaculture in Thailand and the challenges of improving water quality in an area with many point and nonpoint sources of pollution. Intensive crop and livestock production occur on more than half the area of the basin, and the operations are characterized by heavy use of fertilizer and pesticides (Schaffner *et al.*, 2009). The region produces 15% of Thailand's pork and 6% of its poultry output, by value. Aquaculture has been increasing in the basin, extending gradually from coastal lands in the south to inland areas along the Thachin River. Many industries also discharge untreated effluent into the Thachin River, thus contributing to a notably polluted waterway with high concentrations of many undesirable constituents (Klayklung *et al.*, 2010).

Given the number and complexity of water pollution sources in the Thachin River basin, a single policy approach or a one-dimensional programme would not be successful in improving water quality. Rather, local officials might consider a programme that includes combinations of regulatory measures and economic incentives. For example, they might implement effluent charges at point source sites, while also requiring the attainment of ambient concentration standards at selected monitoring stations along the river. The rate of the effluent charge might be allowed to vary in accordance with observed concentrations at the monitoring stations. Officials might also consider requiring shrimp farmers to report their effluent discharges and be subject to financial penalties if the reports are not produced. Officials might also impose a charge per ton of sludge discharged from aquaculture operations (Bluffstone *et al.*, 2006).

Other Countries also Combine Economic Incentives with Other Measures

Several countries in Asia rely on combinations of incentives and other regulatory or educational programmes to motivate improvements in water quality. For many years, public officials in rural areas of low- to middle-income Asian countries have relied on awareness and information campaigns to boost demand for clean water and safer sanitation. For example, information campaigns that encourage the uptake of point-of-use technology (such as boiling water) have been used to ensure that the quality of water consumed is better than that at source.

Community-level infrastructure (such as the construction of common wells, with either community financing or co-financing), and joint implementation of water use rules that best suit the terrain and cultural norms of an area, have been encouraged in rural South Asia, with a view toward ensuring and securing the rights of access to improved water quality (Isham & Kahkonen, 2001; Prokopy, 2005). However, such programmes often are donor dependent, and many are implemented in isolation, rather than as part of a comprehensive policy programme.

Policy makers in high-income Asian countries also have experimented with economic incentives in both urban and rural areas. For example, Japanese authorities offer direct payments to farmers who irrigate their rice fields in cascade fashion, such that the runoff from one field becomes irrigation supply to the next. Farmers are also rewarded for reducing fertilizer applications, with the goal of improving water quality in lakes across Japan. The lakes are an important source of drinking water in the country, and thus the public is willing to pay farmers for the service of ensuring that water quality is maintained at high levels (Yamada, 2007; Nakano *et al.*, 2008; Shiratani *et al.*, 2010).

The Republic of Korea has implemented a programme of variable emission standards that recognizes differences in treatment levels and costs between industries and watersheds in an effort to increase the efficiency and efficacy of water quality programmes (Shin, 2007). At the same time, Korea measures the concentrations of nonpoint source pollutants and compiles data regarding abatement technology, with the goal of establishing guidelines for the construction, operation, and maintenance of pollution abatement facilities (Shin, 2007; Yamada, 2007).

Poorer countries also have implemented combinations of incentive and regulatory programmes to motivate improvements in water quality. India has offered farmers transitional payments to assist them in converting to a programme of organic farming, with the goal of reducing water pollution (Hope *et al.*, 2008). In New Delhi, public-private partnerships have been promoted to attract investments in the water sector (Ali *et al.*, 2009; Butala *et al.*, 2010). Authorities in urban areas of Cambodia, Thailand, and Iran have combined volumetric pricing and block-rate tariffs in water pricing structures that differentiate between domestic and industrial water uses (Sadr, 2001; Babel *et al.*, 2010; Biswas & Tortajada, 2010). Authorities in rural areas of Laos have launched public-health campaigns to boost demand for sanitation and increase awareness of water quality issues (Lamaningao, 2002; Lahiri & Chantanpone, 2003).

Institutions, Expertise and Political Will are Essential

Technical expertise, judicial recognition, and the support of politicians and public leaders are essential conditions for implementing economic incentives. In addition, there must be a well-developed institutional structure in which public agencies are charged with overseeing incentive programmes with the full support of appropriate legal authorities. Kumar *et al.* (2009) demonstrate that limited staff support, inadequate financial resources, and poorly developed technical expertise limit the effectiveness of solid waste management in India. With such poor baseline conditions, new forms of water quality programmes that rely on economic incentives are not likely to be successful.

In Cambodia, the Phnom Penh Water Supply Authority successfully redesigned its tariff structure, thanks largely to the notable technical expertise of its employees, who maintain a current list of consumers and meter all connections. At the same time, the public utility functions as a business operation, without requiring direct contact with government departments (Biswas & Tortajada, 2010). Similarly, in Thailand, effective corporate governance and an operational management structure were critical in ensuring success of the Malina Water Company and the Bangkok Metropolitan Waterworks Authority (Wu & Malaluan, 2008; Babel *et al.*, 2010). In New Delhi, microfinance has been identified as an important source of funds to support the renovation of infrastructure, with the goal of providing better supply coverage and ensuring improved water quality (Butala *et al.*, 2010).

Perhaps the most important component of a successful effort to implement economic incentives is political will. Public officials must be willing to trust the role of economic incentives in motivating desirable outcomes on the part of individuals and firms, and they must provide the necessary institutional, legal, and financial support. Singapore's ability to improve water quality and extend supply coverage was made possible by a strong political will that produced very effective legal and regulatory frameworks (Tortajada, 2006).

Similarly, China's introduction of an urban water quota management programme has succeeded, in part, due to the political commitment of authorities at the national level. The centralized governance structure that characterizes political leadership in both Singapore and China is conducive to providing the necessary political will. In countries with a more decentralized framework, greater effort might be needed to cultivate and maintain political will across a range of state or provincial governments seeking to implement economic incentives in support of water quality improvements.

Economic Incentives are Consistent with Economic Growth Objectives

Public and commercial support for economic incentives to improve water quality is likely to increase with economic development. During the early stages of development, public agencies might overlook or mildly regulate water-polluting activities in the interest of encouraging economic growth. Over time, as economies expand and household wealth increases, citizens begin to call for improvements in environmental amenities, including water quality. At the same time, many firms and residents will have gained notable experience with economic interactions in commerce and industry. Thus, the notion of designing pollution reduction policies that incorporate economic incentives should find greater public support with increasing economic development.

A policy approach that relies on economic incentives will support sustainable economic growth, provided that policy parameters reflect the pertinent costs and benefits of production and consumption activities. In theory, economic incentives to adopt desirable practices should reflect the incremental benefit that accrues to society. Effluent taxes should reflect the incremental harm that pollution imposes on the public. Selecting policy parameters that reflect accurate estimates of incremental benefits and costs will motivate those who generate pollution to internalize the external impacts of their activities. The resulting production decisions and output levels will then be consistent with the goal of sustaining economic growth while not depleting or destroying environmental amenities.

Effluent charges, by design, allow for economic expansion, while effluent standards can limit economic growth. When an environmental agency implements a regional effluent standard, in terms of either a total load or an ambient concentration, firm-level activity might become constrained by the standard. For example, suppose an agency implements a total load standard of 100 tons of discharge per year into a river. Once that amount of load is reached, economic activity might be unable to expand. Current firms might need to cease production, while new firms might be prevented from establishing operations. In this manner, a regional load standard can restrict economic growth. An ambient concentration standard could have the same impact, as commercial or industrial activities would be constrained to an aggregate level that ensures attainment of the concentration target. At the same time, if cleaner production technology becomes available, then the socially optimal amount of pollution would decrease, all else equal, reflecting the lower incremental cost of abatement. Thus, effluent charges offer greater flexibility to firms and regulators in changing economic environments. Effluent standards, by contrast, do not allow timely responses to changes in abatement technology or in the incremental costs or benefits of polluting activities.

The regional economic impact of a programme of effluent charges would be quite different. Suppose an environmental authority establishes an effluent charge of $2,000 per ton of discharge, based on the agency's estimates of resulting loads and concentrations. Any firm wishing to expand or begin production could do so, provided the firm paid the charge of $2,000 for each ton of effluent discharged. As long as the incremental net revenue from sales is greater than $2,000 per ton of effluent, firms will expand production and pay the charge. Clearly, there is a risk that the resulting sum of discharges will be greater than planned, and the agency might then need to reconsider the level of the effluent charge it has established. Yet when using an effluent charge in place of an effluent standard, agencies have the opportunity to observe firm-level responses that reflect market conditions and the incremental cost of abating pollution, while retaining the authority to modify the effluent charges accordingly. The process of implementing, observing, and adjusting can generate substantial information for the agency, firms, and the public, regarding the incremental costs and benefits of achieving alternative water quality objectives. Such information is less likely to be generated when implementing effluent standards.

Summing Up

Water quality issues in Asia are numerous, complex, and of long standing. The level of effort invested in improving water quality and the nature of programmes implemented vary widely, particularly in the less developed countries. In many areas, firms, farmers, and residents have discharged pollutants in point and nonpoint source settings for many years with little or no regulation. With increasing population density and persistent poverty in many regions, government agencies are unable or reluctant to impose programmes that might reduce water pollution at the cost of restricting economic growth. It is very difficult to regulate the production activities of tens or hundreds of thousands of small-scale producers in a single watershed. It can also be politically unpopular.

Economic incentives are not a panacea for achieving water quality objectives in Asia. Yet they might be of value in some settings and in combination with other regulatory and educational programmes. Positive incentives, such as subsidies for investing in newer production techniques that are less polluting, or payments for achieving effluent load reductions, can motivate desirable improvements while being well received by participating farmers and firms. Negative incentives, such as effluent taxes and penalties for not achieving pollution reduction targets, also can be well received, if the parameter values reflect accurate estimates of the incremental costs of compliance and reasonable estimates of the social values inherent in achieving water quality goals.

The experience to date with economic incentives in Asia is mixed but encouraging. China and Thailand have gained notable experience with several programmes that have provided useful opportunities to observe firm-level responsiveness and the resulting changes in water quality conditions. Japan and Korea have achieved notable successes, but those results might be expected, given the more advanced status of water quality authorities and the higher levels of public and institutional support for environmental improvement programmes in those countries. In all four of these countries, and in others, public officials are turning much of their effort to reducing nonpoint source pollution, as the relative importance of nonpoint sources increases. The degree of success in all countries will depend to a large extent on the levels of institutional and political support for new programmes to improve water quality. Yet, such support is not yet sufficiently strong in many settings.

Looking forward, we should expect to see greater use of economic incentives to improve water quality, both alone and in combination with other regulatory measures. Economic incentives can be designed in ways that are consistent with economic growth objectives, and incentives are likely to gain appreciation by firms and farmers as economies expand. Additional research describing innovative uses of economic incentives will be helpful in encouraging public agencies to implement incentive-based programmes. So, too, will be efforts to encourage greater public awareness of the critical nature of many water quality issues in Asia, and the potential benefits that improvements in water quality will bring to so many residents in the region. Much of humanity will enjoy better health and welfare as the water upon which they depend becomes cleaner and safer for drinking and for use in agricultural production and other livelihood activities.

References

Akbar, F., Ishaq, M., Khan, S., Ihsanullah, I., Ahmada, I. & Shakirullaha, M. (2010) A comparative study of human health risks via consumption of food crops grown on wastewater irrigated soil (Peshawar) and relatively clean water irrigated soil (lower Dir), *Journal of Hazardous Materials*, 179(1–3), pp. 612–621.

Ali, S. I., Hall, K. R., Aronson, K. & Philip, L. (2009) Humanitarian engineering in Mylai Balaji Nagar: an integrated water, environment and public health project for slums in the Indian subcontinent, *Desalination*, 248(1–3), pp. 418–427.

Azizullah, A., Khattak, M. N. K., Richter, P. & Hader, D. P. (2011) Water pollution in Pakistan and its impact on public health: a review, *Environment International*, 37(2), pp. 479–497.

Babel, M. S., Rivas, A. A. & Kallidalkurichi, S. (2010) Municipal water supply management in Bangkok: achievements and lessons, *International Journal of Water Resources Development*, 26(2), pp. 193–217.

Bartram, J., Lewis, K., Lenton, R. & Wright, A. (2005) Focusing on improved water and sanitation for health, *The Lancet*, 365, pp. 810–812.

Bennett, M. T., Mehta, A. & Xu, J. (2011) Incomplete property rights, exposure to markets and the provision of environmental services in China, *China Economic Review*, 22(4), pp. 485–498.

Biswas, A. K. & Tortajada, C. (2010) Water supply of Phnom Penh: an example of good governance, *International Journal of Water Resources Development*, 26(2), pp. 157–172.

Bluffstone, R. A., Anantanasuwong, D. & Ruzicka, I. (2006) Mixing economic and administrative instruments: the case of shrimp aquaculture in Thailand, *Environment and Development Economics*, 11(5), pp. 651–667.

Butala, N. M., VanRooyen, M. J. & Patel, R. B. (2010) Improved health outcomes in urban slums through infrastructure upgrading, *Social Science & Medicine*, 71(5), pp. 935–940.

Cai, X. (2008) Water stress, water transfer and social equity in northern China: implications for policy reforms, *Journal of Environmental Management*, 87(1), pp. 14–25.

Chen, M., Chen, J. & Sun, F. (2008) Agricultural phosphorus flow and its environmental impacts in China, *Science of the Total Environment*, 405(1–3), pp. 140–152.

Cheng, H. & Hu, Y. (2011) Improving China's water resources management for better adaptation to climate change, *Climatic Change*, published online 5 March. DOI: 10.1007/s10584-011-0042-8.

Dasgupta, P. (2004) Valuing health damages from water pollution in urban Delhi, India: a health production function approach, *Environment and Development Economics*, 9(1), pp. 83–106.

Dasgupta, P., Shyamsundar, P. & Maler, K. (2004) The economics of environmental change and pollution management: issues and approaches from South Asia, *Environment and Development Economics*, 9(1), pp. 9–18.

Fu, B. (2008) Blue skies for China, *Science*, 321(5889), p. 611.

Holm, P. E., Marcussen, H. & Dalsgaard, A. (2009) Fate and risks of potentially toxic elements in wastewater-fed food production systems: the examples of Cambodia and Vietnam, *Irrigation & Drainage Systems*, 24(1), pp. 1–16.

Hope, R., Borgoyary, M. & Agarwat, C. (2008) Smallholder preferences for agri-environmental change at the Bhoj wetland, India, *Development Policy Review*, 26(5), pp. 585–602.

Huang, Q., Wang, J., Easter, K. W. & Rozelle, S. (2010) Empirical assessment of water management institutions in northern China, *Agricultural Water Management*, 98(2), pp. 361–369.

Isham, J. & Kahkonen, S. (2001) Institutional determinants of the impact of community-based water services: evidence from Sri Lanka and India, Available at: SSRN: http://ssrn.com/abstract=279061. DOI: 10.2139/ssrn.279061.

Jaffe, A. B., Newell, R. G. & Stavins, R. N. (2003) Technological change and the environment, in: K. G. Maler & J. R. Vincent (Eds) *Handbook of Environmental Economics: Environmental Degradation and Institutional Responses*, pp. 461–507. (Amsterdam: Elsevier, North-Holland).

Jiang, Y., Jin, L. & Lin, T. (2011) Higher water tariffs for less river pollution: evidence from the Min River and Fuzhou City in China, *China Economic Review*, 22(2), pp. 183–195.

Jiang, Y. L., Chen, Y. S. & He, H. P. (2008) Studies on principle of quota management of water resources, *China Water Resources*, 17, pp. 6–8 [in Chinese].

Jin, M. H., Tang, W. J. & Qi, L. L. (2004) Water quota principle for industrial enterprises products, *China Standardization*, 2, pp. 47–49 [in Chinese].

Khan, A. H., Rasul, S. B., Munir, A. K. M., Alauddin, M., Habibuddowlah, M. & Hussam, A. (2000) On two simple arsenic removal methods for groundwater of Bangladesh, in: M. F. Ahmed (Ed.) *Bangladesh Environment-2000*, pp. 151–173, (Bangladesh Poribesh Andolon).

Khan, S., Cao, Q., Zheng, Y. M., Huang, Y. Z. & Zhu, Y. G. (2008) Health risks of heavy metals in contaminated soils and food crops irrigated with wastewater in Beijing, China, *Environmental Pollution*, 152(3), pp. 686–691.

Klayklung, R., Tingsbadh, C. & Gajaseni, N. (2010) Surface water pollution control by appropriate effluent taxation: the Thachin River Basin Study, Thailand, *Journal of Applied Sciences*, 10(15), pp. 1492–1510.

Kumar, S., Bhattacharya, J. K., Vaidya, A. N., Chakrabarti, T., Devotta, S. & Akolkar, A. B. (2009) Assessment of the status of municipal solid waste management in metro cities, state capitals, class I cities, and class II towns in India: an insight, *Waste Management*, 29(2), pp. 883–895.

Lahiri, D. & Chanthapone, S. (2003) Water, sanitation and hygiene: a situation analysis paper for Lao PDR, *International Journal of Environmental Health Research*, 13, pp. S107–S114.

Lamaningao, P. (2002) HASWAS Project implementation, paper accepted for the 28th Water, Engineering and Development Centre (WEDC) Conference, 18–22 November, Kolkata (Calcutta).

Nakano, T., Tayasu, I., Yamada, Y., Hosono, T., Igeta, A., Hyodo, F., Ando, A., Saitoh, Y., Tanaka, T., Wada, E. & Yachi, S. (2008) Effect of agriculture on water quality of Lake Biwa tributaries, Japan, *Science of the Total Environment*, 389(1), pp. 132–148.

Ongley, E. D., Zhang, X. & Yu, T. (2010) Current status of agricultural and rural non-point source pollution assessment in China, *Environmental Pollution*, 158(5), pp. 1159–1168.

Ooi, G. L. (2009) Challenges of sustainability for Asian urbanization, *Current Opinion in Environmental Sustainability*, 1(2), pp. 187–191.

Patel, R. B. & Burke, T. F. (2009) Urbanization: an emerging humanitarian disaster, *New England Journal of Medicine*, 361(8), pp. 741–743.

Porciuncula, A. D. (2009) Creative financing solution for water supply and sanitation in the Philippines, *Ocean & Coastal Management*, 52(7), pp. 374–377.

Prokopy, L. S. (2005) The relationship between participation and project outcomes: evidence from rural water supply projects in India, *World Development*, 33(11), pp. 1801–1819.

Qadir, M., Wichelns, D., Raschid-Sally, L., McCornick, P. G., Drechsel, P., Bahri, A. & Minhas, P. S. (2010) The challenges of wastewater irrigation in developing countries, *Agricultural Water Management*, 97(4), pp. 561–568.

Qi, F., Cheng, G. D. & Masao, D. (1999) Water resources in China: problems and countermeasures, *Ambio*, 28(2), pp. 202–203.

Qu, F., Kuyvenhoven, A., Shi, X. & Heerink, N. (2011) Sustainable natural resource use in rural China: recent trends and policies, *China Economic Review*, 22(4), pp. 444–460.

Rammont, L. & Amin, A. T. M. N. (2010) Constraints in using economic instruments in developing countries: some evidence from Thailand's experience in wastewater management, *Habitat International*, 34(1), pp. 28–37.

Raschid-Sally, L., Carr, R. & Buechler, S. (2005) Managing wastewater agriculture to improve livelihoods and environmental quality in poor countries, *Irrigation and Drainage*, 56, (Suppl. 1) pp. S11–S22.

Roomratanapun, W. (2001) Introducing centralized wastewater treatment in Bangkok: a study of factors determining its acceptability, *Habitat International*, 25(3), pp. 359–371.

Sadr, K. (2001) Water markets and pricing in Iran, In: N. I. Faruqui A. K. Biswas & M. J. Bion (Eds) *Water Management in Islam*, (International Development Research Council: IDRC/UNU Press).

Schaffner, M., Bader, H. & Scheidegger, R. (2009) Modeling the contribution of point sources and non-point sources to Thachin River water pollution, *Science of the Total Environment*, 407(17), pp. 4902–4915.

Scheierling, S. M., Bartone, C. R., Mara, D. D. & Drechsel, P. (2011) Towards an agenda for improving wastewater use in agriculture, *Water International*, 36(4), pp. 420–440.

Shao, W. (2010) Effectiveness of water protection policy in China: a case study in Jiaxing, *Science of the Total Environment*, 408(4), pp. 690–701.

Shin, H. S. (2007) Water resource policies and management in Korea, *Water, Science and Technology: Water Supply*, 7(2), pp. 49–56.

Shiratani, E., Munakata, Y., Yoshinaga, I., Kubota, T., Hamada, K. & Tahayoshi, H. (2010) Scenario analysis for reduction of pollutant load discharged from a watershed by recycling of treated water for irrigation, *Journal of Environmental Sciences*, 22(6), pp. 878–884.

Simachaya, W. (2009) Wastewater tariffs in Thailand, *Ocean & Coastal Management*, 52(7), pp. 378–382.

Skinner, M. W., Joseph, A. E. & Kuhn, R. G. (2003) Social and environmental regulation in rural China: bringing the changing role of local government into focus, *Geoforum*, 34(2), pp. 267–281.

Srinivasan, J. T. & Reddy, V. R. (2009) Impact of irrigation water quality on human health: a case study in India, *Ecological Economics*, 68(11), pp. 2800–2807.

Sujaritpong, S. & Nitivattanonon, V. (2009) Factors influencing wastewater management performance: case study of housing estates in suburban Bangkok, Thailand, *Journal of Environmental Management*, 90(1), pp. 455–465.

Tortajada, C. (2006) Water management in Singapore, *International Journal of Water Resources Development*, 22(2), pp. 227–240.

Wang, C. & Maclaren, V. (2012) Evaluation of economic and social impacts of the sloping land conversion program: a case study in Dunhua County, China, *Forest Policy and Economics*, 14(1), pp. 50–57.

Wang, J., Da, L., Song, K. & Li, B. L. (2008a) Temporal variations of surface water quality in urban, suburban and rural areas during rapid urbanization in Shanghai, China, *Environmental Pollution*, 152(2), pp. 387–393.

Wang, M., Webber, M., Finlayson, B. & Barnett, J. (2008b) Rural industries and water pollution in China, *Journal of Environmental Management*, 86(4), pp. 648–659.

Wang, X., Zhang, W., Huang, Y. & Li, S. (2004) Modeling and simulation of point-non-point source effluent trading in Taihu Lake area: perspective of non-point sources control in China, *Science of the Total Environment*, 325(1–3), pp. 39–50.

Weckenbrock, P., Evans, A., Majeed, M. Q., Ahmad, W., Bashir, N. & Drescher, A. (2011) Fighting for the right to use wastewater: what drives the use of untreated wastewater in a periurban village of Faisalabad, Pakistan? *Water International*, 36(4), pp. 522–534.

Wei, Y., Chen, D., Hu, K., Willet, I. R. & Langford, J. (2009) Policy incentives for reducing nitrate leaching from intensive agriculture in desert oases of Alxa, *Inner Mongolia, China, Agricultural Water Management*, 96(7), pp. 1114–1119.

Wichelns, D., Owaygen, M. & Redwood, M. (2011) Developing country farmers need more than financial incentives to reduce the risks of wastewater irrigation, *Water International*, 36(4), pp. 467–475.

Wu, X. & Malaluan, N. A. (2008) A tale of two concessionaires: a natural experiment of water privatisation in metro Manila, *Urban Studies*, 45(1), pp. 207–229.

Xie, J. (2009) *Addressing China's water scarcity: recommendations for selected water resource management issues* (Washington, DC: World Bank).

Yamada, K. (2007) Diffuse pollution in Japan: issues and perspectives, *Water Science & Technology*, 56(1), pp. 11–22.

Yu, D. Y., Shi, P. J., Han, G. Y., Zhu, W. Q., Du, S. Q. & Xun, B. (2011) Forest ecosystem restoration due to a national conservation plan in China, *Ecological Engineering*, 37(9), pp. 1387–1397.

Zhang, H., Wang, X., Ho, H. H. & Yong, Y. (2008) Eco-health evaluation for the Shanghai metropolitan area during the recent industrial transformation (1990–2003), *Journal of Environmental Management*, 88(4), pp. 1047–1055.

Zhang, J., Mauzerall, D. L., Zhu, T., Liang, S., Ezzati, M. & Remais, J. V. (2010) Environmental health in China: progress towards clean air and safe water, *The Lancet*, 375, pp. 1110–1119.

Exploring the Boundaries of Water Quality Management in Asia

JAMES E. NICKUM

International Water Resources Association

ABSTRACT   *Beginning with the case of iodine-131 detection in Tokyo's water supply in March 2011, this paper explores the boundaries of water quality management, with focus on Asian cities. Boundaries include those of definition, of measurement, of the significance of measurements, of public perceptions and trust, of disjunctures between human and natural systems, of dis-integrated water resources management, and of social and political marginality. Delineating these boundaries, most of them well known, is not a call for inaction or despair, but for clarity and recognition of the difficult road ahead.*

A Hard Rain Might Have Fallen: The Prelude

This paper is an attempt to think through some of the critical limitations, or boundaries, on urban water quality management and governance in Asia—and by extension, elsewhere. Urban water quality management is a challenge everywhere, but especially in the rapidly growing and transforming cities of Asia. For example, to address urban water quality, it is increasingly necessary to reach beyond the conventional administrative boundaries of the cities. Watershed activity cannot always be shut out by protected zones; urban wastes flow downstream, or into adjoining fields as wastewater irrigation (Wichelns & Dreschel, 2011). But there are other problems beyond those that beset those who wish to manage water quality—problems of definition, of measurement, of public perception, of limits of administrative systems, and of equity. The task at hand in this article is to explore some of these boundaries of the management of water quality.

I begin with an example from my recent experience, of a rare instance when one city's water supply evoked worldwide concern. On 23 March 2011, nearly two weeks after the 9.0 magnitude East Japan Earthquake, the Tokyo government reported that iodine-131 was detected at a level of 210 Becquerels per litre (Bq/l) in a sample of treated water at a plant (the Kanamachi) supplying much of the city with water from the Edo River. This was in excess of the newly fixed government limit of 100 Bq/l deemed safe for infants, if consumed over the course of a year, but below the 300 Bq/l maximum recommended for adults.[1] These are extremely conservative standards, an order of magnitude below the 3,000 Bq/kg set by the International Atomic Energy Agency, so the warning was an excellent example of the precautionary principle in practice.[2] The government mobilized to supply bottled water to parents of infants (although apparently not to pregnant women, who were not covered by the standards).

Nonetheless, this news triggered a run on bottled water in the stores (but, at least momentarily, not in the ubiquitous public vending machines). The following day, the government announced that the measured levels had fallen back to a safe level, where they have remained ever since, it is reported. Bottled water stayed off the shelves well into April.

This example may seem a bit out of the ordinary, but it illustrates a number of issues I wish to address here, such as the nature and role of standards and problems of public perception. It is also a demonstration of the inevitable occurrence of the extraordinary and usually unforeseen, which is one of the most significant consequences of a number of "boundary problems" in urban water quality management. Other well-known instances come to mind from Asia:

- *Japan*: During the rapid economic growth period of the 1960s, largely rural Shiga Prefecture and downstream urban-industrial areas, especially Osaka, negotiated the Lake Biwa Comprehensive Development Plan, wherein the flow from Lake Biwa would be augmented for downstream uses in exchange for financial and other support for infrastructure projects in Shiga. Almost immediately upon the finalization of the agreement in 1972, the rapid-growth era came to an end, downstream industrial demand for water fell (in part due to new environmental regulations), and algal outbreaks unexpectedly began to occur in the lake, degrading water quality (Nakamura & Nakajima, 2002; Nickum & Greenstadt, 1998). The plan had been formulated in quantity and, as the name implies, developmental terms; while it retained these, environmental concerns forced themselves onto the agenda.
- *China*: A massive spill of benzene into the Songhua River due to an industrial accident in November 2005, followed by a clumsy attempt by authorities to cover it up while taking remedial action, brought intense domestic and international attention to the hazards posed by China's 21,000 riparian and coastal chemical plants and by government opacity (Watts, 2010).[3]
- *Bangladesh*: Naturally occurring arsenic in drinking water from shallow tube wells, dug to provide a safe alternative to heavily polluted surface sources, was discovered only after many years of consumption had damaged the health of many users.

The boundary problems addressed here are those of definition, of measurement, of the significance of measurements, of public perceptions and trust, of disjunctures between human and natural systems, of dis-integrated water resources management, and of social and political marginality. The purpose is not to provide a guide to management, but to explore critical intrinsic problems of water quality management that may place bounds on management under current practice. The intent is not to discourage, but to clarify the boundaries so that they may be tested.

Boundary Problem #1: Definition

Among water specialists, it is often said that water is "too much, too little, or too dirty". One could add that it is often in the wrong hands and in many cases has already been used. Water quantity—too much or too little—is difficult enough to work with, but at least it has one form (H_2O, or oxidane) and three phases (steam, water, and ice). It is easy and costless to measure—every cook does it, and much of the metric system is based on water (e.g. 1 litre of water weighs 1 kg, while 0°C and 100°C bracket the liquid state of water under standard conditions). Water quantity is not at all easy to manage, of course, because of, for example, multiple sources (impoundments, rivers, groundwater), variability of supply (leading to floods [too much] and drought [too little]), and shifting public and private goods characteristics as it passes through the hydrological cycle. Management tends to be supply side first, based upon civil engineering works such as dams, canals, and flood-control works. Yet demand and institutions matter very much.

Water quality—the "dirty" part—is another matter altogether. It is multidimensional, and the number of dimensions is large and continuously increasing with advances in technology and knowledge.[4] Water quality therefore tends to be shunted off to separate analytical and administrative tracks while the mainstream of the water community discourses in terms such as fresh water availability.

Yet water quantity and quality are inextricably linked. As Loucks *et al.* put it three decades ago (1981, pp. 426, italics added):

> While water quality cannot be separated from water quantity, and surface-water quality cannot be considered independently of groundwater quality and quantity, analyses of water quantity and quality problems are often carried out assuming a fixed set of boundary conditions. This is done to simplify the analyses and sometimes to *conform to institutional policies and responsibilities that typically do not include both quantity and quality management.* Still, it is essential to recognize that these two aspects of water resources planning are integrated in nature.

Especially at a policy/management scale, they go together; (usable) quantity is a function of quality. Water outside of the laboratory is rarely unaccompanied. For better as well as for worse, it almost always has something in it, be it minerals, particles, chemicals, nuclides, or disease vectors. At the same time, quality is often a function of quantity, since quality characteristics are usually dimensionalized in concentrations.

Quantity is linked to human or environmental uses, which are in turn dependent on quality. Quality is in turn defined in terms of uses. For example, water that is not potable can still be used for bathing. Many countries have established graded systems linking water quality to acceptable uses, usually with five grades. These are not uniform across systems, however, as can be seen in Table 1, which compares China's five-plus-one-grade system of environmental standards for surface waters with India's five-grade classification.

Differences become even more striking in the highly variable choice of parameters that are used to determine the grade of water quality. Both China and India include pH value, ammonia, sulphates, chlorides, iron, copper, zinc, nitrates, dissolved oxygen, biochemical oxygen demand, total coliforms, fluoride, arsenic, and lead; China also includes temperature, permanganates, chemical oxygen demand, total phosphorus, selenium, mercury, cadmium, hexavalent chromium, cyanide, phenol, petroleum, and anionic surfactants; India also includes total dissolved solids, chlorides, colour, sodium absorption, boron, conductivity, and iron. Hence there is concurrence in only 14 of the 31 parameters underlying the standards in the two countries.

Malaysia also has a five-class system of environmental standards for surface water, where classes I and II can be used for drinking water after treatment, while Class V is suitable only

Table 1. Surface water environmental standards in China and India.

China: Environmental Standards for Surface Water Bodies		India: Central Pollution Control Board Standards for Inland Surface Waters	
I	Water sources and nature reserves	A	Drinking water source without conventional treatment but after disinfection
II	Class A protected area sources of drinking water, habitats of valued aquatic organisms, spawning grounds, and fish nurseries	B	Outdoor bathing (organized)
III	Class B protected area sources of drinking water, wintering grounds for fish, etc.	C	Drinking water source with conventional treatment followed by disinfection
IV	Industrial water supply and non-contact recreation	D	Propagation of wild life, fisheries
V	Agriculture and landscape	E	Irrigation, industrial cooling, controlled waste disposal
> V	Unusable		

Sources: Xia *et al.*, 2011 (China); MEP 2007 (China); Wate, 2011 (India).

for navigation. The classes are determined by a water quality index (WQI) and Malaysia's Interim National Water Quality Standards (Department of Environment, Government of Malaysia, n.d.). The WQI is determined by six parameters[5] (Chan, 2011). Not included are heavy metals, phenols, coliforms, or more exotic items such as micropollutants or nuclides, or the weights given to the parameters. The more parameter-dense Chinese and Indian classification systems use a "one-ballot veto" or barrel-stave approach, where the standard is set at the level of the poorest performing single parameter.

Japan has separate environmental quality standard systems with varying numbers of classes (from two to six) for rivers, lakes, reservoirs, and coastal waters, and within those categories, for different types of parameters: (1) pH, biochemical oxygen demand (BOD), suspended solids (SS), dissolved oxygen (DO), and total coliform; (2) total nitrogen and total phosphorus (for lakes and coastal waters); and total zinc (Ministry of the Environment, Government of Japan, n.d.).

The Chinese standards include 24 parameters, the Indian 19. While important, these are only a small number of the dimensions that could be considered, especially if one includes habitats in the studied environment. For example, Malaysia also includes flotables, odour, salinity, taste, total suspended solids, turbidity, and faecal coliform in its surface water quality criteria, but, as noted, no heavy metals (Department of Environment, Government of Malaysia, n.d.).

Which dimensions of quality are to be monitored evolves, and grows, over time, based upon advances in knowledge, public concern and monitoring capacity. As implied by the term "dirty", sediment perhaps lays claim to being the longest-established parameter of concern, followed in the environmental era by heavy metals and industrial effluent and nonpoint sources, especially agricultural and urban runoff. Presumably in response to limitations of measurement and data availability, a small subset of hopefully representative parameters may be resorted to for large-scale comparisons, especially of ambient waters. China's integrated water assessment of rivers relies on two critical parameters, COD and ammonia nitrogen, to reflect water quality as affected by these sources (Xia, 2011).

These criteria apply to waters that flow into and out of cities, and therefore relate generally to urban water use. Most countries also have specific water quality standards for drinking water (e.g. China) or human health (e.g. Japan). These are usually quite a bit more numerous, but with even more variation among countries: for example 80–85 in China for surface water sources (Guojia Huanjing, 2002); 60–67 in India (Bureau of Indian Standards, 2009); and 26 "standards" plus 27 "monitored substances" in Japan (Ministry of the Environment, Government of Japan, n.d.).[6] Over the past decade, there has been increasing concern regarding micropollutants such as persistent organic pollutants (POPs) and PPCPs (pharmaceutical and personal care products)—for the latter, see Eckstein and Sherk (2011). Then there are nuclides.

Boundary Problem #2: Measurement

Once the important dimensions have been determined, the next problem is measuring them. Because of the cost of monitoring and the large number of dimensions of water quality, information can be spotty at best, both in what is measured and where it is measured. In the Tokyo case, daily measurements had been taken of radioactivity only for the previous week, and clearly covered the water only once it entered the Tokyo water supply system, and not actually at the tap. Often data availability, not impact, drives regulation (for the United States, see GAO, 2011).[7]

Due to cost and staffing limitations, monitoring has to be done at a limited number of sites, usually fixed points. Significant "hot spots" may be missed. The problem of monitoring is particularly salient with groundwater, due to the additional complexity of aquifer systems. Thus, in greater Bangkok, there were 144 monitoring stations in 2008 with 462 wells, but sampling was only done once a year at irregular times, and only 18 parameters were monitored. Sampling practices were questionable, quality data were not synchronized with piezometric level data, the database was not regularly updated (and access to it was limited), and the monitored parameters were fewer than were subject to standards (Babel, 2011).

At the same time, because water quality issues fall within multiple domains, there is often a plenitude of incompatible data. In 1993, in the United States, over 165 programmes at the federal level alone were tasked with dealing with water quality (GAO, 1993, pp. 3). Since then, growing attention to nonpoint sources and total quality assessments have increased data collection and coordination burdens considerably (GAO, 2011).

Groundwater systems are poorly understood, more often than not because they are not easily observed or measured—witness the arsenic found in much of Bangladesh's groundwater or the widespread contamination of the shallow aquifers of the North China plain by both industrial and agricultural pollutants (Wang, 2010). Yet groundwater is a primary and increasing source of supply for the world's cities and farms.

Technical advances are lowering the costs of monitoring (e.g. using gas chromatography–mass spectrometry or GIS systems) and processing, so the quality and quantity of data is improving over time. Still, there are significant gaps in our understanding of areas such as the long-term health effects of persistent organic pollutants or synergistic effects.[8] Also, for parameters whose critical values are set at the level of detection, improved monitoring technologies can lead to a further increase in the objects of regulation (GAO, 2011).[9]

One way with dealing with definition and measurement problems is by adopting treatment methods that capture all items within a category. Yet more comprehensive treatment methods (e.g. for sewerage) tend to be more expensive and therefore inadequate in the occurrence of extreme events such as storm surges, because their scale is limited by economic and technical feasibility constraints.

Boundary Problem #3: Significance of Measurements

Even if the measurement problem is solved, there is an issue of making sense of the results, which is related to the process of standard setting, and the model of health (or environmental) effects. Is there a threshold level—how is it determined?—and if not, how can we interpret an exceedance of the standard? What do measures measure, and which ones should we pay attention to? For example, both BOD (biological oxygen demand) and COD (chemical oxygen demand) measure oxygen depletion, but there is no general correlation between the two. Some countries only include one in their water quality standards (e.g. India and the Republic of Korea, both BOD); others include both (e.g. China and Malaysia). When the two measures diverge, it points to additional puzzles and complexities of water quality degradation. In Lake Biwa, for example, BOD values have declined for quite some time while COD has increased, indicating an increase in organic matter that does not readily decompose, but the nature of that matter was not immediately apparent until recently (Takemoto *et al.*, 2009).

Standards are a way of providing meaning, as policy triggers, but tend to be arbitrary lines in the sand. They often depend on measurement capabilities, especially for substances that are difficult to detect. When there are too many, they may overwhelm administrative capacity, or be subject to benign neglect for economic or political reasons. They are rarely fully enforced.

Setting standards (or not setting them) is often a political act. Here I can offer two examples from field visits to China. In a 1980 field survey of the proposed eastern route of the south-to-north transfer, we were informed that the Nansi Lake water was good, because it met all the criteria values set for industrial pollution. When we actually went to the site, it was immediately evident from the slippery rocks along the shore that nutrients from agricultural runoff were not included in the tests. In 1991, in the prosperous heavy industrial village of Daqiu Zhuang, on the outskirts of Tianjin, our briefer assured us that since none of the 226 steel, building materials, and ferrous metals factories in the village polluted, there was no need to measure the rust-coloured water flowing through the fields for anything except pH. Since the wastewater was acid and the groundwater used was alkaline, the water passed this test.

Pathways are not always well understood, either in nature or between source and health effects. In the Japanese case, the crippled nuclear power plants in Fukushima were almost certainly the source of the iodine, conveyed by a north-easterly rain the two days before. Nonetheless, the specific pathway into the Tokyo water supply was far from clear for quite some time, until circulation models had been developed both in Japan and abroad. The iodine might have fallen directly with the rain into the open settling tanks, or it might have come from runoff from terrestrial "hot spots" within the watershed. Such hot spots have since been discovered in fields further removed from the power plants than Tokyo. Many local governments responded to citizen concerns over the validity of the airborne radioactivity readings, issued regularly from a number of fixed monitoring stations by the Ministry of Education, Culture, Sports, Science and Technology (MEXT), by taking supplementary measurements at a greater variety of locations. Not surprisingly, given that they were monitoring at a much finer scale, they found spots with higher readings than the MEXT reports, but an order of magnitude below those found in Fukushima, and unlikely to be harmful to health (*Tokyo Shimbun*, 2011). Subsequent reports of hot spots, including more durable nuclides such as caesium, did little to allay citizen concern, however.

Boundary Problem #4: Perceptions and Trust

Even were the problems of measurement to be solved and realistic standards set that satisfy the experts that they cautiously protect people's health or the environment, there is the problem of public perception. This in turn is related to "cultural models" of pollution and health and of governance in general—that is, the level of trust of the populace in government and the corporate sector. It can take a long time to build public trust in water quality. That trust can dissipate overnight, as illustrated by the Tokyo case.[10] An incident can easily feed into a cultural model of incompetent government or greedy corporations.

"Risk communication" and transparency are often advocated as means for specialists and officials to overcome the sometimes diametrically opposite concerns of the experts and the populace. If it were only so simple! Referring again to the Tokyo case, Yukio Edano, then chief cabinet secretary, pointed out correctly that the standards for infants were "very conservative" and based on longer-term consumption than "a few drinks of water", and asked people to "respond calmly" (Jolly & Grady, 2011). His words did not reassure the public.

For many, Tokyo tap water was no longer a trustworthy source of drinking water after a radioactive element was discovered in it following the Fukushima nuclear mishap. Yet unfiltered tap water was not popular before—a 2001 *Asahi Shimbun* survey found that only 50% of Japanese drank tap water as it was supplied; 38% bought bottled water, while 29% used water filters or purifiers. The main concern at that time, however, was taste, not health: 64% said it did not taste good, but 78% considered it safe to drink (*Asahi Shimbun*, 2001).

A 2010 Gallup survey indicated that more than a quarter of the world's adult population is dissatisfied with water quality in their communities. In Asia the regional median was slightly higher, at 30%. In this poll, the level of dissatisfaction in Singapore was lowest in the world (0%), followed in Asia by Malaysia (13%), Sri Lanka and South Korea (14%), Laos and the Philippines (15%), Japan (17%), Indonesia and Hong Kong (18%), and Vietnam (19%). In China, 24% expressed dissatisfaction, in India 30%, and in Taiwan 31%. These attitudes clearly appear to be affected as much by perception and cultural values (and possibly sampling bias) as by objective measures of quality. Levels of dissatisfaction tended to be higher in western and central Asia than in South, Southeast or East Asia (English & Ray, 2010).

There are many reasons to mistrust any organization, government or corporate, that has a monopoly over information and an interest in the outcome—and it is rare for an organization to collect irrelevant information unless it is required to. The first question that often comes to the public's mind is "If this is what they are telling us, what are they keeping secret?" The rise in popularity of bottled water is due in part to a lack of trust in the safety of the public water supply, despite reassurances of utility management (Gleick, 2010).

In this context, the efforts by the Singapore government to promote NEWater are a bold experiment in trust-building. Casual observations and conversations indicate that the public is not yet entirely convinced of its desirability. Households who have come to accept reclaimed water for household irrigation in Tuscon are not yet ready to accept treated water for drinking (Campbell & Scott, 2011).

Announcements such as in the Tokyo case also may serve as a signal that the situation may become more serious. But if the government does not release data, especially that showing exceedance of standards, its credibility is also at stake. One of the most serious problems of the 2005 Songhua River spill was not that the government put people's lives at risk. In that regard, its response to the crisis was quick and apparently effective: the water supply to downstream Harbin was shut off and alternative sources of water provided for the interim. The problem was that authorities initially tried to cover up the extent or even the existence of the spill for 10 days.[11]

Boundary Problem #5: Disjunctures between Coevolving Natural and Human Systems

The relationship between natural systems and human systems, including that of management, add yet another layer of complexity. The tsunami disrupted both, but one of the more disturbing aspects of the Tokyo case is that the existing administrative system was unable (at least at first) to provide an explanation of how the iodine had moved through the natural system into the city's water supply. Even where the situation is more stable, despite intensive study, natural processes (e.g. in lakes or groundwater aquifers) are not fully understood, and where they are, the time scales of degradation and recovery are poorly aligned with the capacity of human management systems to respond.

Falkenmark notes (2011, p. 17) two types of delays to pollution mitigation in river basins, which together can "be quite long":

> the social response time, from the first suspicion to taking the necessary technical measures; and the hydrophysical response time, … the time it takes for pollution to build up … in a water body, and … the time it takes to flush away the accumulated pollutants.

The hydrophysical response mentioned by Falkenmark reflects a *hysteresis* effect that is even more pronounced in the lentic (lake and reservoir) systems where most of the world's fresh surface water is located at any given time, in part because the renewal time tends to be much longer there. The "first suspicion" there can come with an algal bloom, as in Lake Biwa in 1977, or with a sudden collapse in an indigenous species due to a change in lake ecology, overfishing, or the introduction of exotic rivals. These events are the culmination of a long period of degradation, often linked to growing or changing levels of economic activity and related political forces. Resistance from these sectors can contribute to inertia in the political and management systems that delays and sometimes impedes the "social response time". Then, once efforts are made to address the problem, the response of the water body toward restoration is also delayed, so results are not immediately visible and it becomes difficult to sustain commitments. Some things, such as the original ecology, are unlikely to ever be restored completely.

Many human systems, including governments, markets, and civil society, may have historically been strongly affected by certain hydrological imperatives, but those needs were usually of the nature of too much (flooding) or too little (irrigation). For the most part, especially today, human systems evolve in response to a number of imperatives that have little relationship to the hydrological cycle or water quality. As noted at the outset, those that evolve to deal with water quality have usually been isolated from those that deal with water quantity.

Boundary Problem #6: Dis-integrated Water Resources Management

Within the human system, there is a close relationship between water, especially water quality, and other key sectors. Food security is a typical example that has long been linked with water quantity, but with important quality characteristics. Increasingly, as food production "industrializes" with large commercial enterprises, especially relying on factory production of meat and fish, and marketing expands beyond national borders, food security has taken on a qualitative dimension that is directly linked to the quality of the water used and released from production. This is exemplified by the use of urban wastewater to irrigate nearby agricultural lands to provide fresh vegetables for street food vendors (Wichelns & Dreschel, 2011). This urban agriculture can be a significant source of food to cities in developing Asia. Where the water is organic waste, it can provide valuable nutrients to the crops while offering a source of water to unentitled farmers where no other is available. This is actually not new in East Asia, where before the advent of chemical fertilizer, night soil was collected from urban areas and transported to farms. Even in more recent times, the Qing ("Clean") River in northwest Beijing was used to divert raw sewage from residential areas to the fields, aerating it as it went to improve its safety.[12] Yet in most cases the linkage between wastewater and irrigation occurs "spontaneously", without government oversight, raising the likelihood that the water used will contain dangerous non-organic pollutants, especially from industry.

Legislation does not always have the intended effect in improving water quality, due to poor design or implementation failures. India's water pollution regulations have had no statistically observable effect on infant mortality (Greenstone & Hanna, 2011). Even in the United States, with its long history of water quality regulation, the Safe Drinking Water Act of 1974 has often been honoured in the breach, due, among other factors, to unrealistic mandates (Tiemann, 2006).

The Tokyo iodine case demonstrates some bureaucratic and administrative delimitations that were also limitations on effective water quality management, as is the mix of institutions (public, private, other, or none) that lie at the core of management and governance. Within the Japanese government, the Ministry of Health and others issued the health standards, while the Ministry of Education and others monitored the air, and the Ministry of the Environment was nowhere to be seen, because (unlike the US Environmental Protection Agency) it has no mandate to deal with radioactivity.[13] Similar stews of overlapping and absent bureaucratic turf over water are common elsewhere (e.g. the case of the 165-plus US federal water quality programmes mentioned above). In Bangkok, the four main agencies concerned with groundwater quality (the Departments of Groundwater Resources, Pollution Control, and Environmental Quality Promotion, and the National Environment Board) are within the Ministry of Natural Resources and the Environment, as is the Wastewater Management Authority, but it is not certain that this guarantees coordinative success (Babel, 2011). In many cases, the agency in charge of development is also given regulatory authority, putting the fox in the chicken coop. As a rule, government structures are not set up to deal well with cross-cutting issues such as water quality, especially novel ones under emergency conditions.

In China's urban areas, an attempt has been made to address the phenomenon of "nine dragons contending over the water" (*jiulong zhengshui*) by establishing integrating water service bureaus. These have had some apparent success, but relationships between the urban areas and their upstream and downstream "citysheds" are not always harmonious or coordinated (Nickum & Lee, 2006). Shifting to a focus on integrated river basin management would not always be helpful, as many large cities go outside the basin for their supply.

At a supra-urban level, federal systems such as in India and Malaysia seem to be particularly prone to dis-integration (Chan, 2011; Wate, 2011), but even "unitary" states such as China, and to some degree Japan, have similar problems of interadministrative coordination.

Nor is privatization a clear alternative. Tokyo Electric (Tepco), the operator of the Fukushima nuclear power plants, is a private company that because of its size and importance, and the power of the "nuclear lobby", has usually been able to regulate its regulators. The Tokyo water supply is public, but it is not clear that water quality would be any better if it were provided by a private company.

Boundary Problem #7: Social and Political Marginality

Marginal peoples are almost by definition poorly served by both state and market. By the same token, it is difficult to address marginality by either the state (which responds to organized interest groups) or the market (which responds to purchasing power). Recent economic trends have only exacerbated the global gated community (internal north-south) phenomenon of economic and social polarization.

Significant efforts are being made to improve the quality of the water supply to much of the world's poor and poorly accessed, both in response to Millennium Development Goal #7 of the UN and through development of low-cost technologies. For example, the development of inexpensive methods to remove arsenic from groundwater, especially in Bangladesh, has been something of an international cottage industry for the past decade, as a quick Internet search can verify. Unfortunately, the subtext of the continuing development and reportage of magic solutions indicates that none appears to have been widely adopted.[14]

Technical "solutions" may exacerbate the global gated community phenomenon, for example by allowing those households who are connected to the public (or privatized) water supply to obtain highly purified water, but at a cost that inhibits the extension of the system to the less economically fortunate or geographically remote. Improvements in measurement, monitoring, and treatment technologies, while exciting and promising in many ways, may also lead to a wider separation of the entitled from the unentitled. Entire communities, especially rural and semi-rural, may be excluded if they are too small and remote to afford advanced treatment facilities.

Recently there has been a lot of attention to "urban footprints", including in water. In the case of water quality, it might be better termed an urban boot-print: it is more likely to be local and less likely to stretch across international borders. The aforementioned urban wastewater applied to nearby fields, often untreated, is a clear example, especially when it includes industrial waste (Wichelns, 2011). Wichelns (and Wichelns & Dreschel, 2011) recommend a solution in considering effluent as a resource, recovering that resource, adopting business models, relying on markets, and focusing on value chains. The ultimate solution to marginality is to "mainstream" those affected, economically and politically, so this is the right direction, if appropriate entitlements can be established. The problem in many systems, however, is that both state and market tend to favour the already entitled.

Conclusion

Delineating boundaries can be daunting, but it also leaves one with an appreciation for the accomplishments of those who deal with water quality issues. Water quality cannot be separated from water quantity or end uses, either conceptually or in practice. Because they cover so many more dimensions, though, water quality problems will always be more complex than water quantity ones, which are serious enough. Successful water quality management is very technical but also highly political. Monitoring and finding meaning for the results are significant problems, but even if these could be settled scientifically, there is also the necessity to communicate risks to the public accurately and in a timely manner, especially in times of emergency. Yet, while necessary, that has serious drawbacks, especially where the public does not entirely trust the government or the corporate sector, which is just about everywhere. It is easy to call for political will and social justice in addressing some of the problems of uneven exposure, or marginality, but most political structures are not well set up to deal with those problems. Well-known and nearly universal maladies of vertical and horizontal coordination within the government administration come to the fore in trying to address a plethora of water quality management challenges. At the same time, quality problems of all types are frequently identified and addressed. There are a variety of valuable experiences in Asian urban areas. Monitoring, modelling, and management capabilities are improving at a breath-taking pace. The boundaries themselves are constantly shifting, and not always beyond our grasp.

Notes

1. According to the "Indices Relating to Limits on Food and Drink Ingestion" formulated by the Nuclear Safety Commission of Japan (orig. 1980, with periodic updates), incorporated into the "Manual for Measuring Radioactivity of Foods in Case of Emergency" produced by the Ministry of Health and Labour in March 2002 as an "office memo", and established by that ministry (now the Ministry of Health, Labour and Welfare) as provisional regulation values in a notice of 17 March. At this point they became "official", but they appear to have existed as working guidelines for much longer. In December 2011, the Japanese Ministry of Education, Culture, Sports, Science and Technology (MEXT) replaced the "temporary" standards for radiation in food and drinking water that were the basis of the 23 March health alert with new, revised values that were much stricter (Yamamoto, 2011). This would appear to reflect a policy of extreme caution in the face of public scepticism, since as noted the temporary standards were themselves conservative by international standards.
2. Professor Richard Wakeford at Manchester University "calculated that drinking water for a year at the Japanese limit would give an infant a dose of 0.4 mSv" (millisieverts). Average background dose per year in the UK is about 2.7 mSv, and goes up to 7.8 mSv in Cornwall (Walsh, 2011).
3. An even more significant tipping point may have been a 1994 pollution event in the Huai River, already one of the most polluted rivers in China, when a heavy rainfall forced the release of impounded waters containing high levels of industrial and municipal wastewater (Wang & Ongley, 2004; Xia, 2011).
4. In the latest volume of *The World's Water*, Palaniappan *et al.* (2012) specify 10 broad categories of factors affecting water quality: nutrients, erosion and sedimentation, water temperature, acidification, salinity, pathogenic organisms, trace metals, human-produced chemicals and other toxins, introduced species and other biological disruptions, and emerging contaminants (including pathogens). Radionuclides miss mention.
5. BOD, COD, NH_3N, pH, DO, and suspended solids.
6. The US Environmental Protection Agency lists primary (legally enforceable) drinking water standards for 6 microorganisms, 3 disinfectants, 3 disinfection by-products, 16 inorganic chemicals, 53 organic chemicals, and 4 radionuclides, as well as 15 secondary (non-enforceable) standards (EPA, n.d.).
7. "EPA's selection of contaminants for regulatory determination in 2003 and 2008 was driven by data availability—not consideration of public health concern. EPA does not have criteria for identifying contaminants of greatest public health concern" (GAO, 2011, inside front cover).
8. Thanks to Patricia Holm for this observation.
9. "EPA ... based most of its final determinations to not regulate 20 contaminants on the rationale of little or no occurrence of the contaminants in public water systems" (GAO, 2011, inside front cover).
10. Thanks to Peter Gleick for this observation. Actually, at a general level, there may not have been a high level of trust in the government in Japan even before the incident.

11. A vice-director of the State Environmental Protection Administration (SEPA) was quoted as saying, "There are many ways to spread information. Notifying the people is one way, and notifying local governments and affected enterprises is another way" (Spaeth, 2005). In January-February 2012, another major industrial spill, this time of cadmium in the southern province of Guangxi, tested the environmental and political response system.
12. Witnessed in field visit, 1990.
13. At the same time, victims of Minamata Disease from the 1960s protest to the Ministry of the Environment, because it is responsible for overseeing certification and compensation, even though it was not set up until 1971 and has no control over industrial processes.
14. The latest intriguing example from the news is a "super sand" combining inexpensive graphite oxide with ordinary coarse sand to create a rapid but more effective sand filter to clear out heavy metals and much more (Moskvitch, 2011).

References

Asahi Shimbun (2001) Poll: 47% don't drink tap water. 10 April, p. 21 (in English); 7 April, p. 1 (in Japanese).
Babel, M. S. (2011) [In this volume.]
Bureau of Indian Standards (2009) IS 10500:2004. Draft Indian Standard: Drinking Water - Specification (Second Revision of IS 10500). Available at: http://bis.org.in/sf/fad/FAD25(2047)C.pdf. (viewed 29 March 2012).
Campbell, A. C. & Scott, C. A. (2011) Water reuse: policy implications of a decade of residential reclaimed water use in Tucson, Arizona, *Water International*, 36(7), pp. 908–923.
Chan, N. W. (2011) [In this volume.]
Department of Environment, Government of Malaysia (n.d.) Interim national quality standards for Malaysia. Available at: http://www.nahrim.gov.my/download/pkkaas/Table 2_INTERIM NATIONAL WATER QUALITY STANDARDS FOR MALAYSIA.pdf (accessed 31 December 2011).
Eckstein, G. & Sherk, G. W. (2011) *Alternative Strategies for Managing Pharmaceutical and Personal Care Products in Water Resources* (Lubbock, TX: Texas Tech University School of Law).
English, C. & Ray, J. (2010) 1.3 billion adults worldwide unhappy with water quality, *Gallup*. Available at: http://www.gallup.com/poll/127187/billion-adults-worldwide-unhappy-water-quality.aspx (accessed 7 November 2010).
EPA (N.d.) Drinking Water Contaminants (US Environmental Protection Agency). Available at: http://water.epa.gov/drink/contaminants/#List (accessed 15 December 2011).
Falkenmark, M. (2011) Water: a reflection of land use. Understanding of water pathways and quality genesis, *International Journal of Water Resources Development*, 27(1), pp. 13–32.
Gleick, P. (2010) *Bottled and Sold: The Story Behind Our Obsession with Bottled Water* (Washington, DC: Island Press).
Government Accountability Office [GAO] (1993) *Environmental Protection: EPA Faces Formidable Challenges Managing Water Quality Data*, GAO/T-AIMD-93-2 (Washington, DC: GAO).
Government Accountability Office [GAO] (2011) *Safe Drinking Water Act: EPA Should Improve Implementation of Requirements on Whether to Regulate Additional Contaminants*, GAO-11-254 (Washington, DC: GAO).
Greenstone, M. & Hanna, R. (2011) *Environmental Regulations, Air and Water Pollution, and Infant Mortality in India*, Working Paper No. 17210 (Cambridge, MA: National Bureau of Economic Research).
Guojia Huanjing Baohu Zongju (State Environmental Protection Administration) and Guojia Zhiliang Jiandu Jianyan Jianyi Zongju (State Quality Monitoring, Inspection and Quarantine Administration) (2002) Dibiao shui huanjing zhiliang zhibiao (Environmental quality standards for surface water). GB 3838-2002. Available at: http://www.es.org.cn/download/35-1.pdf (accessed 12 December 2011).
Jolly, D. & Grady, D. (2011) Japan considers importing bottled water, *International Herald Tribune*, 25 March p. 3.
Loucks, D. P., Stedinger, J. R. & Haith, D. A. (1981) *Water Resource Systems Planning and Analysis* (Englewood Cliffs, NJ: Prentice-Hall).
Ministry of the Environment, Government of Japan (n.d.) Environmental quality standards for water pollution. Available at: http://www.env.go.jp/en/waQ6 ter/wq/wp.pdf (accessed 15 December 2011).
Ministry of Environmental Protection [MEP] (2007) *Environmental quality standards for surface water*, GB 3838-2002 (Ministry of Environmental Protection, People's Republic of China) [in Chinese]. Available at: http://english.mep.gov.cn/standards_reports/standards/water_environment/quality_standard/200710/W020061027509896672057.pdf (accessed 29 June 2011).
Moskvitch, K. (2011) "Super sand" to help clean up dirty drinking water, *BBC News* [online], 24 June. Available at: http://www.bbc.co.uk/news/business-13895077 (accessed 30 June 2011).

Nakamura, M. & Nakajima, T. (Eds) (2002) *Lake Biwa and Its Watershed* (Otsu: Lake Biwa Research Institute).

Nickum, J. E. & Greenstadt, D. (1998) Transacting a commons: the Lake Biwa Comprehensive Development Plan, in: J. Donahue & B. Johnston (Eds) *Water, Culture and Power: Local Struggles in a Global Context*, pp. 141–161 (Washington, DC: Island Press).

Nickum, J. E. & Lee, Y. F. (2006) Same longitude, different latitudes: institutional change in urban water in China, north and south, *Environmental Politics*, 15(2), pp. 231–247.

Palaniappan, M., Gleick, P. H., Allen, L., Cohen, M. J., Christian-Smith, J. & Smith, C. (2012) Water quality, in: P. H. Gleick (Ed.) *The World's Water, Volume 7*, pp. 45–72 (Washington, DC: Island Press).

Spaeth, A. (2005) *China's toxic shock, Time Magazine World* [online], 5 December. Available at: http://www.time.com/time/magazine/article/0,9171,501051205-1134807,00.html (accessed 29 June 2011).

Takemoto, K., Ichise, S., Ichikawa, M., Namba, H. & Kihara, H. (2009) X-ray imaging of picoplankton in Lake Biwa by soft X-ray microscope at Ritsumeikan University SR Center, *Journal of Physics: Conference Series*, 186(1), pp. 1–3. Available at: http://iopscience.iop.org/1742-6596/186/1/012097 (accessed 31 December 2011).

Tiemann, M. (2006) *Safe Drinking Water Act: Implementation and Issues* (Washington, DC: Congressional Research Service).

Tokyo Shimbun (2011) Fuan no oya sokutci tanomi [Uneasy parents request measurements], 26 June, p. 29.

Walsh, F. (2011) Japan nuclear leak and tap water, *BBC News* [online], 23 March. Available at: http://www.bbc.co.uk/blogs/thereporters/ferguswalsh/2011/03/japan_nuclear_leak_and_tap_water.html (accessed 29 June 2011).

Wang, C. & Ongley, E. (2004) Transjurisdictional water pollution management: the Huai River example, *Water International*, 29(3), pp. 290–293.

Wang, Q. (2010) Most northern plain groundwater unsafe to drink, *China Daily* [online], 5 November. Available at: http://www.chinadaily.com.cn/china/2010-11/05/content_11505372.htm (accessed 27 June 2011).

Wate, S. R. (2011) [In this volume.]

Watts, J. (2010) *When a Billion Chinese Jump: How China Will Save Mankind—or Destroy It* (New York: Scribner).

Wichelns, D. (2011) [In this volume.]

Wichelns, D. & Dreschel, P. (Eds) (2011) *Water International, 36(4): special issue on Wastewater Use in Agriculture: Economics, Risks, and Opportunities*.

Xia, J. (2011) [In this volume.]

Xia, J., Zhang, Y. Y., Zhan, C. & Ye, A. Z. (2011) Water quality management in China: the case of the Huai River basin, *International Journal of Water Resources Development*, 27(1), pp. 167–180.

Yamamoto, R. (2001) Hōshanō kijun nyūjishoku 50 bekureru [50 bequerel radiation food standards for infants], *Asahi Shimbun*, day ed., 21 December, p. 1.

Emerging Contaminants and the Implications for Drinking Water

Introduction

As the technology for chemical analysis has advanced over the past decade, the capability to identify and measure trace levels of organic chemicals in environmental media, particularly water, has also increased significantly. As a consequence, there are many reports of a range of substances, mostly anthropogenic contaminants, being identified in wastewater, river, lake, and groundwater, and drinking water, at concentrations that are usually in the low nanogram-per-litre range. Some of these are familiar substances and others less familiar, but most become contaminants through their use by humans with subsequent entry into wastewater from domestic use or as a result of excretion or bathing and showering. Some arise as a consequence of wider use by industry and some from specific sources of pollution. The US Geological Survey (USGS) has defined emerging contaminants (ECs) as any synthetic or naturally occurring chemicals or microbial constituents that have not historically been considered to be contaminants (USGS, 2011). The presence of these substances, some of which are known to be biologically active, in water raises a number of questions regarding their significance for aquatic organisms and particularly drinking water and what needs to be done to mitigate any significant risks to the environment and to human health. Often these groups of compounds are not covered by current regulations. Many of these substances have probably been present for a long time, probably over decades, and it is only now that they can be identified in water and their concentrations quantified. As such, the term "emerging contaminants" can be misleading; a better description would be "contaminants of emerging concern".

Types of Substances

There are numerous substances that are used for a variety of purposes in modern life.

These range from cleaning products of various types, through cosmetics and personal care products, to the wide range of medicines, both over-the-counter remedies and prescribed pharmaceuticals, which are extensively used around the world. Other ECs that have been included in recent lists are artificial sweeteners, nanoparticles, perfluorinated compounds, flame retardants, and other more well-known contaminants such as the fuel additive methyl tertiary butyl ether (MTBE). There are also natural substances that are excreted by humans, such as hormones, which are biologically very active. Some of these substances possess endocrine activity, which has raised concerns because of the observed changes in fish in waters containing treated wastewater effluent.

The several types of ECs, generally grouped by their initial use but sometimes by structure or mechanism of action, include the following:

1. *Endocrine disrupting compounds* (EDCs). The WHO defines an endocrine disruptor as "an exogenous substance or mixture that alters function(s) of the endocrine system and consequently causes adverse health effects in an intact organism, or its progeny" (WHO, 2002). EDCs are a diverse group of substances that include human hormones and a range of industrial chemicals. They may mimic, inhibit, or modulate synthesis, release, or metabolism and interfere with the normal physiological activities of the reproductive system. These substances were the first of the emerging contaminants to draw the attention of the media, primarily because of the observed feminization of male fish immediately downstream of wastewater discharges. EDCs have in common the ability to act as or mimic hormones or to interfere with the endocrine system at varying concentrations (Watts *et al.*, 2002). However, little is known about their effects in the environment other than oestrogenicity. The human oestrogens that are naturally excreted in the urine and the artificial oestrogens used in oral contraceptives are the most potent of the EDCs, while there are a number of other industrial substances such as some organotins, detergent building blocks such as the alkylphenols, and bisphenol A (Lam *et al.*, 2011). While these have been of concern for aquatic life in limited stretches of water, they are hydrophobic and readily adsorb to particulate matter and sediment. Many EDCs have been found to possess some form of endocrine activity in *in vitro* assays, but often there are few data regarding their potential for affecting intact organisms at environmentally relevant concentrations.

2. *Pharmaceuticals* are a very broad range of chemicals used in both human and animal medicine. They are chemicals (either synthetic or natural) that can be found in prescription medicines and over-the-counter therapeutic drugs for treatment or prevention of diseases in humans. They have a significant variation in chemical structure and behaviour, both in terms of metabolism and in the environment. Pharmaceuticals also vary significantly in their structure and action. Their presence in water needs to be considered on a country-by-country

basis because there is considerable variation in what is used in different countries and in the circumstances through which they might reach water sources (WHO, 2011a). Numerous surveys have been conducted on the occurrence of pharmaceuticals in municipal wastewater and effluents. Their presence has been identified in major sources of drinking water and some have been identified at trace concentrations in drinking water. For Asian developing countries, pharmaceutical waste discharge into rivers and lakes as high as over 30 mg/L has been reported close to factory outlets, and it is of concern that the water may be used for agriculture and in households (Lubick, 2009).

3. *Veterinary medicines* are widely used to prevent and treat animal disease. Some drugs are also used as growth promoters that increase growth rate and allow animals to be brought to market faster and at lower cost. There is a wide range of drugs, including antimicrobials, anti-protozoals, anti-parasiticides, and flavophospholipol, that are commonly used in livestock feed supplements. Recently, low levels of these medicines have been detected in soil, surface water, and groundwater in different parts of the world (Boxall *et al.*, 2003). As a result, questions have arisen about the potential for these substances to have adverse effects on non-target organisms in the environment, and, similarly to human pharmaceuticals, on human health, following long-term exposure to low doses in water. There have also been questions as to whether the presence of antimicrobials in the environment could increase antibiotic resistance in human pathogens. However, this latter issue is less likely to be affected by environmental concentrations of antibiotic residues than by the excretion of antibiotic-resistant organisms into the environment that then pass on their resistance genes through plasmid exchange where there are large concentrations of organisms, such as in slurry or in sewage treatment plants.

4. *Personal care products* are often grouped with pharmaceuticals in "pharmaceuticals and personal care products" (PPCPs). Nevertheless, they are made up of a very wide range of substances used in toiletries, make-up, domestic cleaning and air-freshening products, and for other purposes such as in sunscreen and insect repellent. Compounds for disinfection purposes, such as triclosan and chlorophene, are commonly used on a larger scale than pharmaceuticals. Triclosan for example has been used for decades in a wide variety of consumer products, ranging from toothpaste and hand soap to toys. Personal care products enter the environment via treated sewage effluent as a result of showering, bathing, and clothes washing. They also can be released into surface waters during recreational activities such as swimming. Personal care products are observed regularly in effluents and surface waters in different parts of the world (Daughton & Ternes, 1999; Kasprzyk-Hordern *et al.*, 2008; Kuster *et al.*, 2008; Rahman *et al.*, 2009). Some of these compounds may accumulate in exposed organisms; for example triclosan and chlorophene were reported in bile from bream in the Dutch River Dommel (Houtman *et al.*, 2004).

5. *Perfluorinated substances* such as perfluorooctanoic acid (PFOA) and perfluorooctane sulfonate (PFOS) have been widely used as building blocks in dirt-repellent coatings, non-stick coatings such as grease-repellent coatings and sprays for leather and textiles, polytetrafluoroethylene (PTFE) non-stick cookware, and fire-fighting foams. They are persistent in the environment and

are found in water, often groundwater, where they can accumulate: they are unusual in that they are quite water soluble. Concern about perfluorinated compounds is growing because of their persistence, their potential for accumulation in organisms, and their toxic properties, including developmental toxicity and possibly carcinogenicity (Skutlarek *et al.*, 2006; McLachlan *et al.*, 2007). Perfluorinated compounds have been reported in surface waters throughout Europe (Ahrens *et al.*, 2009; Loos *et al.*, 2010; Kwadijk *et al.*, 2010) and they pose a particular problem for groundwater, where they can remain for a very long time, even if the source is stopped.

6. *Nanomaterials* (NMs) have been classified by the US Environmental Protection Agency (EPA) as emerging contaminants. Because of their unique properties they are increasingly used in a wide range of scientific, industrial, and medical applications. Although there are no data on their occurrence as nanoparticles in the environment there is concern about the lack of environmental health and safety data for nanomaterials, which are difficult to study because of the problems in assessing their potential for causing adverse effects by traditional means. So far, there are insufficient scientific data to determine whether NMs under realistic exposure conditions may present adverse health effects to humans, and currently there are no specific standards or guidelines that regulate NMs. Major NM sources with potential impacts to surface and groundwater result from industrial production, including silica, carbon black and fullerenes, and titanium and zinc oxides (Borm *et al.*, 2006). Some NMs may generate reactive oxygen species (ROS) which can lead to membrane or cell damage (Li *et al.*, 2010).

Entry into the Water Environment

These compounds may enter the water environment through a wide variety of portals, including agricultural, industrial, and urban channels (Figure 1). One of the primary routes is by discharge to surface waters in treated wastewater effluent (treated sewage effluent). However, some may reach groundwater from poorly maintained and leaking sewers and also from poorly designed landfills. Industrial wastewater may also be an important source of these contaminants in both surface water and groundwater but primarily on a localized basis that can be very specific. Use in animal husbandry is a potential source of some animal drugs, which can be present in animal manures and slurries; of course in some circumstances the use of such substances in fish farming in freshwater systems is potentially a more direct route into surface waters.

However, these substances mostly enter the sewer system from domestic or industrial sources and there is the potential for removal or degradation in wastewater treatment. Some that are ingested, such as pharmaceuticals, will be excreted, either as the parent compound or as metabolites; others will enter wastewater in the process of washing or showering while others will come from their use in a range of domestic activities including cleaning and clothes washing. In wastewater treatment, biological processes will degrade many of these substances; however, some will be broken down only partially or not at all and so will reach surface water in the treated wastewater discharge. Some substances, such as hormones that are excreted as glucuronides or sulphates to make them water-soluble, will be metabolized back to the parent compound in wastewater treatment and the solubility will be significantly reduced. However, the efficiency of wastewater treatment

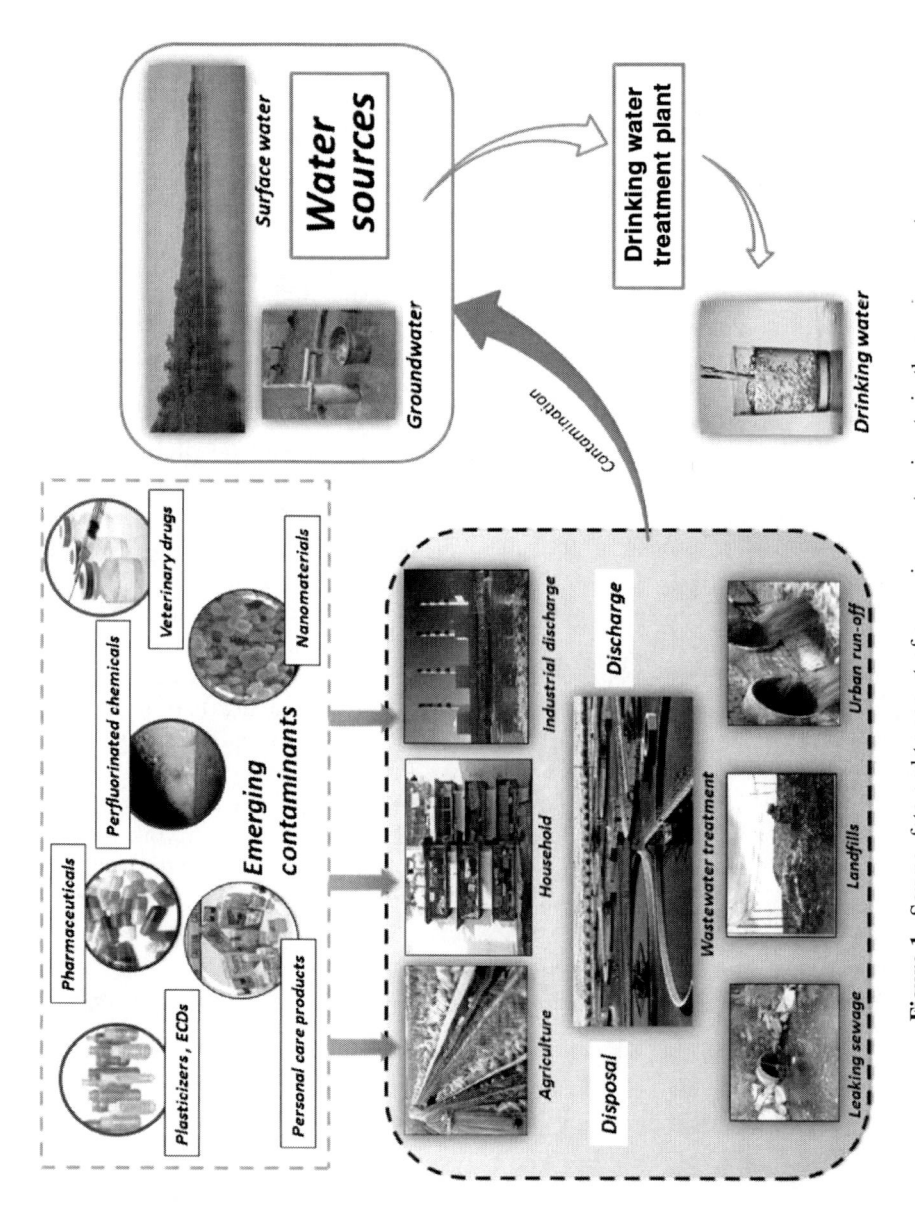

Figure 1. Source, fate and transport of emerging contaminants in the environment.

varies significantly, according to the technology employed; biological systems may also vary in efficiency with temperature and dilution by storm water. Those substances of low water solubility with a high octanol/water partition coefficient will tend to adsorb to the solid phase in the treatment process. These processes of biodegradation and adsorption will continue in surface water systems so there will continue to be amelioration of the concentrations in the environment. Where there is minimal treatment, much higher concentrations of the active compounds will potentially be present and glucuronides and sulphates will allow the hormones to remain in solution for much longer. In addition, there is evidence, in some Asian countries in which there is an industry for the manufacture and formulation of generic pharmaceuticals with only limited controls on discharges, that concentrations of these pharmaceuticals may be very much higher than usual and some specific substances can be present in significant concentrations. In terms of drinking-water treatment there is significant variation in the ability of different treatments or combinations of treatments to remove emerging contaminants and some drinking-water treatment may be inadequate to completely eliminate some of these substances, particularly some pharmaceutical compounds. This has been demonstrated by the fact that trace levels of a few substances have been found in drinking water (Kolpin *et al.*, 2002; Kuster *et al.*, 2008; Benotti *et al.*, 2009; Cooney, 2009; Daughton & Ruhoy, 2009).

Pharmaceuticals and other emerging contaminants are widely used all over the world. Clearly, the higher the population density, the greater the potential for their being present in treated wastewater. It is estimated that in Europe alone there are more than 4,000 pharmaceuticals registered for use in human and veterinary medicine (Hayward, 2011), although how many of these are likely to reach the aquatic environment is uncertain. The growth of cities and the evolution of megacities is an important consideration in assessing whether such substances are present in surface waters. In addition, the pressure on water resources from the growth of cities and the increasing concentration of population there imply a significantly increased reliance on surface water for drinking. In some areas there is also a move to more planned re-use of wastewater for water supply and it is important that where the dilution will be less, proper consideration is made of the substances that might be present. The WHO has proposed and promoted the use of water safety plans as a means of assuring drinking water safety and one of the key steps is identifying the hazards that might be present and the risks those hazards pose to health (WHO, 2011b).

Other substances regarded as emerging contaminants may follow the same route, for example human hormones, which we all excrete, and synthetic hormones such as ethinyl oestradiol (used as a contraceptive). Others such as the alkyl phenols may reach wastewater from industrial wastewater discharged to sewers or in direct discharges. An example of a group of emerging contaminants that reach groundwater through their use in the environment as detergent building blocks are fluorinated substances such as PFOS and PFOA. One particular source was their use in fire-fighting foams at airports, where they were used regularly in certain areas for practice. This has resulted in a significant build-up in the groundwater underneath some airports and aerodromes. However, such circumstances are relatively localized.

What Are the Concentrations in Water?

Although there is an increasing number of reports on the presence of pharmaceuticals and other emerging contaminants in source water or drinking water, they are usually from ad hoc surveys or targeted research projects. So far, there are no systematic investigations that provide a good overview of the occurrence and concentrations of different substances in different parts of the water cycle over time. In addition, routine monitoring to measure pharmaceuticals and other emerging contaminants in drinking water is difficult and expensive, and is not required by most regulatory agencies. It is, therefore, difficult to generalize about the presence of specific substances or their concentrations. The concentrations, except in some specific circumstances, are very low and will vary according to dilution in receiving waters and with the extent of use, for example seasonality. The WHO expert working group on pharmaceuticals in drinking water concluded that "available studies have reported that concentrations of pharmaceuticals in surface waters, groundwater and partially treated water are typically less than $0.1 \, \mu g \, l^{-1}$ and concentrations in treated *drinking* water are generally below $0.05 \, \mu g \, l^{-1}$" (WHO, 2011a). However, these concentrations so far represent the highest levels seen, and most substances that are present are there only at much lower concentrations. Not all drinking water and source waters will contain emerging contaminants; where contaminants are present, they will vary significantly in number and concentration according to location and circumstance (Bull *et al.*, 2011; Focazio *et al.*, 2008; Ternes, 2001; Mons *et al.*, 2003).

The rapid expansion of large-scale animal feeding operations to cope with the increase of population has resulted in increases of environmental contaminations by various veterinary medicines in the water bodies. In the US, antimicrobial compounds of different classes could be detected in waste storage lagoons at concentrations greater than 100 μg/L (Boxall *et al.*, 2003). Of more significance was their detection in surface water and groundwater samples collected proximal to swine and poultry farms at concentrations below 1 μg/L in the former and trace levels in the latter.

Other emerging contaminants, such as the natural and synthetic hormones, may be found at concentrations in the low nanogram-per-litre range. However, most of these substances are very hydrophobic and will tend to adsorb to particulate matter and sediment. Thus bioavailability to pelagic organisms will be reduced, but they may be bioavailable to sediment-dwelling organisms. Adsorption to particulate matter means that they mostly reduce in concentration as they travel downstream and are unlikely to be present in most groundwater unless very shallow, or in drinking water unless it receives no or very limited treatment.

Substances such as the alkylphenols nonylphenol and octylphenol, which are primarily the breakdown products of alkylphenol ethoxylates used in detergents, may be found in microgram-per-litre concentrations in wastewater effluents and effluents from industrial facilities using these materials, but will also be rapidly associated with particles and sediment. Other substances may be found in surface waters close to discharges at microgram-per-litre concentrations but usually rapidly reduce with dilution, breakdown, and association with sediments. However, it must be emphasized that knowledge is incomplete and there are many parts of the world for which there minimal data, if any, and there will almost certainly be localized hotspots. For most of the developed countries, concentrations in groundwater are generally much less because many groundwaters are well protected or there is significant attenuation potential in the soil and rock through which water must percolate to reach the groundwater. Again, there will be hotspots where there is a direct route to groundwater through fissuring and fracturing or where the groundwater is very shallow and vulnerable to surface contamination. Any groundwater that is rapidly influenced by surface rainfall, for example, will be vulnerable.

So far, the concentrations in drinking water have received limited attention compared with effluents and surface waters. However, data from Europe and the US indicate that the levels detected are generally well below the concentrations that would be of concern for health (Bull *et al.*, 2011; Watts & Crane Associates, 2007; WHO, 2011a).

In contrast to pharmaceuticals, over the last decade, extensive studies have been conducted on perfluorinated organic compounds (PFCs) in several Asian countries. Among the various PFCs that can be detected, perfluorooctanic acid (PFOA) was the most dominant compound found in surface water and aquatic animals (Shi *et al.*, 2011; Kunacheva *et al.*, 2011; Nguyen *et al.*, 2011). Most of the findings suggested that human and industrial activities showed close correlations to the concentrations found in the waters. The concentrations detected in river, lake and reservoir water were usually in the range of 1–100 ng/L (Zhang *et al.*, 2011; Nguyen *et al.*, 2011), and the concentrations were generally higher during dry weather than during storm water flow (Nguyen *et al.*, 2011). Perfluorooctane sulfonate (PFOS) was also detected in Asian water bodies, as well as in surface water in Europe (Ericson *et al.*, 2009). It was estimated that the concentration of PFOS and PFOA in drinking water in various Chinese cities ranged from 0.12 to 0.92 ng/L. The estimated daily intake of PFOA and PFOS via drinking water ranged from 0.006 to 0.15 ng per kg body weight per day (Sun *et al.*, 2011). The authors concluded that drinking water was a minor source of PFC exposure among adults in those cities studied. Results from 62 samples of potable water collected from 34 locations across Australia came to a similar conclusion: the combined PFCs from drinking water was generally low, below 2–5 ng per kg body weight (Thompson *et al.*, 2011).

Where pharmaceuticals have been studied, there are only a few individual substances that have been found in drinking water, and those that have been identified in the US and Europe are many orders of magnitude below the lowest clinical dose (Reddersen, 2002; Loos *et al.*, 2010).

Risks to Health and the Environment

The first step in considering risks to aquatic populations and to public health is to assess the extent of exposure and the dose, in particular for mixtures of different types of contaminants. Based on currently available data, typical levels of emerging contaminants detected are of low concentrations (nanograms to micrograms per litre). Acute toxicity for most of these compounds can be observed only at relatively high doses; they are not expected at low environmental concentrations (Schriks *et al.*, 2009), and risk assessment will be technically highly demanding because of the need for data on long-term exposure. In general, mixtures at low concentrations are unlikely to show any specific impact other than additive effects and then usually only when the substances concerned have similar mechanisms of physiological action or toxicity.

Aquatic life has a much greater risk for adverse effects because the total dose has the potential to be much greater in organisms exposed through the medium in which they live all the time and throughout the life cycle. In addition, sediment-dwelling organisms may absorb substances adsorbed to the sediment and this can potentially be magnified through the food chain if the substance is not metabolized. Although there is clear evidence for the impact of endocrine disrupting substances on the development of feminization in male fish or amphibians, additional evidence is needed to verify whether this has had a significant impact on their populations. In terms of the question of mixtures, the studies on fish exposed to mixtures of EDCs from wastewater effluent do reflect an additive effect from similar mechanisms of action (Fick *et al.*, 2010; Barber *et al.*, 2011).

While the supposition for aquatic populations is that organisms close to the source of wastewater effluent will be exposed to the concentrations in the diluted flow, for humans there is the opportunity for further attenuation (physical, chemical, and biological) in surface water, as well as drinking water treatment, which will also mitigate the concentrations that might reach drinking water. Certainly there is evidence that concentrations of some pharmaceuticals in surface waters may be close to concentrations that would be toxic to some aquatic organisms. The risks to aquatic life, therefore, remain uncertain but of possible concern in some parts of some receiving waters. However, the overall impact on the aquatic ecosystem may be difficult to detect and may be negligible, unless the affected species are key to the functioning of that particular ecosystem and are not readily replaced, either by recruitment from upstream or downstream or by another species that can fill the niche that has been vacated.

Among the most intensively studied groups of substances are the oestrogens and their mimics and their effects on fish populations in surface waters. While it is difficult to generalize, there appears to be no significant impact on aquatic populations from these emerging contaminants. However, where sewage treatment is minimal, or is regularly bypassed, concentrations are likely to be much greater and the risks of adverse effects on aquatic populations will be increased.

The contribution of potential risk from drinking water can differ between compounds and depends on the concentrations relative to those in other matrices, exposure volumes, and efficiency of uptake after exposure. Although at this stage it is not possible to be absolutely sure that there are no effects resulting from human exposure to trace levels of ECs in drinking water, any effects would be extremely difficult to detect against the background of natural disease in the human population. In addition, a recent comparative study on exposure to oestrogenic activity and trace contaminants in US municipal drinking water with food, beverage, and air demonstrated that water consumption represents only a small fraction of pharmaceuticals, personal care products, and endocrine disruptors (Stanford *et al.*, 2010). The study further suggested there was no clear evidence of adverse human health effects based on the concentrations present in US drinking waters and the consumption pattern. Studies in the US and Europe support these conclusions (Bull *et al.*, 2011; Watts & Crane Associates, 2007; Mons *et al.*, 2003). Several other investigations also present exposure assessments of the contribution of drinking water for the general population for PFOA and PFOS in Germany and for oestrogenic hormones in the US, finding only on the order of 0.7–2% of the total daily intake of the general population (Fromme *et al.*, 2009). If we take pharmaceuticals as an example, they are normally governed by relatively stringent regulatory processes and require preclinical and clinical studies to assess their efficacy and safety to a greater extent than many commercial products. Thus they are generally better characterized than other environmental contaminants such as personal care products or some endocrine disruptors. Based on our review, the reported concentrations of individual pharmaceutical compounds in drinking water, except perhaps in one or two specific locations of exceptionally high input and no treatment, are too low to cause acute or even sub-acute effects (Bull *et al.*, 2011; Watts & Crane Associates, 2007; WHO, 2011a). However, there are gaps in our knowledge with regard to very long-term exposure to substances normally only used for short-term treatment and to some population subgroups such as the foetus or developing child not normally exposed to some substances. With regard to EDCs, the evidence also suggests that concentrations in drinking water, if detectable, are normally too low to be of any concern (Wenzel *et al.*, 2003; Fawell & Chipman, 2000). However, where there is only minimal sewage treatment and/or minimal water treatment the extent of exposure remains unclear.

It is worth mentioning that risk assessment for emerging contaminants is expensive and technically demanding, as their presence is usually in very low concentrations and close to detection limits. New methods for screening of chemicals in water will definitely lead to discovery of additional emerging compounds in the water. But the presence of these compounds does not necessarily mean they will constitute a health risk; they will need to be present in sufficient concentrations and over sufficient periods of time at that concentration to cause effects.

In terms of trying to prioritize monitoring, particularly investigative monitoring, for emerging contaminants, the development of new and innovative methods to enable the early detection of biological activity can be valuable. Biomonitoring methods enable the measurement of biological effects of both detected and undetected compounds in water. These methods can be used to detect the presence of compounds with a wide scope of specific effects, such as genotoxicity, cytotoxicity, or hormonal activity, prior to analysis using chemical techniques. Furthermore, these tools provide a means of looking at the potential impact of mixtures of substances with similar mechanisms of action, and may in some cases provide an integration of response over time. Vitellogenin is an egg yolk protein normally only found at significant concentrations in females and is extremely sensitive to exogenous oestrogens and so provides a means of integrating exposure. It is regarded as a useful biomarker to monitor oestrogenic activity (Tong *et al.*, 2004) and has been successfully applied for source water monitoring and to track activity downstream from a source (Fawell *et al.*, 2001). In addition, it is fortunate that vitellogenin production follows sub-acute exposure and so means that it provides a useful and meaningful screening tool. However, such tools must be used with great care because many require that samples be concentrated prior to testing and this changes the nature of the sample content as well as the matrix. In addition, care must be taken because biological tests can be difficult to control and will vary from laboratory to laboratory and so the reliability of data can be a significant issue.

Over the past decade there has been increasing interest in biomonitoring systems as a means of integrating exposure (Petrovic *et al.*, 2007). The objective is to try to increase the detection of uncharacterized or unknown contaminants by their combined biological action and enhance the confidence in water quality (Lam *et al.*, 2008). Unlike traditional chemical analysis, the use of an animal model may better reflect the toxicological effects of contaminants and allow inference of human health impact, at least theoretically. Such systems have been used successfully as acute warning systems for high levels of pollutants that threaten public supplies. Although long-term and continuous exposure of fish in particular can provide a means of checking whether there may be something that has been missed, it does require intensive and detailed biochemical and pathological investigation and with small fish this is quite difficult. Nevertheless it can provide an additional means of public reassurance because it is monitoring an integrated vertebrate physiology and histology—even though the extrapolation from fish to humans may not be simple (Sukardi *et al.*, 2011). To date, numerous studies have been conducted using zebra fish as a model for emerging contaminants and the overall findings have reflected well that biomonitoring complemented with chemical assays provides a more robust system for risk assessment than chemical concentration by itself. Nevertheless, it is worth pointing out that many of these studies were carried out with high exposure ranges, usually in micromolar concentrations. More systematic investigations are urgently needed for better risk assessment of low-level chronic exposure with realistic concentrations. In addition, some substances that affect fish may not be of significance for mammals, and vice versa. Monitoring does not solve problems, it only provides information about the status of a problem.

The Way Forward

Emerging contaminants are a problem resulting from the increase in population and the increasing size of cities with high human population in a small area. This creates an increasing demand for water and for food to be produced for these urban populations. All of this leads to the presence of varying amounts of trace substances, such as pharmaceuticals in sewage, with other inputs including intensive animal rearing for veterinary medicines and industrial discharges to sewer or to surface water. The range of substances identified as emerging contaminants has increased steadily with advances in the analytical capability to identify and quantify nanogram-per-litre concentrations (or less) of a wide range of chemical types. The technologies needed to remove, transform, or treat organic trace contaminants in drinking water are generally costly and energy-intensive. In addition, most technologies available today are still unable to completely remove many of the ECs to below the detection limits of advanced analytical instruments. On the other hand, overemphasis on routine monitoring and continual upgrading is not a sustainable, optimal use of resources, as the list of ECs will continue to evolve.

Nevertheless, the potential risk of emerging contaminants in the water needs to be carefully and systematically evaluated. It is most likely that new emerging contaminants will be identified in the future and trying to deal with such issues on a case-by-case basis is not really an appropriate long-term or cost-effective solution. Further, these effects on aquatic ecosystems are extremely difficult to assess in a scientific and meaningful way. While a more comprehensive assessment of the potential impact on human health calls for all possible routes of exposure including food, air, and lifestyle behaviour to be considered, epidemiological investigations to determine possible effects of low-level exposure against the natural background of human disease is expensive, very slow, and very uncertain. Therefore, waiting until adverse effects from a continuously changing exposure scenario can be proven does not seem to be a sensible or effective way forward, particularly considering that if such effects are proven, interventions will also take a significant time to put into place.

In the WHO Guidelines for Drinking Water Quality, the framework for assuring safe drinking water is centred around the development of water safety plans, which represent a proactive and preventive approach to risk management. Water safety plans are based on comprehensive risk assessment and risk management from source to tap, with the first barrier to hazards being prevention of source contamination (WHO, 2011b). It is, therefore, appropriate to consider the prevention of contamination of the source as the first and most comprehensive means of addressing the problem in the long term. This approach addresses both drinking water and the aquatic ecosystem at the same time.

The three primary sources of contamination are wastewater from cities, towns and villages, wastewater discharges from industry, and diffuse inputs from agriculture, industry, and human dwellings. Each requires a different approach but there are several different strands required for each.

One overarching step in prevention is the need to reduce or prevent the use and release of persistent substances that can result in widespread contamination and that have the potential for biological effects. There are already steps in place for dealing with some existing groups of contaminants such as the alkylphenols and perfluorinated compounds such as PFOS by international agreements to abolish, or at least minimize, their use. Although this will take time to be effective at least progress is being made. It is, however, important that all countries and regions participate and unloading such substances cheaply on poorer countries must also be prevented for the agreements to be truly effective. Nevertheless, better identification of possible future problems is also important and at least there are indications that efforts are being made in this direction through chemical management programmes in Europe and the US and with the nanomaterials. The rush to economic development must also be sustainable; some caution applied at an early stage may mean that developing countries do not have to go through the expensive remediation that arises from the mistakes made in many highly developed and wealthy countries.

The most important source of emerging contaminants in terms of both number and quantity of substances is sewage. Collecting sewage is an important step to ensure hygienic disposal of waste and was one of the major steps in improving health in the cities in the 19th century, allowing sewage disposal and abstraction for drinking water to be separated. The introduction of both sewage treatment (now more accurately termed wastewater treatment) and drinking water treatment were also key steps in improving the health of city dwellers. However, the developments of the past 200 years mean that it is not just microbiological contamination that is important. In the 20th century it became apparent that the removal of plant nutrients in the form of nitrate and phosphate was important to prevent problems with excessive algal growth; then metals were seen as an issue, and we now recognize that a series of more complex substances at low concentrations need to be considered. It is also recognized that current approaches to treating wastewater cannot guarantee the complete removal of such substances or even sufficient levels of mitigation to be sure that there is no threat to aquatic life or human health. This means that we need to develop newer and less energy-intensive treatments that will provide a measure of surety that possible future problems will also be dealt with. This will require considerable coordinated research effort and the willingness to consider new and unusual ideas. Of course such an approach will take time but the overall assessment for health means that we probably have time to follow this road (and it is difficult to see what the alternative might be). This approach also helps to level the position between developed and developing countries because all will be, in effect, starting from the same baseline. The costs are likely to be substantial, but so are the costs of following the current approach and surely we should be looking to the future rather than relying on the past.

In the interim there are of course necessary actions that will help overall, both for sources that are not centralized, such as agriculture and industrial discharges, and for centralized wastewater collection and treatment. Establishing some wastewater treatment where there is none, and ensuring that existing wastewater and drinking water treatment are optimized at all times to achieve the best result possible, are important considerations and there are cost-effective means of achieving them. Carrying out risk assessments for surface and ground water can identify the need for action to control discharges; this does not necessarily involve advanced analytical monitoring but proper and thorough inspection on the ground and the introduction and enforcement of suitable environmental legislation. Education is an important part of this process. In the past in parts of Europe it was common practice to dispose of chlorinated solvents onto the ground or into pits to allow evaporation. We now know that the solvents did not evaporate but moved down into groundwater, and such practices are no longer considered to be acceptable.

The need to control the use of persistent substances has been discussed above but minimizing the use of a range of substances that are emerging contaminants would also be important. Unwanted drugs are often flushed away into the sewer system; it would be more effective if these substances were not released in the first place. Although eliminating this has been estimated by Daughton (2001) to result in a reduction of only about 10% of the pharmaceutical load, where it can be achieved sensibly and in a cost-effective manner it does reduce the input. Such programmes and the education to go with them also help to begin a change in attitude in consumers and in those involved in the health care industry. Policies promoting or regulations governing disposal practices at point sources (e.g. health care and veterinary facilities) can reduce the amount of expired or unused pharmaceutical waste entering water bodies. In addition, take-back programmes, guidance, and enhanced consumer education will support efforts for the proper disposal of medicines and reduce the impact of pharmaceuticals entering our water sources.

A second point of control is to reduce the amount used by not over-prescribing drugs and not using them inappropriately as is often considered to be the case in some veterinary uses. Responsible prescribing also requires education and some thought on the part of health care professionals and consumers. In this respect guidance from central sources can be a vital step in reducing the amount and the doses of drugs prescribed.

Another long-term approach is the introduction of "green" chemistry in the development and manufacture of chemicals, including pharmaceuticals (Clark et al., 2010). This means the design of chemicals and pharmaceuticals that do not persist in the environment and so are much more amenable to treatment.

It has been suggested that the way forward is to introduce regulation for emerging contaminants. However, to date there has been little or no significant movement in this respect. It may be possible to regulate a few individual substances, but it seems unlikely that a wide range or a substantial number of emerging contaminants could be addressed in this way. For example, setting standards for a small number of pharmaceuticals in surface waters has been proposed in Europe but it is unclear how values could be achieved without banning the use of important pharmaceuticals, or installing add-on treatment to wastewater treatment plants that would be expensive in terms of running costs and energy, as well as capital costs—without the overall problem being solved. Likewise, the introduction of standards for drinking water would result in a piecemeal approach. Health guidance values can be developed to determine whether specific circumstances constitute a risk to a particular ecosystem or drinking water to inform localized preventive action. However, it would appear that to address a problem this diverse requires a different approach from our traditional means of addressing such problems.

Conclusions

New findings of contaminants in water sources and drinking water at very low concentrations continue to raise questions regarding the impact of a range of contaminants and mixtures of contaminants on aquatic life and human health. These "emerging contaminants" are mostly recognized only because of new analytical methods and so should be termed "contaminants of emerging concern". In most cases they are present at concentrations that appear to pose no significant threat to human health, although there still remain uncertainties in assessing the risks. However, there are local circumstances where concentrations of individual compounds or some mixtures may be of immediate concern. There remain questions over the potential impact on aquatic organisms, although currently there is little evidence of significant effects on aquatic populations.

The source of most of these contaminants is sewage from human habitations and industries, although this is not exclusive and there are other sources. The water sources most likely to be affected are surface waters impacted by sewage effluent and diffuse agricultural inputs. Some of these contaminants are found in groundwater but mostly on a more localized basis.

Groups of substances such as pharmaceuticals and personal care products are attracting considerable attention. These substances primarily reach sewage through excretion by humans taking pharmaceuticals or drainage of personal care products in grey water from domestic premises and industry. Many are broken down, at least partially, in sewage treatment but some are resistant. Many are also removed in drinking water treatment depending on the treatment stages present.

It is probable that further unrecognized contaminants will be identified in the future and so a different approach is needed to address the problem of trace contaminants such as pharmaceutical residues in water sources and drinking water.

The most important steps are, therefore, to do as much as possible to prevent contamination occurring in the first place. Several steps were discussed above, including establishing and enforcing environmental protection legislation, installing and operating wastewater treatment at its optimum, and reducing the unnecessary use of substances that are emerging contaminants or could become emerging contaminants. It is also important to ensure that drinking water treatment is operated at its optimum at all times. For the future we need to improve wastewater treatment to remove much more of the trace organic matter present, but this needs to be based around sustainable, environmentally sound systems that are not energy-intensive.

By taking this approach we can improve the protection of aquatic life and protect aquatic ecosystems, as well as protecting human health, which should be the twin goals of environmental protection. To achieve this will require determination, coordination, and long-term planning by governments, utilities, and industry and will be in the best interests of all three and their people.

Acknowledgements

We thank Shaomin Huang for the illustration. This work is partially supported by the School of Public Health and the Environmental Research Institute, NUS.

References

Ahrens, L., Felizeter, S. & Ebinghaus, R. (2009) Spatial distribution of polyfluoroalkyl compounds in seawater of the German Bight, *Chemosphere*, 76, pp. 179–184.
Barber, L. B., Brown, G. K., Nettesheim, T. G., Murphy, E. W., Bartell, S. E. & Schoenfuss, H. L. (2011) Effects of biologically-active chemical mixtures on fish in a wastewater-impacted urban stream, *Science of the Total Environment*, 409(22), pp. 4720–4728.

Benotti, M. J., Trenholm, R. A., Vanderford, B. J., Holady, J. C., Stanford, B. D. & Snyder, S. A. (2009) Pharmaceuticals and endocrine disrupting compounds in US drinking water, *Environmental Science and Technology*, 43, pp. 597–603.

Borm, P. J., Robbins, D., Haubold, S., Kuhlbusch, T., Fissan, H., Donaldson, K., Schins, R., Stone, V., Kreyling, W., Lademann, J., Krutmann, J., Warheit, D. & Oberdorster, E. (2006) The potential risks of nanomaterials: a review carried out for ECETOC, *Particle and Fibre Toxicology*, 14(3), pp. 11–19.

Boxall, A. B., Kolpin, D. W., Halling-Sørensen, B. & Tolls, J. (2003) Are veterinary medicines causing environmental risks? *Environmental Science and Technology*, 37(15), pp. 286A–294A.

Bull, R. J., Crook, J., Whittaker, M. & Cotruvo, J. A. (2011) Therapeutic dose as the point of departure in assessing potential health hazards from drugs in drinking water and recycled municipal wastewater, *Regulatory Toxicology and Pharmacology*, 60, pp. 1–19.

Clark, J. H., Breeden, S. W. & Summerton, L. (2010) Green(er) pharmacy, in: K. Klaus & M. Hempel (Eds) *Green and Sustainable Pharmacy*, pp. 37–60 (Berlin: Springer).

Cooney, C. M. (2009) Study detects trace levels of pharmaceuticals in US drinking water, *Environmental Science and Technology*, 43(3), pp. 551–551.

Daughton, C. G. (2001) Pharmaceuticals and personal care products in the environment: overarching issues and overview, in: C. G. Daughton & T. L. Jones-Lepp (Eds) *Pharmaceuticals and Care Products in the Environment*, pp. 2–38 (Washington, DC: American Chemical Society).

Daughton, C. G. & Ruhoy, I. S. (2009) Environmental footprint of pharmaceuticals: the significance of factors beyond direct excretion to sewers, *Environmental Toxicology and Chemistry*, 28(12), pp. 2495–2521.

Daughton, C. G. & Ternes, T. A. (1999) Pharmaceuticals and personal care products in the environment: agents of subtle change? *Environmental Health Perspectives*, 107, pp. 907–937.

Ericson, I., Domingo, J. L., Nadal, M., Bigas, E., Llebaria, X., van Bavel, B. & Lindström, G. (2009) Levels of perfluorinated chemicals in municipal drinking water from Catalonia, Spain: public health implications, *Archives of Environmental Contamination and Toxicology*, 57(4), pp. 631–638.

Fawell, J. K. & Chipman, K. (2000) Endocrine disrupters, drinking water and public reassurance, *Water and Environmental Management*, 5(6), pp. 4–5.

Fawell, J. K., Sheahan, D., James, H. A., Hurst, M. & Scott, S. (2001) Oestrogens and oestrogenic activity in raw and treated water in Severn Trent Water, *Water Research*, 35(5), pp. 1240–1244.

Fick, J., Lindberg, R. H., Parkkonen, J., Arvidsson, B., Tysklind, M. & Larsson, D. G. (2010) Therapeutic levels of levonorgestrel detected in blood plasma of fish: results from screening rainbow trout exposed to treated sewage effluents, *Environmental Science and Technology*, 44(7), pp. 2661–2666.

Focazio, M. J., Kolpin, D. W., Barnes, K. K., Furlong, E. T., Meyer, M. T., Zaugg, S. D., Barber, L. B. & Thurman, M. E. (2008) A national reconnaissance for pharmaceuticals and other organic wastewater contaminants in the United States. II: Untreated drinking water sources, *Science of the Total Environment*, 402, pp. 201–216.

Fromme, H., Tittlemier, S. A., Völkel, W., Wilhelm, M. & Twardella, D. (2009) Perfluorinated compounds: exposure assessment for the general population in Western countries, *International Journal of Hygiene and Environmental Health*, 212(3), pp. 239–270.

Hayward, K. (2011) Emerging contaminants: the need for a sound-science solution, *Water*, 21, 13(3), pp. 17–18.

Houtman, C. J., van Oostveen, A. M., Brouwer, A., Lamoree, M. H. & Legler, J. (2004) Identification of estrogenic compounds in fish bile using bioassay-directed fractionation, *Environmental Science and Technology*, 38, pp. 6415–6423.

Kasprzyk-Hordern, B., Dinsdale, R. & Guwy, A. (2008) The occurrence of pharmaceuticals, personal care products, endocrine disruptors and illicit drugs in surface water in South Wales, UK, *Water Research*, 42(13), pp. 3498–3518.

Kolpin, D. W., Furlong, E. T., Meyer, M. T., Thurman, E. M., Zaugg, S. D., Barber, L. B. & Buxton, H. T. (2002) Pharmaceuticals, hormones, and other organic wastewater contaminants in U.S. streams, 1999–2000: a national reconnaissance, *Environmental Science and Technology*, 36(6), pp. 1202–1211.

Kunacheva, C., Tanaka, S., Fujii, S., Boontanon, S. K., Musirat, C. & Wongwattana, T. (2011) Determination of perfluorinated compounds (PFCs) in solid and liquid phase river water samples in Chao Phraya River, Thailand, *Water Science and Technology*, 64(3), pp. 684–692.

Kuster, M., de Alda, M. J., Hernando, M. D., Petrovic, M., Martin-Alonso, J. & Barcelo, D. (2008) Analysis and occurrence of pharmaceuticals, estrogens, progestogens and polar pesticides in sewage treatment plant effluents, river water and drinking water in the Llobregat river basin (Barcelona, Spain), *Journal of Hydrology*, 358, pp. 112–123.

Kwadijk, C. J., Korytar, P. & Koelmans, A. A. (2010) Distribution of perfluorinated compounds in aquatic systems in the Netherlands, *Environmental Science and Technology*, 44, pp. 3746–3751.

Lam, S. H., Hlaing, M. M., Zhang, X., Yan, C., Duan, Z., Zhu, L., Ung, C. Y., Mathavan, S., Ong, C. N. & Gong, Z. (2011) Toxicogenomic and phenotypic analyses of bisphenol-a early-life exposure toxicity in zebrafish, *PLoS ONE*, 6(12): e28273.

Lam, S. H., Mathavan, S., Tong, Y., Li, H., Karuturi, R. K., Wu, Y., Vega, V. B., Liu, E. T. & Gong, Z. (2008) Zebrafish whole-adult-organism chemogenomics for large-scale predictive and discovery chemical biology, *PLoS Genetics*, 4(7): e1000121.

Li, J. J., Hartono, D., Ong, C. N., Bay, B. H. & Yung, L. Y. (2010) Autophagy and oxidative stress associated with gold nanoparticles, *Biomaterials*, 31(23), pp. 5996–6003.

Loos, R., Locoro, G., Comero, S., Contini, S., Schwesig, D., Werres, F., Balsaa, P., Gans, O., Weiss, S., Blaha, L., Bolchi, M. & Gawlik, B. M. (2010) Pan-European survey on the occurrence of selected polar organic persistent pollutants in ground water, *Water Research*, 44(14), pp. 4115–4126.

Lubick, N. (2009) India's drug problem, *Nature*, 457, pp. 640–641.

McLachlan, M. S., Holmstrom, K. E., Reth, M. & Berger, U. (2007) Riverine discharge of perfluorinated carboxylates from the European continent, *Environmental Science and Technology*, 41, pp. 7260–7265.

Mons, M. N., Hoogenboom, A. C. & Noij, T. H. M. (2003) *Pharmaceuticals and Drinking Water Supply in the Netherlands*, Kiwa Report BTO 2003.040 (Nieuwegein, the Netherlands: Kiwa Water Research).

Nguyen, V. T., Reinhard, M. & Karina, G. Y. (2011) Occurrence and source characterization of perfluorochemicals in an urban watershed, *Chemosphere*, 82(9), pp. 1277–1285.

Petrovic, M., Sole, M., de Alda, M. J. L. & Barcelo, D. (2002) Endocrine disruptors in sewage treatment plants, receiving river waters, and sediments: integration of chemical analysis and biological effects on feral carp, *Environmental Toxicology and Chemistry*, 21, pp. 2146–2156.

Rahman, M. F., Yanful, E. K. & Jasim, S. Y. (2009) Endocrine disrupting compounds (EDCs) and pharmaceuticals and personal care products (PPCPs) in the aquatic environment: implications for the drinking water industry and global environmental health, *Journal of Water and Health*, 7, pp. 224–243.

Reddersen, K., Heberer, T. & Dunnbier, U. (2002) Identification and significance of phenazone drugs and their metabolites in ground- and drinking water, *Chemosphere*, 49(6), pp. 539–544.

Schriks, M., Heringa, M. B., van der Kooi, M. M., de Voogt, P. & van Wezel, A. P. (2009) Toxicological relevance of emerging contaminants for drinking water quality, *Water Research*, 44, pp. 461–476.

Shi, Y., Pan, Y., Wang, J. & Cai, Y. (2011) Distribution of perfluorinated compounds in water, sediment, biota and floating plants in Baiyangdian Lake, China, *Journal of Environmental Monitoring*, 14(2), pp. 636–642.

Skutlarek, D., Exner, M. & Farber, H. (2006) Perfluorinated surfactants in surface and drinking waters, *Environmental Science and Pollution Research International*, 13, pp. 299–307.

Stanford, B. D., Trenholm, R. A., Holady, J. C., Vanderford, B. J. & Snyder, S. A. (2010) Estrogenic activity of US drinking waters: a relative exposure comparison, *Journal of the American Water Works Association*, 110(11), pp. 55–65.

Sukardi, H., Chng, H. T., Chan, E. C., Gong, Z. & Lam, S. H. (2011) Zebrafish for drug toxicity screening: bridging the in vitro cell-based models and in vivo mammalian models, *Expert Opinion on Drug Metabolism & Toxicology*, 7, pp. 579–589.

Sun, H., Li, F., Zhang, T., Zhang, X., He, N., Song, Q., Zhao, L., Sun, L. & Sun, T. (2011) Perfluorinated compounds in surface waters and WWTPs in Shenyang, China: mass flows and source analysis, *Water Research*, 45(15), pp. 4483–4490.

Ternes, T. (2001) Pharmaceuticals and metabolites as contaminants of the aquatic environment, in: C. G. Daughton & T. L. Jones-Lepp (Eds) *Pharmaceuticals and Care Products in the Environment*, pp. 39–55 (Washington, DC: American Chemical Society).

Thompson, J., Eaglesham, G. & Mueller, J. (2011) Concentrations of PFOS, PFOA and other perfluorinated alkyl acids in Australian drinking water, *Chemosphere*, 83(10), pp. 1320–1325.

Tong, Y., Shan, T., Poh, Y. K., Yan, T., Wang, H., Lam, S. H. & Gong, Z. (2004) Molecular cloning of zebrafish and medaka vitellogenin genes and comparison of their expression in response to 17beta-estradiol, *Gene*, 328, pp. 25–36.

USGS (2011) *Toxic Substances Hydrology Program: Emerging Contaminants in the Environment* (US Geological Survey). Available at: http://toxics.usgs.gov/regional/emc/ (accessed 7 March 2012).

Watts and Crane Associates (2007) *Desk Based Review of Current Knowledge on Pharmaceuticals in Drinking Water and Estimation of Potential Levels: Final Report to DWI (Defra Project Code: CSA 7184/WT02046/DWI70/2/213)* (Faringdon, UK: Watts and Crane Associates).

Watts, M. M., Pascoe, D. & Carroll, K. (2002) Population responses of the freshwater amphipod Gammarus pulex (L.) to an environmental estrogen, 17α-ethinylestradiol, *Environmental Toxicology and Chemistry*, 21, pp. 445–450.

Wenzel, A., Müller, J. & Ternes, T. (2003) *Study on endocrine disrupters in drinking water: Final Report ENV.D.1/ETU/2000/0083* (Smallenberg: European Commission).

WHO (2002) *Global Assessment of the State-of-the-Science of Endocrine Disruptors, WHO/PCS/EDC/02.2* (Geneva: World Health Organization).

WHO (2011a) *Pharmaceuticals in Drinking Water* (Geneva: World Health Organization).

WHO (2011b) *Guidelines for Drinking-Water Quality*, 4th ed. (Geneva: World Health Organization).

Zhang, T., Sun, H., Lin, Y., Wang, L., Zhang, X., Liu, Y., Geng, X., Zhao, L., Li, F. & Kannan, K. (2011) Perfluorinated compounds in human blood, water, edible freshwater fish, and seafood in China: daily intake and regional differences in human exposures, *Journal of Agriculture and Food Chemistry*, 59(20), pp. 11168–11176.

An Overview of Policies Impacting Water Quality and Governance in India

S. R. WATE

National Environmental Engineering Research Institute, Nagpur, India

ABSTRACT   *Water is one of the most crucial elements in developmental planning of India for the 21st century. The growth of urban megalopolises, increased industrial activity and dependence of the agricultural sector on chemicals and fertilizers has resulted in the overcharging of the carrying capacity of the water bodies to assimilate and decompose wastes. Several ambitious legal and institutional measures and projects like the Water Pollution Act, Pollution Control Boards, and the National River Action Plan have yielded no significant results. There is a need to bring about a perceivable shift in philosophy and address water problems to meet the demands of a growing population by improving efficiency, prioritizing the water demand sector-wise, and adopting policies and practices that check resource degradation.*

Water Resources of India

India is rich in water resources, being endowed with a network of rivers and blessed with snow cover in the Himalayan range that can meet a variety of water requirements of the country. However, with the rapid increase in the population of the country and the need to meet the increasing demands of irrigation, human, and industrial consumption, the available water resources in many parts of the country are being depleted and water quality has deteriorated. About 85% of the rural population in India is solely dependent on groundwater, which is being depleted at a high rate. NASA's Gravity Recovery and Climate Experiment (GRACE) satellites have determined that groundwater in north-western India is being depleted at an average rate of 4 cm equivalent height of water per year (Rodell *et al.*, 2009). This amounts to around 18 km^3 of water per year. In the urban areas, though, about 60% of the population is dependent on surface water sources; however, the availability and quality are questionable. Studies put the amount of available aggregate annual utilizable water in India, surface and ground together, at about 1,100 billion m^3. Population growth is expected to result in a decline in the per capita availability of fresh water. In 1947, this was measured at 5,150 m^3. By the year 2000, it was around 2,200 m^3. It has been recently estimated that by 2017 India will be "water stressed": per capita availability will decline to 1,600 m^3 (Rodell *et al.*, 2009).

Annually, India receives 4,000 km^3 of water through rainfall. Three-quarters of this occurs during the monsoon. The surface flow is estimated as 1,880 km^3 (CPCB, 2009).

The annual replenishable groundwater resources are assessed to be about $600\,km^3$, of which the annual usable resources are estimated at $420\,km^3$. The inland water resources of the country are classified as rivers and canals; reservoirs; tanks and ponds; beels, oxbow lakes, and derelict water; and brackish water. Other than rivers and canals, total water bodies cover an area of about 7 million hectares. There are a few desert rivers, which flow for some distance and get lost in deserts. There are completely arid areas where evaporation equals rainfall and hence there is no surface flow. The medium and minor river basins are coastal rivers. The Brahmaputra, Ganga, Indus, and Godavari put together serve more than half of the area of the country. The whole of the west coast, stretching 1,500 km between Surat in Gujarat and Cape Comorin in Tamilnadu, is fed by 14 medium and 18 minor river basins, leaving important cities like Bombay, Panaji, Cochin, and Trivandrum out of major river basins. On the east coast of Peninsular India there are three areas which are out of any major river basins. These are the area south of River Cauvery from Madurai to Cape Comorin; the area between Pennar and Cauvery basin in which Chennai and Pondicherry are located; and the area between Mahanadi and Godavari basins on the Orissa coast. There is a significant variation both in the quantity of discharge from a major basin to minor one and also in the quality of discharge from region to region.

Surface Water

Not all the major river basins are perennial. Only 4 of the 13 major basins possess areas of high rainfall. The Brahmaputra, Ganga, Mahanadi, and Brahamani have annual average discharge of a minimum of 0.47 million m^3 per km^2; they are perennial. Six basins (Krishna, Indus, Godavari, Narmada, Tapi, and Subarnarekha) occupy the category of medium rainfall and have annual average discharge of a minimum of 0.26 million m^3 per km^2; the remaining four (Cauvery, Mahi, Sabarmati, and Pennar) occupy the category of low rainfall and have annual average discharge between of 0.06 and 0.24 million m^3 per km^2. Thus, many of the major river basins also go dry during summer, leaving no available water for dilution of the waste water discharged into them (CPCB, 2009).

Groundwater

The replenishable groundwater potential of the country has been estimated by the Ministry of Water Resources as $431\,km^3$ per year. The potential available for irrigation is $360\,km^3$ per year; the remaining 16% is available for drinking, industrial and other purposes. The figure for net draft of groundwater considering the present utilization indicates that a substantial portion (about 68%) of the total potential remains untapped. However, the development of groundwater in different areas of the country has not been uniform. Highly intensive development of groundwater in certain areas in the country has resulted in over-exploitation, leading to decline in the levels of groundwater and scarcity of drinking water during summer (Rao *et al.*, 2011).

Water Quality Issues

The shortage of water in India is slowly affecting the lives of people as well as the environment around them. Some of the major issues are:

- As a result of excessive extraction of groundwater to meet agricultural, industrial, and domestic demands, drinking water is not available during the critical summer months in many parts of the country.
- About 10% of the rural and urban population does not have access to regular safe drinking water and many more are threatened. Most of them depend on unsafe water sources to meet their daily needs. Moreover, water shortages in cities and villages have led to large volumes of water being collected and transported over great distances by tankers and pipelines.
- Chemical contaminants (fluoride, arsenic, and selenium) pose a very serious health hazard in the country. It is estimated that about 70 million people in 20 states are at risk due to excess fluoride and around 10 million are at risk due to excess arsenic in groundwater. Apart from this, increases in the concentration of chloride, TDS, nitrate, and iron in groundwater are of great concern for a sustainable drinking water programme. All these need to be tackled holistically. With over-extraction of groundwater the concentration of chemicals is increasing regularly. West Bengal had been using surface water and shallow ponds as drinking water sources. As the state shifted to groundwater sources, reports of arsenic contamination began coming in from the right bank of the Ganga. Similarly, over-extraction of groundwater has also resulted in increases in fluoride concentration in the states of Andhra Pradesh, Assam, Gujarat, Karnataka, Madhya Pradesh, and Rajasthan.
- Ingress of seawater into coastal aquifers as a result of over-extraction of groundwater has made water supplies more saline and unsuitable for drinking or irrigation.
- Pollution of ground and surface waters from agrochemicals (fertilizers and pesticides) and from industry poses a major environmental health hazard, with potentially significant costs to the country. The World Bank has estimated that the total cost of environmental damage in India amounts to US$9.7 billion annually, or 4.5% of the gross domestic product. Of this, 59% results from the health impacts of water pollution (MoEF, 1999).

Water Quality Policy

In India, laws related to use of water date back to the period when Code of Manu was prescribed, over 3,000 years ago. Water was considered public property, subject to public administration; several penalties were prescribed for unauthorized use, for causing harm to water-holding structures, and for causing pollution of water. Upstream points along a river were reserved for drawing drinking water; *in situ* uses of water such as bathing and laundry were permitted only downstream.

In 1974, the Parliament enacted the Water (Prevention and Control of Water Pollution) Act per the provisions of Article 249, and Article 250, and Clause 1 of Article 252 of the Constitution. "The Act is for the prevention and control of water pollution and the maintaining or restoring of wholesomeness of water, for the establishment, with a view to carrying out the purposes aforesaid, of Boards for the prevention and control of water pollution, for conferring on and assigning to such Boards powers and functions relating thereto and for matters connected therewith" (Cullet, 2007).

According to the Constitution of India, Water is in the "state list". Therefore, states can enact any legislation regarding water, that is to say water supplies, irrigation and canals, drainage, embankments, water storage, and water power, excepting the regulations and development of inter-state rivers and river valleys.

While the intervention of the central government in water regulation is limited by the constitutional scheme, the importance of national regulation in water has already been recognized in certain areas. The Water Act gives powers to water boards to set standards and regulations for prevention and control of pollution. Besides statutory frameworks, a number of common-law principles linking access to water and rights over land still prevail in India. These include separate rules for surface and groundwater. With regard to surface water, existing rules still derive from the early common rule of riparian rights. Thus, the basic rule was that riparian owners had a right to use the water of a stream flowing past their land equally with other riparian owners, to have the water come to them undiminished in flow, quantity, or quality. In recent times, the riparian right theory has increasingly been rejected as the appropriate basis for adjudicating water claims. Further, common law rights must today be read in the context of the recognition that water is a public trust. If the latter principle is effectively applied in the future, it would have important impacts on the types of rights and privileges that can be claimed over surface water.

The Pollution Control Boards

In India, the Central Pollution Control Board (CPCB) was established under the provision of the 1974 Water (Prevention and Control of Pollution) Act. This follows the recommendations of the special committee that was set up in 1962 to draft an act for the prevention of water pollution. The CPCB was a response that was sought to curb the pollution of various water resources in the country that was already affecting the quality of potable water and the overall ability of water to sustain the rapid level of pollution by development activities. The Water Cess Act of 1977 (Cullet, 2007) provided the central and state pollution control boards with a funding tool, enabling them to charge the water user with a cess designed as a financial support for the board's activities. The Environment Protection Act of 1986 is umbrella legislation that provides a single focus in the country for the protection of environment and seeks to plug the loopholes of earlier legislation relating to environment.

As explained earlier, the composition of the pollution control boards (PCBs) was first defined in the Water Act of 1974. The boards are usually composed of a qualified chairman; a full time secretary; five official members; three official members each coming from the fields of agriculture, fishing, and industry or trade respectively; two persons representing government corporations; members of the state pollution control boards. PCBs are given the following powers:

- approval of applications for the establishment of operational facilities; making, varying, or revoking orders to prevention and control of water pollution
- ordering construction, modification, alteration, or extension of safe disposal systems
- ordering remedial measures necessary to prevent and control pollution
- planning; advising
- collecting information; inspecting
- setting standards; participating in investigation and research.

Ever since 1974, many polluters have disregarded the directions of pollution control boards and violated the conditions of consent with impunity. This is because, from the start, PCBs have not been fully empowered to exercise coercive powers of their own. For the most part this comes from the clash of jurisdiction of powers. Overdependence of the legal system is perhaps one of the major problems engulfing enforcement actions by the PCBs. In India, to prosecute polluters, PCBs are required to approach the judiciary. This often encourages legal wrangling by polluters. The CPCB does not have sufficient teeth for pollution control and its infrastructure resources are not adequate to deliver the mandate.

Water Quality Management

Water quality management in India is accomplished under the provision of the Water (Prevention and Control of Pollution) Act of 1974. The basic objective of this act is to maintain and restore the wholesomeness of national aquatic resources by prevention and control of pollution. It was considered ambitious to maintain or restore all natural water bodies at a pristine level. Planning pollution control activities to attain such a goal is bound to deter developmental activities and to be cost prohibitive. Since the natural water bodies are used for various competing as well as conflicting demands, the objective is to restore and/or maintain natural water bodies or their parts to just the quality needed for their best uses. Thus, a concept of "designated best use" (DBU) was developed. According to this concept, out of the various uses a water body is put to, the use which demands the highest quality of water is the "designated best use", and accordingly the water body is designated. Primary water quality criteria for different uses have been identified. A summary of the use-based classification system is presented in Table 1.

Water Quality Monitoring

The CPCB, in collaboration with concerned SPCBs, established a nationwide network for water quality monitoring comprising 1,019 stations in 27 states and 6 union territories. The monitoring is done monthly or quarterly in surface waters and twice a year in the case of groundwater. The monitoring network covers 200 rivers, 60 lakes, 5 tanks, 3 ponds, 3 creeks, 13 canals, 17 drains and 321 wells. Of the 1,019 stations, 592 are on rivers, 65 on lakes, 17 on drains, 13 on canals, 5 on tanks, 3 on creeks, and 3 on ponds; 321 are groundwater stations.

Presently the inland water quality monitoring network is operated under a three-tier programme—that is the Global Environment Monitoring System (GEMS), Monitoring of Indian National Aquatic Resources System (MINARS), and the Yamuna Action Plan (YAP). Water samples are being analyzed for 28 parameters, consisting of 9 core parameters plus 19 other physico-chemical and bacteriological parameters apart from the field observations. Besides this, 9 trace metals and 22 pesticides are also analysed in selected samples. Biomonitoring is also carried out on specific locations. In view of limited resources, limited numbers of organic pollution–related parameters are monitored; that is micropollutants (toxic metals and persistent organic compounds) are analyzed once per year to assess the water quality.

Water Cess Act

The government has introduced, as a supplementary measure, major economic incentives for pollution abatement, besides the "command and control" regulatory mechanism. The Water Cess Act was introduced in 1977, empowering the state pollution control boards to levy

Table 1. Classification of inland surface waters (CPCB standards). A: Drinking water source without conventional treatment but after disinfection. B: Outdoor bathing (organized). C: Drinking water source with conventional treatment followed by disinfection. D: Propagation of wild life, fisheries. E: Irrigation, industrial, cooling, controlled waste disposal.

Characteristics	A	B	C	D	E
Dissolved oxygen, mg/L, min	6	5	4	4	-
Biochemical oxygen demand, mg/L, max	2	3	3	-	-
Total coliform organisms, MPN/100 mL, max[1]	50	500	5,000	-	-
Total dissolved solids, mg/L, max	500	-	1,500	-	2,100
Chlorides (as Cl), mg/L, max	250	-	600	-	600
Colour, Hazen units, max	10	300	300	-	-
Sodium absorption ratio, max	-	-	-	-	26
Boron (as B), mg/L, bax	-	-	-	-	2
Sulphates (as SO_4), mg/L, max	400	-	400	-	1,000
Nitrates (as NO_3), mg/L, max	20	-	50	-	-
Free ammonia (as N), mg/L, max	-	-	-	1.2	-
Conductivity at 25°C, micromho/cm, max	-	-	-	1,000	2,250
pH	6.5–8.5	6.5–8.5	6.5–8.5	6.5–8.5	6.5–8.5
Arsenic (as As), mg/L, max	0.05	0.2	0.2	-	-
Iron (as Fe), mg/L, max	0.3	-	50	-	-
Fluorides (as F), mg/L, max	1.5	1.5	1.5	-	-
Lead (as Pb), mg/L, max	0.1	-	0.1	-	-
Copper (as Cu), mg/L, max	1.5	-	1.5	-	-
Zinc (as Zn), mg/L, max	15	-	15	-	-

[1] If the coliform count is found to be more than the prescribed tolerance limits, the criteria for coliforms shall be satisfied if not more than 20% of samples show more than the tolerance limits specified, and not more than 5% of samples show values more than 4 times the tolerance limits. Further, the faecal coliform should not be more than 20% of the coliform. Source: Indian Standard (IS:2296-1982).

a cess on local authorities supplying water to consumers and on consumption of water for certain specified activities. The act also provides for a rebate on the cess payable if the local authority or industry concerned installs a plant to treat sewage or trade effluent. The cess rates were increased three-fold in February 1992. A rebate of 25% on the cess payable has been provided to those industries whose wastewater discharge does not exceed the quantity declared by them and which also comply with the effluent standards prescribed under the Water Act and the Environment Protection Act. The act was further amended in 2003.

Special Schemes

Common effluent treatment plants schemes. Pollution from small-size industries (SSIs) puts the Indian regulators in front of a difficult arbitrage between economic development and environmental sustainability. Indeed, 40% of the wastewater generated by India's most polluting industries comes from small-size industries. With the adoption of the Water Act, those small-size industries had in theory the obligation to treat their effluent in order to reach a pollution concentration respecting the minimum acceptable standards laid down by the SPCBs. Nevertheless, the size of these facilities makes the installation of a standard effluent treatment plant (ETP) unaffordable because of the important fixed cost of an individual ETP. Therefore, public authorities have taken the initiative to promote common effluent treatment plant (CETP) schemes, allowing small industries to jointly treat their effluents. The CETP concept was originally promoted by the Ministry of Environment and Forests (MoEF) in 1984. The first CETP in India was constructed in 1985 in Jeedimetlha near Hyderabad, Andhra Pradesh, to treat waste water from pharmaceutical and chemical industries. As of 1999, 82 CETPs had been set up around the country.

Although CETPs are mainly seen as a means to take advantage of scale economies, these schemes also act as subsidies from public powers to small industries in order to allow them to respect the standards. The minimum participation asked from SSIs in the CETP schemes implemented in India is 20%. The rest is funded through subsidies from central and state governments as well as loans from international organizations such as the World Bank or Indian institutions such as the Industrial Development Bank of India or Infrastructure Leasing & Financial Services.

The subsidy effect in favour of SSIs may be increased in some cases when an industrial area gathers SSIs as well as larger polluting industries. In these case, some cross-subsidies may be set up by asking the larger industries to contribute to the development of the CETP while treating their effluent before releasing them in the common drain.

There are in fact diverging opinions on the relevance of CETPs in a national pollution abatement policy. Per the CPCB report, it has been clearly shown that compared to individual ETPs, CETPS are more cost-effective in reaching the effluent concentration standards (CPCB, 2005). However, treating the effluents is not the only way to meet the standards, and process changes induced by regulatory pressure have proved to give good results in several studies (CPCB, 2005), and can even enhance the company's competitiveness. In a seminal article published in 1991, Michael Porter formulated what is usually referred to as the Porter hypothesis: "Strict environmental regulations do not inevitably hinder competitive advantage against foreign rivals; indeed, they often enhance it" (Porter, 1991).

The National River Action Plan. The National River Conservation Directorate (NRCD), under the Ministry of Environment and Forest, Government of India, is in charge of coordinating several river conservation plans. Under the National River Action Plan (NRAP), certain stretches of major rivers with high or intermediate levels of pollution were identified by the CPCB. These plans basically lay the framework for setting up sewage diversion and treatment facilities, along with action directed toward mitigation of industrial pollution through the setting up of individual or common effluent treatment plants.

The first large-scale action plan oriented towards conservation and rehabilitation of water resources was the Ganga Action Plan (GAP), launched in 1985. The Ganga River basin is one of the most populous in the world, with five Indian states relying on the Ganga for their water needs (Haryana, Delhi, Uttar Pradesh including Uttarakhand, Bihar, West Bengal). The main elements of the strategy adopted for the first phase of the Ganga Action Plan were a combination of diversion and treatment of sewage from the major cities in the river basin, as well as provision of low-cost sanitation for rural areas, and other interventions such as river bank development and the setting up of electric crematoria. In the GAP, 29 towns were selected along the river and 261 schemes of pollution abatement sanctioned. The GAP has led to an observable enhancement of river quality in the Ganga. Along with the actions directed toward domestic pollution, 68 high polluters were identified along the Ganga River Basin and were asked to conform with the standards by setting up ETPs. At present, 156 towns are being considered under the NRAP, out of which about 74 towns are located on the river Ganga, 21 on the Yamuna, 12 on the Damodar, 6 on the Godavari, 9 on the Cauvery, 4 each on the Tungbhadra and Satlej, 3 each on the Subarnarekha, Betwa, Wainganga, Brahmini, Chambal, and Gomti, 2 on the Krishna, and 1 each on the Sabarmati, Khan, Kshipra, Narmada, and Mahanadi (MoEF, 1999).

National Drinking Water Mission. The Accelerated Rural Water Supply Programme (ARWSP) was introduced in 1972–73 by the Government of India to assist the states and union territories in accelerating the pace of coverage of drinking water supply.

The Water Technology Mission of Drinking Water and Related Water Management, also called the National Drinking Water Mission (NDWM), was launched in 1986 (concurrently with the GAP). It was one of the five Societal Missions launched by the Government of India. The NDWM was renamed the Rajiv Gandhi National Drinking Water Mission in 1991 for covering states where the supply of potable water is problematic due to the presence of excessive iron and manganese, chloride and sulphate, fluoride, dissolved solids, and nitrates. The National Drinking Water Mission faced the problem of developing inexpensive treatment technologies as well as testing and treatment kits. The mission has been quite successful due to effective water quality management in rural India. High concentrations of arsenic in the groundwater in many districts of Bengal in India has become problematic during the last few years and has led to a high incidence of skin diseases as well as cancer. Fortunately, concerted efforts—such as tapping a deeper third layer beyond 100–150 meters below ground level; utilizing surface water from rivers, lakes, and ponds, which are normally free from arsenic contamination; sanitary protected ring-wells tapping the shallow aquifers; and arsenic removal techniques through domestic filters, attached hand pumps, and arsenic removal plants in piped water supply schemes—have resulted in development of solutions for this problem. The Government of India introduced an Arsenic Sub-mission in 1994 under the Rajiv Gandhi National Drinking Water Mission to tackle the arsenic problem in West Bengal on a 75:25 cost-sharing basis between the centre and the state.

Management of lakes and wetlands. Natural and human-made lakes happen to be a major source of water supply in many regions in India. Excessive siltation, variation in run-off, and changing land use in the watersheds have contributed to depletion of these water bodies. The water quality in lakes is also affected by run-off loaded with fertilizers, insecticides, and pesticides, coupled with discharges from industries, as well as human settlements. Major interventions for improving the lake systems in the country include watershed management, dredging operations, emphasis on treatment of effluents before discharge into the lakes, and disposal of solid wastes away from the shores of the lakes. Major efforts of the central and state governments have been directed towards clean-up of such problematic lakes as the Dal in Kashmir, Naini in Uttar Pradesh, Chilka in Orissa, Hussain Sagar in Andhra Pradesh, Poondy in Tamil Nadu, and Lok Tak in Manipur (Jumbe *et al.*, 2007).

Groundwater management. The policy guidelines and the groundwater regulatory framework encompass various aspects relating to groundwater ownership, environment, monitoring, abstraction, subsidy, power tariff, licensing, registration, and community participation. The present-day law stipulates that an owner of land is also the owner of the underlying water. But groundwater is a common resource moving under the ground. A person pumping from underground always draws water from his neighbours as well. Ownership of groundwater is therefore a complicated and contentious issue.

Ownership is an important issue to be resolved before implementation of any strategy for managing groundwater resources. The absolute ownership concept, embodied in the Indian Easements Act of 1882, has paved the way for unlimited extraction of groundwater by landowners. One of the consequences of this law is the overexploitation of groundwater by landowners, which may lead to the development of water quality problems such as nitrate, fluoride, and arsenic.

The contribution of groundwater for drinking, industrial, and irrigation use has been on the increase during the last two decades. Indiscriminate extraction of groundwater already poses the threat of aquifers going dry in some parts of the country. The central and state groundwater boards have, therefore, prepared groundwater availability maps and prescribed extraction rates in a bid to ensure that extraction is balanced with recharge. The country has been zoned depending upon whether water is available in plenty, or it has already become scarce in the region. Accurate determination of groundwater reserves can be done through actual borehole data in a given region. Extraction of groundwater is prohibited in some regions where water depletion has already become critical.

Implementation of Water Policy and Acts

The existing water law framework in India is characterized by the coexistence of a number of different principles, rules, and acts adopted over many decades. These include common-law principles and irrigation acts from the colonial period as well as more recent regulation of water quality and the judicial recognition of a human right to water. The lack of umbrella legislation at the national level has ensured that the different state and central legal interventions and other principles do not necessarily coincide and may in fact be in opposition in certain cases.

In general, water law is largely state based. This is due to the constitutional scheme, which since the Government of India Act of 1935 (Cullet, 2007) has in principle given power to the states to legislate in this area. Thus, states have the exclusive power to regulate water supplies, irrigation and canals, drainage and embankments, water storage, hydropower, and fisheries. There are nevertheless restrictions with regard to the use of inter-state rivers. Further, the central government is entitled to legislate on certain issues. These include shipping and navigation on national waterways as well as powers to regulate the use of tidal and territorial waters. The Constitution also provides that the central government can legislate with regard to the adjudication of inter-state water disputes. Besides statutory frameworks, a number of common-law principles linking access to water and rights over land still prevail in India. These include separate rules for surface and groundwater. With regard to surface water, existing rules still derive from the early common rule of riparian rights. Thus, the basic rule was that riparian owners had a right to use the water of a stream flowing past their land equally with other riparian owners, and to have the water come to them undiminished in flow, quantity, or quality.

Water law includes a number of other laws and regulations that are directly or indirectly concerned with water. One example concerns dams. Two major aspects of dam building are regulated by laws and regulations which are only partly concerned with water. The Environmental Impact Assessment Notification provides a framework for assessing the environmental impacts of planned big hydropower and irrigation projects. Further, there are Guidelines for Environmental Impact Assessment of River Valley Projects, which provide a general framework since 1985 for assessing the impacts of planned big dam projects which affect the river water quality downstream of the dam because of the reduction in flow, thereby reducing the waste-assimilation capacity of the water body (MoEF, 1999).

The general picture which emerges is that of a multiplicity of principles and rules, a multiplicity of instruments, and the lack of an overall framework. While certain principles have remained relatively constant until recently, such as the assertion of the state's right to use surface waters in the public interest, there have been a number of changes.

There have also been progressive calls for changes in the law and policy framework concerning water. This is due to two broad factors. First, the water law and policy framework was for a long time the object of relatively little attention. While many water-related laws were adopted over several decades, comparatively little was done to provide a broader integrated framework for water. Secondly, the recognition that there is a water crisis in most countries of the world and that availability of and access to fresh water will be a challenge for nearly all countries in coming decades has led to a number of international initiatives to reform water governance, law, and policy in most developing countries. In other words, domestic and international factors have contributed to ongoing water law and policy reforms. This is taking the form of reforms, which are changing and will change existing water law as well as expand the scope of regulation. Stringent law and heavy penalties for water polluters and prohibiting the extraction of groundwater will definitely help in improving the quality of surface and groundwater sources.

Water sector reforms have been proposed as a way to address diminishing per capita availability, increasing problems in water quality, and increasing competition for control, access, and use of available fresh water. They seek comprehensive reform of governance in the water sector. Current reforms seek in particular to reduce the role played by the public sector and to emphasize the direct contributions of individuals to their water needs and the participation of the private sector. Increasing use of water has led to a number of suggestions to remedy the situation. These include new strategies to cope with all the various water-related issues. Water pollution has been addressed through the introduction of environmental measures to control and reduce it. Access to domestic water has been the object of various governmental and other programmes. The provision of irrigation water and water to cities, for instance, have been taken up in the context of the construction of large dams.

Over the past couple of decades, a more coordinated effort at changing water law has been put in place.

Groundwater Policy and Practice

India does not have any specific law defining ownership and rights over water sources. Several court judgments in post-Independence India have affirmed that all natural resources—resources that are by nature meant for public use and enjoyment—are held by the State in public trust. However, the legal position on whether groundwater is a resource meant for public use is fuzzy, and India has no law that explicitly defines groundwater ownership. Section 7(g) of the Indian Easement Act states that every landowner has the right to "collect and dispose" of all water under the land within his or her own limits, and all water on its surface that does not pass in a defined channel. Hence, by this act, the owner of a piece of land does not, strictly speaking, own the groundwater under the land or surface water on the land; he or she only has the right to collect and use the water. However, it is customarily accepted across India that a well on a piece of land belongs to the owner of that land, and others have no right to extract water from the well or restrict the landowner's rights to use the water. So groundwater is mostly controlled by the private sector. The National Water Policy (Cullet, 2007) clearly specifies that water is a state subject; therefore its legislation and enforcement are within the purview of state governments. Further groundwater protection–related issues are often linked with public-interest litigations and court judgments. There is a need to ensure uniformity in monitoring stands and avoid some duplication.

Regulation is enforced in the form of bore well registration and licensing in designated or notified areas. Indirect means of regulation (through incentives and disincentives) include subsidy, electricity pricing, taxation, quotas, and community participation. Groundwater pollution is controlled through regulatory rules for compliance by polluting industries and municipalities. The guiding principles are to make the polluter pay and to remediate any contamination of groundwater aquifers. Special care with respect to drinking water in terms of well-head protection zones has also been defined. However, indirect enforcement does not yet yield significant results.

With continued over-exploitation and declining groundwater levels, the Supreme Court of India on the basis of public interest litigation passed several orders in 1996, and issued directions to the Government of India for setting up the Central Groundwater Authority (CGWA) under the Environment (Protection) Act of 1986 for the purposes of regulation and control of groundwater development. The court further ordered that the CGWA regulate indiscriminate boring and withdrawal of groundwater in the country and issue necessary directions with a view to preserving and protecting the groundwater. Under the Supreme Court notification, the CGWA as a statutory body has been granted the powers, amongst others, to regulate, control, manage, and develop groundwater in the entire country and to issue necessary directions. The CGWA, in consultation with the Ministry of Law, has opined that, though the states are competent to make their own laws pertaining to groundwater and constitute state groundwater authorities, the provisions of the Environment (Protection) Act of 1986 override the state under Article 253 (Cullet, 2007).

Ganga Action Plan

The Ganga Action Plan (GAP) was launched in 1985 with the objective of bringing the water quality of the Ganga and its tributaries to bathing levels. The GAP aimed to tackle 2,794 million litres per day (MLD) of sewage: 882 MLD under the GAP-I and 1,912 MLD under the GAP-II. NRCD records put the estimates of total sewage generation in towns along river Ganga and its tributaries at 5,044 MLD. Delhi alone accounts for 2,270 MLD. The GAP-II was to tackle only 20 MLD in Delhi, and the Delhi government was to handle the balance of 2,250 MLD separately through augmentation of its own available installed capacity.

To achieve the objective of pollution abatement, the GAP took up core and non-core schemes. The core sector schemes consist of interception and diversion schemes and sewage treatment plants designed to tackle point pollution. Non-core schemes comprise low-cost sanitation schemes, riverfront development schemes, and electric and improved wood crematoria, and tackle non-point, non-measurable pollution, such as dumping of solid waste, open defecation, and the dumping of unburnt or half-burnt dead bodies.

However, the GAP was not able to achieve its objectives, despite a total expenditure of INR 9017.1 million over a period of 15 years. There were shortfalls in the allocation of resources. Of the total domestic sewage of 5,044 MLD in 110 towns selected for pollution abatement along the banks of river Ganga and its tributaries, the GAP addressed itself to process only 2,794 MLD. The reported achievement of the participating states was 1,095.69 MLD, only 39% of the truncated target. The assets created in the scheme suffered impairment and closure because of technical design flaws, mismatched between schemes and their components, problems in land acquisition, contract mismanagement, lack of adequate maintenance, and in general because of the lackadaisical attitude of the states and their implementing agencies. Technologies adopted by the NRCD for construction of sewage treatment plants were often questionable inasmuch as they could not adequately address the problem of reducing bacterial load in the river to the desired level.

Water Policy Gaps

The major bottleneck in an effective policy formulation for water quality and management and its implementation is the current institutional set-up involving various government agencies. As many as eight agencies are involved in collecting data on the following water-related parameters: quality of surface water, groundwater quality, monitoring of drinking water quality, sanitation, and drinking water supply. Such a fragmented approach, both at the central and state levels, results in duplication and ambiguity of functions and discourages unitary analysis of this scarce resource.

Water being a state subject, the states are empowered to enact laws or frame policies related to water. Even so, only some of the states have set up organizations for planning and allocating water for various purposes. Though water policy for the country has been prepared by the Ministry of Water Resources, only a few states have their own respective state water policies.

The water cess in industries is potentially an effective instrument for inducing abatement, but the rates of raw water are so low that the rebate has been not much of an incentive so far. It was realized during the later stages of implementation of the Ganga Action Plan that the local authorities were not able to operate and maintain these assets due to inadequate resources and skills. The level of commitment required from the state agencies was also missing. The pollution arose from a number of diffused sources either urban or rural.

Recommendations

River Basin Approach

With water being a subject under the state list, the present approach to water-related matters restricts the issue only to political boundaries, involving a number of agencies and ministries with overlapping responsibilities. Instead, a river basin or sub-basin–based approach to water management is called for. This would ensure that aspects such as water allocation, pollution control, protection of water resources, and mobilization of financial resources are not dealt with in isolation and decisions on the overall development process and land use planning flow from this. The administrative mechanisms of these authorities need to be defined and operationalized in coordination with relevant state government departments, the central government, and representatives from the community, ensuring that the delegation of authority from the existing departments is consistent and avoids any overlapping.

Plug Weaknesses in the Current Policy and Legal Framework

State-specific water policies need to be prepared for all issues concerning a state. Various individual development projects and proposals, water allocation priorities, and guidelines for resource management need to be area-specific and formulated by the states within the framework of such an overall plan. Groundwater legislation aiming at equity and sustainability in access to groundwater and its development needs to be enacted in all states.

Incentives under the Water Cess Act, for instance, have to be made more attractive to make the industries undertake pollution control measures. It is well known that the consumption of water for industrial cooling and boilers is thrice that of process water. Wastewater from cooling and heating systems is less polluted and with a little treatment can easily be recirculated within the same system. With appropriate regulations or incentives, it is possible in most cases to have closed-cycle systems for cooling and heating. The industries can be motivated to implement the pollution control measures by providing financial incentives to promote cleaner technology, process change and providing financial assistance to common facilities such as CETP.

Resource Conservation

Together with the measures towards pollution abatement it is imperative to further intensify efforts for conservation of water to prevent over-exploitation of existing resources and reduce the quantity of wastewater generated. As water tariffs are very low, the consumer has little incentive to conserve water. Industrial water tariffs from public supplies in India are typically based on average cost pricing (rather than marginal cost pricing) and ignore the opportunity cost of water (i.e. the benefits foregone in alternative use). Similarly, the effects of damages caused by industries in polluting surface water and groundwater are ignored in determining water tariffs. Consequently, there are no pollution taxes or effluent charges to be paid by industrial polluters. As a result, from an economic viewpoint, excessive quantities of water are used, and excessive pollution is caused. There is a need to take a fresh look at the existing water pricing structure. Additionally, there is a need to develop and implement cost-effective water appliances such as low-flow cisterns and faucets and formulate citizen forum groups to encourage and raise awareness on water conservation. Besides the Water Cess Act, efforts have to be made to introduce and implement the zero discharge concept, which would enhance recycling and reuse of treated effluent.

Resource Degradation

In order to enhance effective treatment of wastewater, there is a need for better collection and interception of sewage. The existing large number of scattered sources of pollution from high-density, low-income communities needs to be converted into concentrated point sources that are easier to monitor and intercept for treatment. Many low-cost and effective technologies for waste water treatment (e.g. upflow anaerobic sludge blanket (UASB), duckweed ponds, and horizontal filters) have been developed in other parts of the world but are applied to a limited extent in India. There is a need to explore the associated advantages in terms of the negligible amount of energy required, beneficial uses of by-products (sludge as manure and biogas), lower operation and maintenance costs, and so on. Adoption of cleaner technologies by industry would go a long way in safeguarding the quality of scarce resources. Policy initiatives—such as change in emphasis from crisis management to ordered control, regulation, and management; establishing the principles of "precautionary prevention" and "polluter pays"; strong support from the judiciary; and a strong role for local government—can aid the diffusion and implementation of clean technologies by encouraging their procurement by the public sector and other government-owned organizations, leading to development of a domestic market demand for the product.

Community Management

Community management is the key to the successful overall performance of the water sector. It has been amply demonstrated that projects with community inputs are more successful in reaching the greatest number of affected people with long-lasting services. Other benefits include lower costs, greater acceptance of the technology, and better maintenance of facilities by the users. In order to regulate pollution, changes in government policies are required; community participation is also necessary to ensure the success of NRAP.

NGOs can provide a very important link between the community and government institutions. The NGOs can offer their services in capacity-building of the relevant stakeholders, R&D for low-cost and effective water supply and sanitation facilities, and timely enforcement of policies.

References

Central Pollution Control Board (CPCB) (2005) *Performance Status of Common Effluent Treatment Plants in India* (New Delhi: Ministry of Environment & Forests, Government of India).

Central Pollution Control Board (CPCB) (2009) *Status of Water Quality in India* (New Delhi: Ministry of Environment & Forests, Government of India). Available at http://www.whoindia.org/ .../SDE-Workshop_Water_Quality_in_India_MOH.pdf.

Cullet, P. (2007) *Water Law in India: Overview of Existing Framework and Proposed Reforms.* IELRC Working Paper 2007-01 (Geneva: International Environmental Law Research Centre). Available at http://www.ielrc. org/content/w0701.pdf.

Department of Drinking Water Supply (2007) *Guidelines For Preparation of Legislation for Framing Drinking Water Regulations, Rajiv Gandhi National Drinking Water Mission* (New Delhi: Ministry of Rural Development, Government of India).

Jumbe, A. S., Nandini, N. & Tandon, S. (2007) Legal aspects of surface water pollution in India: an overview of existing statutory frameworks in management of lake ecosystems, in: M. Sengupta & R. Dalwani (Eds) *Proceedings of Taal 2007, 12th World Lake Conference*, pp. 1142–1148.

Ministry of Environment and Forests (MoEF) (1999) *The State of the Environment Report* (New Delhi: Government of India).

Ministry of Environment and Forests (MoEF) (2001) *The State of the Environment Report* (New Delhi: Government of India).

Porter, M. E. (1991) America's green strategy, *Scientific American*, 168.

Rao, S. V. N., Grøn, C. & Gupta, A. (2011) *Groundwater Protection: Policy and practice in the EU and India* (EU-India Action Plan Support Facility – Environment, DHI, and Euroconsult Mott MacDonald). Available at: http://www.indiaenvironmentportal.org.in/reports-documents/groundwater-protection-policy-and-practice-eu-and-india (accessed 4 April 2012).

Rodell, M., Velicogna, I. & Famiglietti, J. S. (2009) Satellite-based estimates of groundwater depletion in India, *Nature*, 460, pp. 999–1002.

Water Quality Management in China

DAJUN SHEN

School of Environment and Natural Resources, Renmin University of China, Beijing

ABSTRACT   *This paper analyzes water quality management in China in terms of legislation, institutions, and management instruments, and provides suggestions on improving the system. China has developed a separate, sectoral water quality management system where instruments including standards, function zones, permits, and charges are extensively applied. Nevertheless, problems such as lack of integrated frameworks, overlapping functions, focus on pollution control, poor implementation, and inadequate capacity limit its effectiveness. China should fully implement and reform the current system, restructure water quality management institutions, manage its water resources in a river basin context, and encourage market-based approaches.*

Introduction

Water quality has become a very critical issue in China. The rapid social and economic development during the last 30 years and the increasing discharge of pollutants into its water bodies have had a very negative effect on the overall quality of the waters of the country. In spite of the overall deterioration of the water quality, China still has not managed to develop a management system that considers legislation, institutions, and management tools altogether.

According to the Ministry of Water Resources (MWR), in 2008, 75.8 billion tons of wastewater were discharged into the water bodies of the country, polluting rivers, lakes, and aquifers (MWR, 2008b). The length of the rivers which were classified as Class I, Class II, Class III, Class IV, Class V, and over Class V accounted for 3.5%, 31.8%, 25.9%, 11.4%, 6.8%, and 20.6% respectively in the approximately 150,000 km of rivers evaluated (Table 1). The classification of surface water quality is based on the Environmental Quality Standard for Surface Water, GB2002-3838 (State Environmental Protection Administration and General Administration of Quality Supervision, Inspection and Quarantine of the People's Republic of China, 2006).

The inter-provincial waters with water quality classified as better than Class III and over Class V represented 44.6% and 27.5%, respectively, based on 298 inter-provincial sectors evaluated. The main parameters exceeding the standards were COD, COD_{Mn}, ammonia nitrogen, BOD_5, and volatile phenol.

The proportion achieving the water quality objective of the different bodies of water was only 42.9% among 3,219 zones monitored (the zones are classified upon their use or usability, see definitions in the later section on function zones), of which the first was

Table 1. River water quality in China in 2008.

Water resources zones	River length evaluated (km)	Percentage of river length					
		Class I	Class II	Class III	Class IV	Class V	Over Class V
The State	**147,727.5**	**3.5**	**31.8**	**25.9**	**11.4**	**6.8**	**20.6**
Songhua River	13,562.4	0.8	17.0	29.2	25.2	6.3	21.5
Liao River	5,496.7	1.5	27.1	17.4	10.8	13.1	30.1
Hai River	12,996.2	2.4	19.6	13.2	10.7	2.2	51.9
Yellow River	13,847.7	5.2	12.7	21.3	13.5	10.5	36.8
Huai River	14,130.5	0.5	15.6	23.3	18.1	11.3	31.2
Yangtze River	41,176.6	3.7	36.2	29.2	9.0	7.5	14.4
Tai Lake*	3,028.7	0.0	4.2	10.6	13.6	15.9	55.7
Southeast rivers	5,035.2	5.2	38.3	20.7	12.1	8.9	14.8
Pearl River	18,541.5	0.0	38.8	29.8	11.0	6.8	13.6
Southwest rivers	13,406.7	0.2	48.0	46.1	2.8	0.2	2.7
Northwest rivers	9,534.0	21.2	65.8	7.0	3.5	1.7	0.8

Note: Tai Lake is included in the Yangtze River.

53.2% (excluding the development zone) and the second was 36.7%. Among the so-called first-level bodies of water, the ratio of the protection zone was 65.5%, the reserve zone was 67.7%, and the buffer zone was 25.9%.

Given the degradation of water quality, guaranteeing water supply, particularly for drinking purposes, has become a very complex task. The Standards for Drinking Water Quality, GB5749-2006 (Ministry of Health and Standardization Administration of PR China, 2006) are expected to be fully implemented after 1 July 2012. However, late planning, lack of funds, and the fact that most water treatment plants use traditional treatment processes, mean that most of the urban water supplies will not reach the standards within the time established (Zhang, 2011). In the rural areas it is even more difficult to achieve the appropriate quality of the water supply because of the lack of proper treatment facilities.

Legal Framework

Key legislation for water quality management in China includes the 2008 Water Pollution Control Law (Standing Committee of National People's Congress of PR China, 2008), the 2002 Water Law (Standing Committee of National People's Congress of PR China, 2002), and the 1989 Environmental Protection Law (Standing Committee of National People's Congress of PR China, 1989). These laws are supported by administrative decrees issued by the State Council and by local legislation issued by provinces. There are also departmental regulations and a handful of policies.

The 2008 Water Pollution Control Law focuses on the systems for water pollution control and provides details for industrial, urban, rural, and agricultural water pollution control. For example:

- Water environmental protection targets will be the responsibility of local governments and their leaders, according to the water and environmental responsibility and assessment system (Art. 5).

- Water environmental and ecological protection compensation mechanisms shall be implemented by upstream regions of drinking water source zones, rivers, lakes, and reservoirs (Art. 7).
- Discharged water pollutants shall not exceed the local or national water pollutant discharge standards or the key water pollutant discharge total volumes (Art. 9).
- National water environmental quality standards shall be formulated by the Environmental Protection Administrative Department (EPAD), under the State Council. The provincial government shall formulate local standards for the parameters not included in the national standards (Art. 11).
- National water pollutant discharge standards shall be formulated based on the national water environmental quality standards and economic and technical conditions developed by the EPAD under the State Council. The provincial governments may formulate local standards for the parameters not included in national standards, as well as stricter local standards for the parameters included in the national standards. Water pollutant discharge shall follow local standards, where they exist (Art. 13).
- Water pollution control shall be planned according to river basins or regions (Art. 15).
- Environmental impact assessments shall be conducted for projects which are discharging pollutants into the waters (Art. 17).
- The State shall enforce the total volume control system of the main water pollutants (Arts. 18, 19), and the pollutant discharge permit system (Art. 20).
- Users discharging pollutants directly into the waters shall pay a pollutant discharge fee (Art. 24).
- River basin water resources protection agencies, set up in the state key river basins and lakes, shall be responsible for inter-provincial water environmental quality monitoring. They will report to the EPAD and the Water Administrative Department (WAD) under the State Council (Art. 26).

The 2002 Water Law defines the water resources protection systems as follows:

- The State shall protect the water resources (Art. 9). Whoever, in violation of the plans, degrades the water quality and thus the use of rivers and lakes, overdraws groundwater, or pollutes water, shall bear the responsibility for the related treatment (Art. 31).
- Water function zones shall be formulated for the rivers and lakes by the WAD jointly with the EPAD and relevant departments (Art. 32).
- The WAD shall examine and verify the pollutant loading capacity of waters, in accordance with the water quality objective of the water function zone and with water purification capacity, and shall make suggestions to the EPAD on the pollutant discharge limits of waters (Art. 32).
- The provincial government shall define the drinking water sources protection zones and shall take the necessary measures to protect water sources from depletion and pollution (Art. 33). No wastewater discharge outlet shall be constructed in the drinking water sources protection zones (Art. 34).
- The construction, reconstruction, or expansion of wastewater discharge outlets into rivers and lakes shall be approved by the WAD or river basin management organizations within the jurisdictions (Art. 35).

The 1989 Environmental Protection Law defines water-related environmental protection systems in the country:

- The EPAD under the State Council shall formulate national pollutant discharge standards based on national environmental quality standards and economic and technical conditions (Art. 10).
- The responsibilities for environmental protection shall be elaborated (Art. 24).
- The pollution control facilities of projects must be designed, constructed, and used simultaneously with the main facilities (the "three simultaneousness" system) (Art. 26).

Based on these laws, several State Council decrees detail the water quality management systems:

- The 1994 Decree on Urban Water Supply declares that any activity degrading water quality shall be forbidden (Art. 14). Urban water supply companies shall develop water quality monitoring systems to guarantee that urban water supply meets the national drinking water hygiene standard (Art. 20).
- The 1988 Decree on River Channel Management mentions that the construction and expansion of discharge outlets in rivers or lakes shall be approved by the corresponding administrative departments (Art. 34). These departments shall be responsible for monitoring activities. They shall also help the EPAD supervise water pollution control (Art. 35).
- The 2000 Implementation Detail of Water Pollution Control Law establishes that users discharging pollutants into the waters must submit a Pollutant Discharge Report and Registration Form to the EPAD (Art. 4). The system to control the main water pollutants, based on total volumes, shall be applied in the waters. The system should measure not only environmental quality standards but also discharge standards of the pollutants (Art. 6). Drinking water source protection zones shall include both the primary and secondary protection zones (Arts. 20, 21). Vessels in inland waterways shall be equipped with pollutant control facilities which meet national standards (Art. 25). Water quality from the urban centralized wastewater treatment facilities shall meet the national or local standards (Art.15). Water to recharge groundwater for drinking purposes shall meet drinking water quality standards (Art. 37).
- The 2003 Decree on Pollutant Discharge Fee Collection and Management defines the pollutant type, quantity, collection, and use of discharge fees.
- The 2006 Decree on Water Abstraction Permit and Water Resources Fee Collection and Management establishes that, if water abstraction should deteriorate the water quality and thus affect its use, the approval agency shall object and/or limit water the abstraction volumes (Art. 14).

Based on the laws and the State Council decrees, the ministerial and departmental regulations govern the implementation of the procedures of these systems. These regulations may include the 2008 Water Abstraction Management Method, the 2005 Supervision and Management Method for Discharge Outlets into River, and the 2003 Water Function Zone Management Method by the MWR. Also relevant are the 2006 Urban Water Supply Water Quality Regulation by the Ministry of Housing and Urban-Rural Development (MOHURD); the 1999 Environmental Standard Management Method by the State Environmental Protection Administration (SEPA) (now the Ministry of Environmental Protection or MEP); and the 1989 Management Regulation on Pollution

Control in Drinking Water Sources Protection Zone by SEPA, the Ministry of Health, the Ministry of Construction (now MOHURD), MWR and the Ministry of Mineral Resources.

The legal framework for water quality management in China includes protection of water bodies, wastewater discharge management, and drinking water sources protection. Based on these categories, legislators have tried to develop a framework to solve cross-cutting issues, such as the relation between discharges and water bodies, between river basins and jurisdictions, and between the WAD and the EPAD.

In spite of these efforts, the current legislation faces main problems related to overlap of functions and responsibilities and also, many times, to lack of coherence between them (Li & Cai, 2011). For example, all three laws mentioned before have been approved by the Standing Committee of the National People's Congress, and all of them have the same level of importance. Nonetheless, there are some overlaps between the Water Law and the Water Pollution Control Law. For example, Article 15 of the Water Pollution Control Law establishes that "water pollution control shall be planned at the river basin or region levels", while Articles 14 and 15 of the Water Law state that "development, use, conservation and protection of water resources and control of water disasters shall be planned at the level of the river basins and regions" and that "regional plans shall be subject to river basin plans and special plans shall be subject to the comprehensive plan in the river basins". These definitions raise a question about the relationship between the water pollution plan, the water resources protection plan, and the water disasters plan. Generally, the water resources protection plan includes water pollution considerations. However, with two laws addressing it, it is difficult to decide which law should be considered as a priority. Equally, Article 33 of the Water Law and Articles 56 and 57 of the Water Pollution Control Law define drinking water sources protection zones, which might result in an overlap of responsibilities between MWR and MEP. These overlaps and conflicts result from the own interests of the different institutions and are not dealt with properly from the legal viewpoint.

An additional problem is the lack of coherence between the different laws and the corresponding decrees and regulations. Many decrees and regulations are formulated to support the implementation of laws, but many water quality management decrees and regulations have not been elaborated (such as those related to the pollutant discharge permits), although some of the laws were issued more than 20 years ago. Without systematic, legally binding decrees and regulations, it is very difficult to implement any legal action related to water quality management.

Institutional Arrangements

China has developed a centralized political and administrative system where almost all agencies at the central level have their corresponding agencies at the province, prefecture, and county levels. In this vertical system, regulatory authorities involved in water quality management at the central level, including the MWR, MEP, MOHURD, Ministry of Health, and so on, are able to have their agencies at all different administrative levels.

In terms of responsibilities, according to the Water Pollution Control Law, the MEP is the body responsible for the supervision and management of water pollution prevention and control. Its mandate includes (MEP, 2008):

- Develop and organize the implementation of national environmental protection policies and plans; draft environmental protection laws, regulations, and administrative rules. Organize the formulation of zones for environmental use, environmental protection standards, criteria and technical norms, pollution prevention and control plans in key regions and river basins, as well as environmental protection plans for drinking water source areas.

- Be responsible for implementing national emission reduction targets. Organize the formulation of total emission control systems and pollutant discharge permit system for major pollutants and supervise their implementation; check and supervise the emission reduction tasks of local governments; implement environmental protection targets; examine the outcome of total discharge control and disseminate the results.

- Be responsible for the supervision and management of environmental pollution prevention and control. Develop and implement pollution prevention and control management systems for water, air, soil, noise, light, odour, solid wastes, chemicals, and vehicles; jointly with relevant departments, supervise and administer environmental protection measures for drinking water source areas; organize and guide comprehensive environmental control activities in urban and rural areas.

- Be responsible for environmental monitoring and information release. Develop environmental monitoring systems and norms; organize the implementation of environmental quality and pollution sources monitoring; develop and manage national environmental monitoring networks and information networks.

According to the 2002 Water Law and the stipulations of the State Council, the MWR is responsible for water resource protection in terms of water quality management, including organizing and drafting water resource protection plans; organizing the formulation of and supervising the implementation of water function zones in major rivers and lakes; reviewing and verifying the pollutant loading capacity of waters; making proposals on the total pollutant discharge limit of waters; providing guidance on the protection of drinking water sources and groundwater use as well as management and protection of groundwater in the urban planned areas (MWR, 2008a).

Besides the MWR and MEP, other agencies involved in water quality management include the Ministry of Health, which is responsible for supervising and managing health-related issues of drinking water (Ministry of Health, 2008), and MOHURD, which is responsible for planning and guiding the implementation, construction, and management of urban water supply and wastewater treatment networks and plants (MOHURD, 2008).

In terms of water quality management, the roles of the MWR and MEP have a debate. At present, the MWR is responsible for water quality management in the water bodies, while the MEP is given jurisdiction over the land-based sources of water pollution. This is the "geographic" boundary between the two agencies, regardless of the type of water pollution. Additionally, each agency uses different descriptions for their activities; for instance the MWR uses "water resources protection" and the MEP uses "water environmental management" and "water pollution control".

During the reorganization of the government which took place in 2008, the State Council established that the MWR is responsible for water resources protection and the MEP for water pollution control; the two ministries shall further strengthen their coordination and cooperation, develop ministerial coordination mechanisms, regularly report to each other, and negotiate to solve key problems; the MEP shall release water environmental information and be responsible for data accuracy and timeliness; and the MWR shall release water environmental quality information regarding water resources and hydrological information, and shall be consistent with the MEP (State Council, 2008).

At the local level, with the priorities changing from traditional irrigation to urban water supply and wastewater treatment, the MWR tried to promote management reform looking for integrated urban and rural water issues after the 1990s. The reform aimed to establish water affairs bureaus (WABs) or to increase the roles of the water resources bureaus (WRBs), and to incorporate part or all of the responsibilities related to resources management, service regulation, and environment management from other agencies (Shen & Liu, 2010). Under this reform, part or all of the water quality management functions of the environmental protection bureaus (EPB) and the bureaus of housing and urban-rural development (BHURD) would be merged into WABs or WRBs. In most cases, the role of the BHURDs (responsible for urban water supply and wastewater treatment) would be merged and that of the EPBs would not. After some disagreements related to the reform among the agencies involved, particularly the MWR and the MOHURD, the 2008 governmental reorganization reform gave decision-making power to the local governments.

The government structure in China is built around central institutions and local-level counterparts such as SEPA and the Environmental Protection Agencies (EPAs), respectively. In terms of water quality management, at the central level, the Environmental Protection Administration is responsible for overall pollution policy, while other ministries such as MWR, the Ministry of Construction (MOC), and the Ministry of Agriculture (MOA), contribute in specific fields of responsibility. At the local administrative levels (mainly provinces, cities and counties), the arrangements are a replica of the central structure (World Bank 2006).

In China, the central government has developed six river basin commissions and one lake bureau under the MWR. In terms of water quality management, they are responsible for water resources protection works, including river basin water resources protection planning, inter-province water function zones, discharge outlets management, pollutant loading capacity verification, total pollutant discharge limit proposals, inter-province water quality monitoring, and drinking water sources and groundwater protection (Yellow River Water Resources Commission, 2008).

The river basin water resources protection functions are the responsibility of the river basin water resources protection bureaus. When the bureaus were set up, they were under the dual leadership of MWR and SEPA, but SEPA did not acknowledge them as its subordinate agencies. In the 2008 governmental reorganization, these bureaus were reformed as individual agencies under the river basin water resources commission. At present, the responsibilities of these bureaus are as follows (Tai Lake Water Resources Protection Bureau, 2008):

- Implement water resources protection and water pollution control legislation and policies; mediate inter-provincial water pollution disputes.
- Organize the formulation, supervision and management of water function zones; coordinate and review the provincial water function zones.
- Analyze the pollutant loading capacity of major water bodies, make proposals on the total pollutant discharge limit of waters, supervise and manage pollutant discharge outlets in transboundary waters, and manage certain lakes and rivers, key water resources, and inter-province water transfers; supervise pollutant discharge

control in some drinking water source protection zones; undertake responsibility of water quality management when water abstraction permits are issued.

- Organize the formulation and supervision of the implementation of water resources protection plans; guide and review provincial water resources protection plans; participate in river basin water pollution control plans.
- Manage river basin water quality monitoring; organize and guide water quality and quantity monitoring in provincial boundary waters, key waters, inter-provincial water transfer waters, and major water supply sources; issue river basin water resources quality and water quality bulletins and reports of provincial boundary waters.

Clearly, the vertical and horizontal arrangements for water quality management make institutional arrangements in China relatively complex (Figure 1). Horizontally, two key actors, MWR and MEP, are responsible for most functions. MOHURD and Ministry of Health have specific functions in urban water supply, wastewater treatment, and health-related issues. Vertically, besides from the regional and local administrative agencies, river basin management organizations and their river basin water resources protection bureaus are operated between the central government and the provinces. The water affairs reform is considering at present the changes that will be implemented vertically among the horizontal agencies.

Management Instruments

Standards

There are a number of national water quality standards issued by the PRC's Standardization Administration, and sectoral standards issued by related ministries, covering surface water, groundwater, water supply, wastewater treatment and discharge, and water use benchmarks. These can be grouped into the comprehensive standards, such as those for surface water, groundwater, and wastewater discharge, and the sub-sector standards for drinking, irrigation, and wastewater discharge for specific industries.

Among these standards, the most important and extensively used ones include the following.

- The Environmental Quality Standard for Surface Water (GB3838-2002) is applicable to surface waters and their use. It defines five classes according to their use. Class I is applicable to water sources and national natural reserves. Class II is applicable to the first protection zone of centralized surface drinking water sources, rare aquatic habitats, fish and shrimp spawning areas, and young fish feeding places. Class III is applicable to the secondary protection zone of centralized surface drinking water sources, wintering grounds for fish and shrimps, migration routes, aquaculture zones, and swimming places. Class IV is applicable to industrial water use zones and indirect human body contact such as recreational water use zones. Class V is applicable to agricultural water use and general recreational waters.
- The Discharge Standards of Pollutant for Municipal Wastewater Treatment Plants (GB18918-2002) define the limits of the pollutants for wastewater discharges from municipal wastewater treatment plants.

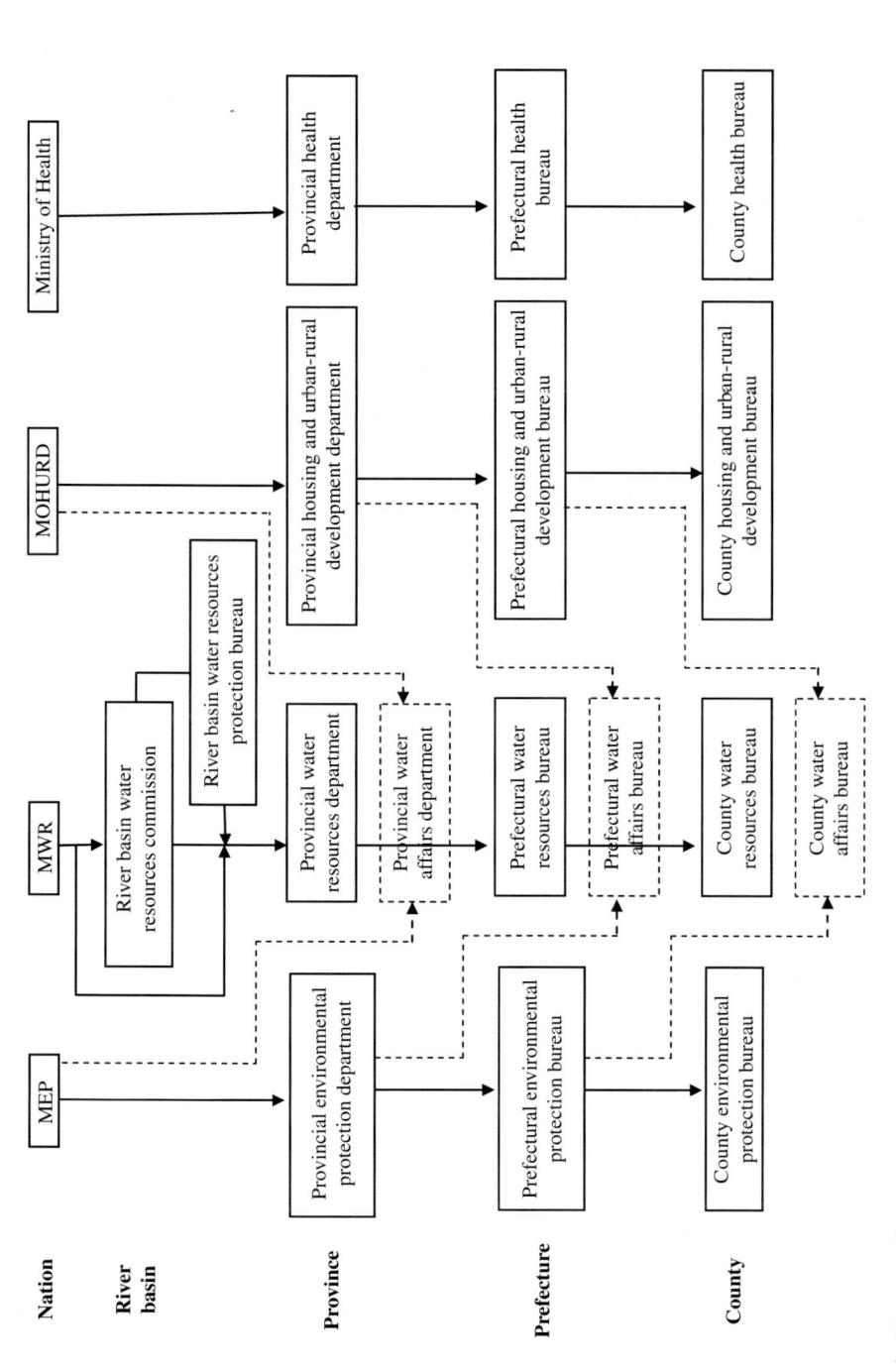

Figure 1. Water quality management institutions in China. *Note:* The dashed lines indicate that the water affairs department or bureau has a connection with MEP or MOHURD.

- The Standards for Drinking Water Quality (GB5749-2006) define the quality requirements of drinking water quality, centralized water supply units, secondary water supply sources, bottled water, and water quality monitoring and methods of analyses. Compared to the previous standard, this one expands water quality requirements to organic materials, microorganisms, and disinfectants; the number of parameters has increased from 35 to 106. It also unifies urban and rural drinking water quality standards and is consistent with international standards (*People's Daily*, 2007).

Standards play a very important role in water quality management. When formulating water quality standards, some of the criteria that must be followed are economic and technological feasibility, enforceability, and suitability to different circumstances in various regions. Therefore, the emphasis should be not only on the formulation of standards, but also on their implementation. In the case of China, a water quality standard system has been developed, but its implementation is still poor. Additionally, the importance of standards has not been fully realized, resulting in only partial implementation.

Some standards are difficult to implement because they are not compatible with the economic and technological conditions. Some are so stringent that companies are not able to meet them due to technological or economic constraints; others are too flexible, without the possibility of controlling the pollution. Standards can also be either too general or too detailed. In the case of China, most of the standards have the objective to be implemented comprehensively at the national level. However, some of them, such as various discharge standards, do not adequately consider the specific conditions of the various regions, their economic development, and the status of their water resources. Some of the standards ignore the existence of other standards and/or indicators.

Function Zones

There are two types of function zone in relation to water quality management: the *water function zone* defined by the Water Law and formulated by the MWR, and the *water environmental function zone* as defined by the Water Pollution Control Law and formulated by the MEP.

Water function zones refer to waters defined by their main use(s) and where relevant water quality standards are implemented. The zones are formulated according to the characteristics of water resources and their use. They are also based on the requirements of a river basin comprehensive plan, as well as water resources protection and socio-economic development plans. The water function zones are formulated to define the use of the waters, verify pollutant loading capacity, and propose pollutants discharge limits, thus providing the basis for water resources development, use, and protection.

There are two levels of classification of water function zones. The first level includes protection, buffer, development and use, and reserve zones. The development and use zone type is further divided into drinking water source, industrial, agricultural, fishery, recreational, intermittent, and pollutant discharge control zones (MWR, 2003). At present, all provinces have developed water function zone plans and these have been approved by the provincial governments (Chen, 2009).

Water environmental function zones are based on not only water use but also water pollution control units. Water environmental function zones consider the water bodies according to their functions as well as the degrees of pollution to determine the appropriate quality objectives. The water pollution control unit combines water use and pollution sources. Overall, both take into consideration regional pollution control, an environmental management target responsibility system, a comprehensive environmental control into the water pollution control unit, and the specific sources of pollution. The zones based on environmental objectives are the basis for the water pollution control.

In fact, the *water function zones* are for water resources protection, and the *water environmental function zones* are for water pollution control. Water bodies are managed by the MWR, and gradually the water zones based on their use override the zones based on environmental objectives. In February 2012, the State Council issued Water Function Zones for the State Key Rivers and Lakes (MWR *et al.*, 2011). However, in most provinces, to avoid conflicts between water environmental zones and water function zones, the water (environmental) function zone, which is a combination of both, has been issued.

Permits

There are four types of permits related to water quality management. These are permits for water abstraction, urban drainage, water pollutant discharge, and wastewater discharge outlet management into rivers.

The water abstraction permit is designed to manage water abstraction activities. Articles 7 and 48 of the 2002 Water Law require that units or individuals who take water directly from rivers, lakes, or groundwater sources must apply for a water abstraction permit, except when taking only a small amount for domestic purposes or for watering livestock. In terms of water quality management, the water abstraction permit requires that the return flow meets the water quality objectives of the zones based on water use.

The urban drainage permit is used to manage urban drainage into the urban sewage network. The 2006 Methods on Urban Drainage Permit Management (MOC, 2006) stipulates that whoever discharges sewage into urban sewage networks and related infrastructure shall apply for an urban drainage permit, and that the construction administrative authority is responsible for the inspection and supervision of the permits. The discharge of sewage will be according to the provisions of the permit, such as type of sewage, total quantity, time limit, locations and amounts of outlets, and types and concentration of sewage.

The water pollutant discharge permit has the objective to manage discharge activities. The 2008 Water Pollution Control Law specifies that a company discharging wastewater into a water body, either directly or indirectly, shall get a pollutant discharge permit. This law is implemented by the EPAD. The permit was introduced in the 1984 Water Pollution Control Law and also in the Water Pollution Discharge for Temporal Permits Methods issued in 1988 (SEPA, 1988). Nevertheless, only in recent years and due to the heavy pollution has the system begun to be implemented in China.

The permit for wastewater discharge outlet management into a river is designed to manage wastewater discharge activities into water bodies. As defined by the Supervision and Management Method for Discharge Outlet into Rivers of the MWR, management activities are conducted by the river basin management organizations and WADs at provincial, prefecture, and county levels.

Among these permits, the MWR is responsible for abstraction permits and wastewater discharge outlet management into a river, the MOHURD is in charge of drainage permits, and the MEP is in charge of pollutant discharge permits. As can be observed, coordination of the tasks related to the four discharge permits remains a problem. Only the abstraction permit and the into-water permits are coordinated more properly because both of them are managed by the MWR.

Fees and Charges

Five types of fees and charges are collected in China with regard to water quality management. They relate to resources, services, and environmental issues. These are the water resources fee (resource charge); water supply tariffs from water infrastructure, urban water supply tariffs, and wastewater collection and treatment tariffs (service charges); and pollutant discharge fees (environmental charges).

Among these charges, water resources fees, water supply tariffs from water infrastructure, and urban water supply tariffs relate to water quality protection, even if not directly, because they have an impact on water quality.

Article 15 of the Water Pollution Control Law defines the pollutant discharge charge. The 2003 State Council Decree on Pollutant Discharge Fee Collection and Management establishes that the polluter who discharges directly into the environment shall pay a pollutant discharge fee. However, the polluter who discharges wastewater into the centralized urban wastewater collection network and pays wastewater collection and treatment fees may be exempt from the pollutant discharge fee. This fee is calculated based on the concentration and volume of specific pollutants, with a fixed-unit fee system applied all over the country. The concentration and volume are decided based on the observations reported by the polluter and the calibration of the EPBs.

The wastewater collection and treatment tariff is a service charge, but in most cities in China it is collected as an administrative fee at present. The tariff is charged based on cost, expenditure, and profit in wastewater collection and treatment. The tariff is normally collected based on volume of tap water use with a transform coefficient.

The most controversial issue within the charging system is the amount of the fees. At present, most opinions, especially among government officials and professionals, are that the price of water is low. However, from the point of view of a water user, the price of water is not considered to be low if income and service levels (such as water supply quality and wastewater treatment quality) are considered.

The problem is also related to the revenues. In all the regulations, pollution charges have been used to cover administrative expenses of environmental protection agencies to invest in pollution abatement. This indicates that the agency could retain the revenues as a financial source. Out of the interests of the different departments, this can motivate the collection of higher revenues regardless of any pollution control, and so can sometimes encourage polluters to discharge more.

The Main Issues in Water Quality Management in China

The main concerns in terms of water quality management in China at present include the lack of an integrated framework, the overlap of roles and conflicts between the various agencies, a focus on pollution control after the water is used rather than on protection of the water resources at the source, poor implementation of the legal framework, and inadequate capacity to manage the quality of the water in the country.

Lack of an Integrated Framework

China has introduced all types of water quality management systems. The characteristics of the current framework are, first, that these systems are designed separately; second, that they are designed for an administrative system rather than based on water quality considerations and on the hydrological cycle; and third, that the implementations of these systems are influenced by factors outside the control of the responsible agencies, such as the zones. The above results in a lack of coordination of the various systems, including the lack of protection of water resources, lack of implementation of water pollution control, and issues relating to the provision of clean water supply.

Overlaps and Conflicts between Agencies

Lack of an integrated framework and lack of coordination between the sectoral departments result in overlaps and gaps in the overall water quality management system. For instance, in the permits system, there are three types of discharge permits based on the place of the discharge. The drainage permit considers urban drainage networks and other parts of the urban areas, such as rivers, lakes, and ponds; discharge outlet management considers rivers and lakes as discharge places; and the pollutant discharge permit considers the environment as a discharge place. Therefore, it might be necessary to issue three permits for only one discharge! Other systems related to water quality management also have overlaps, such as the water resources justification system and the environmental impact assessment (both focus on return flow).

Pollution Control at the End, Rather than Water Resources Protection at the Source

In China, there is a tendency to focus on pollution control after water is used, rather than protecting water quality before its use. Most of the systems focus on how to treat wastewater and how to manage and control wastewater discharges; only the water function zones and the drinking water sources protection zones are directly related to water resources protection. Nonetheless, in a river basin context, the limited area of protection zones could not really protect drinking water sources. Additionally, the water function zones are heavily affected by wastewater discharges and upstream pollution. This completely complicates the purposes of water quality management.

Poor Implementation

Although China has developed a general framework for water quality management, poor implementation has negatively affected its overall effectiveness. Among all the existing systems, the charge system is the best because of its economic incentives. The permit system is not properly implemented because of lack of supervision. The water pollutant discharge permit was introduced in 1980s, but only implemented in the 2000s. The water abstraction permit was implemented after 1993, but at its early stage, the focus was on issuing the permits rather than supervising the permit holders. Finally, regarding standards, one example of complexity is the drinking water standard with its 106 parameters. Even the large water supply companies in the big cities are not able to meet this standard because of treatment processes, networks, and poor water quality at the sources.

Inadequate Capacity

The ability to implement water quality management in China is weak, including an inadequate capacity to monitor the status of the water quality. Even now, not all water-use zones are regularly monitored and not all point sources of pollution are monitored or metered. In the planning system, the consistency among different levels of plans is poor. The net result of a poor capacity is that it affects the implementation of water quality management systems.

Suggestions and Recommendations

Following are some suggestions and recommendations to achieve a more solid water quality management system in China.

Full Implementation of the Current Water Quality System

Even with the associated constraints, the current management systems must be fully implemented. Only then it will be possible to further improve it. At the macro level, China should be able to fully implement the water function zone system to protect the quality of its water resources. At the micro level, all permits should be implemented and supervision should be improved to manage individual activities.

Reforming the Current System

In order to improve water quality, China should strengthen the macro control of water quality management. Only then can the micro-level management instruments be applied effectively.

The relationship between water use and the permits awarded should be strengthened. Mechanisms should be developed to coordinate the current systems when they are implemented by different agencies; for example, the three discharge permits should be consistent with the pollutant loading capacity of the water function zones.

The management system should take into account both the nature of the water quality issues and the administrative system. The current systems, partly developed by, and also to serve, the administrative system, should be improved to reflect the actual situation of water quality problems, such as river basin management, the hydrological cycle, and upstream-downstream relations.

A system to implement the different systems should be developed. The main problem so far is that China lacks a system to promote and guarantee the implementation of the system. A system that considers responsibility, accountability, and follow-up should be developed for all stakeholders involved in water quality management, particularly the government agencies.

Managing Water Quality in a River Basin Context

Water quality should be managed together with water quantity within a river basin context. At present, most of the water quality management systems are designed for jurisdictional management, causing many problems within the river basin.

China should strengthen water quality river basin management in terms of planning (both water quality and water quantity), classification depending on the use of the water bodies, protection tools, and discharge. Water abstraction and wastewater discharge, upstream and downstream, water quality objectives of the water bodies, and drinking water source zoning, should all be considered within a river basin context.

Re-allocating Functions

In China, if we consider the importance of the water sector both at past and present, water quantity should be managed by the MWR in the long term. However, with the very serious existing environmental problems, the MEP will play a more and more important role. Therefore, the co-existence of the MEP and MWR at the central level in the management of water quality and water quantity will have to remain for a long time.

At the local level, the government agencies could reorganize the various institutions. Decision making on water quality management among different agencies could be restructured and water quality monitoring could be built on a single platform. The interrelated and overlapped permits could also be modified. In the urban areas, with the promotion of integrated urban and rural water issues management, the current conflicts between MOHURD and MWR would be solved.

Introducing and Improving Market-based Approaches

At present, except for the charges, most water quality management instruments are control-and-command. Market-based approaches should be introduced and applied more widely in China. This will not only reduce the management cost, but also help the government to be more effective.

Water pricing mechanisms should be improved on the basis of management purposes and characteristics of the resources, their use, and the environment. Water resources fees should reflect the water resources' value both for human demands and ecosystem services. Urban water supply tariffs and wastewater collection and treatment fees should reflect the full costs of providing services, and subsidies on service with public interests, such as domestic water supply. Water pollutant discharge fees should fully cover the environmental damage and restoration costs. Eco-compensation (payment for ecosystem services) should also be introduced in water source areas and upstream areas to protect water quality.

Strengthening Capacity Building

Water quality management should be strengthened in terms of planning, monitoring, and metering, as well as in terms of capacity building. Under the water resources planning framework, an efficient and effective water quality planning system should be developed. At present, water quality planning is divided into the water resources protection plan and the water pollution control plan, which splits the water quality management process. An integrated water quality planning system should be formulated instead.

Monitoring and metering systems are the weakest point in China, particularly when monitoring the concentrations of the pollution loads. Real-time water resources metering and monitoring systems, including water quality monitoring, should be developed. Monitoring and metering of key pollutant dischargers, boundary waters, and water supply systems should be strengthened. A single platform should be developed among different agencies to promote sharing of and consistency of data.

In China, more and more critical water quality problems have been exposed in recent years. In order to deal with water quality management, China has developed a separate, sectoral management system, which has resulted in many problems, including lack of an integrated framework, overlapping functions, focus on pollution control, poor implementation, and inadequate capacity. To solve these problems and improve water quality will be a long and difficult way in China. Nonetheless, a good beginning would be for China to fully implement and reform the current system, restructure water quality management institutions, manage its water resources within a river basin context, and encourage market-based approaches. This will help the country improve not only in terms of its environment but also in terms of its development.

Acknowledgements

The paper is supported by Research on Groundwater Management Systems, Natural Sciences Foundation of China, Project No 71073174; and Research on Water Sector Modernization of China, Social Science Foundation of China, Project No 11AZD007.

References

Chen, L. (2009) Implementing the most stringent water resources management system to guarantee sustainable socio-economic development, Speech to the National Water Resources Conference, 14 February 2009, Guilin, China. Available at: http://www.mwr.gov.cn/ztpd/2009ztbd/2009nqgszygzhy/zyjh/20090214002623b19a1b.aspx [in Chinese] (accessed 28 March 2012).

Li, G. & Cai, S. (2011) Assessment on water environment and water resources protection legislation, *China Legal News Network*, 8 March. Available at: http://www.chinalnn.com/Article/Html/2011/03/78_302570.html [in Chinese].

Ministry of Construction (2006) *The Method on Urban Drainage Permit Management*. Beijing: Ministry of Construction.

Ministry of Environmental Protection (2008) Mission. Available at: http://english.mep.gov.cn/About_SEPA/Mission/200803/t20080318_119444.htm. (accessed 28 March 2012).

Ministry of Health (2008) Organization introduction. Available at: http://www.moh.gov.cn/publicfiles/business/htmlfiles/zwgkzt/pjggk/200804/621.htm [in Chinese] (accessed 28 March 2012).

Ministry of Health and Standardization Administration of PR China (2006) The Standards for Drinking Water Quality (GB5749-2006).

Ministry of Housing and Urban-Rural Development (2008) Main responsibilities, internal organizations and positions. Available at: http://www.mohurd.gov.cn/gyjsb/zyzz/index.html [in Chinese] (accessed 28 March 2012).

Ministry of Water Resources (2003) The water function zone management method.

Ministry of Water Resources (2008a) Main responsibility. Available at: http://www.mwr.gov.cn/zwzc/jgjs/zyzn/ [in Chinese] (accessed 28 March 2012).

Ministry of Water Resources (2008b) Water resources bulletin of People's Republic of China.

Ministry of Water Resources, National Development and Reform Commission, Ministry of Environmental Protection (2011) *Water Function Zones for the State Key Rivers and Lakes*.

People's Daily (2007) New drinking water quality standard implemented with parameters increasing from 35 to 106, *Sohu.com*, 10 July. Available at: http://health.sohu.com/20070710/n250977199.shtml [in Chinese] (accessed 28 March 2012).

Shen, D. & Liu, B. (2010) Integrated urban and rural water affairs management reform in China: affecting factors, *Physics and Chemistry of the Earth*, 33(5), pp. 364–375.

Standing Committee of National People's Congress of PR China (1989) Environmental Protection Law 1989. Available at: www.chinaenvironmentallaw.com (accessed 4 April 2012).

Standing Committee of National People's Congress of PR China (2002) Water Law of the People's Republic of China. Available at: http:// www.china.org.cn/english/government/207454.htm (accessed 4 April 2012).

Standing Committee of National People's Congress of PR China (2008) Water Pollution Control Law 2008. Available at: www.chinaenvironmentallaw.com (accessed 4 April 2012).

State Council (2008) Notice of organization structure. Available at: http://www.zjwater.gov.cn/pages/attachment/40/attachment_908.doc [Microsoft Word document, in Chinese] (accessed 28 March 2012).

State Environmental Protection Administration (1988) *The Water Pollution Discharge for Temporal Permits Methods.*

State Environmental Protection Administration and General Administration of Quality Supervision, Inspection and Quarantine of PR China (2002) *The Environmental Quality Standard for Surface Water (GB3838-2002).*

Tai Lake Water Resources Protection Bureau (2008) Main responsibilities, internal organizations and positions. Available at: http://www.tba.gov.cn:89/web/news_show.jsp?fileId=196386 [in Chinese] (accessed 28 March 2012).

World Bank (2006) *China, Environment and Social Development. East Asia and Pacific Region* (Washington: The World Bank).

Yellow River Water Resources Commission (2008) Main responsibilities. Available at: http://www.yellowriver.gov.cn/zwzc/zjhw/znjg/201108/t20110810_26215.html [in Chinese] (accessed 28 March 2012).

Zhang, Q. (2011) With coming deadline, could water supply quality fully reach standards, *H2O China*, 25 May. Available at: http://news.h2o-china.com/html/2011/05/241306302424_1.shtml [in Chinese] (accessed 28 March 2012).

An Integrated Management Approach for Water Quality and Quantity: Case Studies in North China

JUN XIA

State Key Laboratory of Water Resources and Hydropower Engineering, Wuhan University, and Key Laboratory of Water Cycle and Related Land Surface Process, Chinese Academy of Sciences, Beijing, China

ABSTRACT *This paper presents a systematic concept of integrated water resources quantity and quality assessment and develops a new approach to assess available water resources for water quality management. The method considers not only environmental flow demand in a river system but also water quality objectives as determined by water service function regionalization in the river. The method was applied in North China in basins with different conditions. The results show that this integrated assessment approach provides useful information for decision making concerning allocation of available water resources under the water quality and environmental flow constraints, indicating the need to reduce wastewater loads to reach specific water quality standards.*

Introduction

Efficient water resources management in North China is extremely important. With a growing population, agricultural and industrial development, and urbanization, the discrepancy between supply and demand of water resources becomes serious (Qian & Zhang, 2001; Xia & Chen, 2001; Xia *et al.*, 2009; Zhang *et al.*, 2010). In 2000, the baseline year for China's comprehensive water resources assessment, the North China Plain, with an area of more than 1.5 million km^2, had 437 million inhabitants (35% of the total population). Its gross domestic product (GDP) was CNY3,130 billion (32% of the country's total) and 23 million ha (42%) were occupied by irrigated agriculture (Chen, 2002). In 2010, China's GDP reached CYN39,798.3 billion, four times that in 2000. On the other hand, the water resource per capita in the region is only 305 m^3, less than 1/7th of China's average and 1/24th of the world's average.

The region is currently experiencing serious environmental degradation: groundwater overuse, drying up of rivers, reduced wetlands, and pollution of surface water and groundwater. These problems are associated with a rapid economic development, which has led to runoff decrease and excessive exploitation of water resources (Zhang *et al.*, 2010; Xia *et al.*, 2011; Xia & Zhang, 2008; Xia *et al.*, 2007), jeopardizing water security in this region. Water shortage problems in North China have received considerable attention from the Chinese government, and there has been notable amelioration of the situation (Qian & Zhang, 2001; Xia *et al.*, 2007). However, due to the nature, condition, and complexity of highly intensive human activities in this region, water shortages remain a major problem. Apart from socio-economic factors, the biophysical aspects of the hydrological cycle and its ecosystem interactions require better understanding to provide a sound scientific basis for policy development.

Alongside water shortages, there are also major water-related environmental problems in North China, especially concerning water quality. Poor natural quality of both surface water and groundwater in some areas is aggravated by water pollution, and in some rivers the total pollution load is beyond their carrying capacity. Under such circumstances, water quality management has become a priority issue for water security (Xia *et al.*, 2009; Boxer, 2001; MWR–China Water Conservancy and Hydropower Planning and Design General Institute, 2008; World Bank, 2006; Xia *et al.*, 2011). To tackle water quality-related constraints at the national level, the Ministry of Water Resources (MWR), the Ministry of Environment Protection (MEP), and other water-related institutions have carried out extensive work on environmental monitoring, assessment, and control of water pollution since the nation entered the reform path in 1979, and particularly since industrial growth began in the mid-1980s. China has established a water quality classification system based on water uses and on setting water quality targets by water service function regionalization, following Environmental Quality Standard GB 3838-2002 (China State Environmental Protection Administration, 2002).

Climate change impact adds to human activity altering ecosystems, making the difficult situation still worse. Comprehensive water resources assessment and sustainable water resources management in North China have become key issues for the promotion of social and economic development. Water resources quantity and quality issues have long been treated separately in China, and there is a lack of integrated tools for water quantity and quality assessment, which was emphasized in the 2nd China National Comprehensive Water Resources Assessment document in 2000 (MWR–China Water Conservancy and Hydropower Planning and Design General Institute, 2008). Recently, the Ministry of Water Resources and the Chinese Government developed new strategies for water policy with three "red line" limits: red line I for water resources development in terms of control of total water resources use, red line II for water use efficiency based on water demand management, and red line III for water resources protection through water use management and wastewater control (State Council of PR China, 2012). To realize these policies, integrated assessment and management approaches are required.

The primary objective of this paper is to develop and evaluate a new approach for the integrated assessment and management of water quantity and quality. This integrated assessment method can provide useful information to support decision making concerning allocation of the available water resources under the constraints of water quality and environmental flow, indicating a required reduction of wastewater load to satisfy the national water quality standard. A case study in North China was carried out to demonstrate and evaluate the usefulness of the new approach.

Methodology

Concept of Integrated Water Quality and Quantity Assessment

It is known that coordinated water quality and quantity assessment is a rather difficult task because of the complexity of water systems. Demands for a certain water volume to preserve water quality may change as a result of changing water quality in a river system. Moreover, water storage varies both in time (e.g. during flooding and low-flow periods) and space (e.g. inflow/outflow sites into a reservoir), which leads to quite different final assessment solutions. Thus, it is necessary to first give a clear definition of the available (usable) water resources and introduce an *integrated* water quality and quantity assessment (IWQQA) concept. As illustrated in Figure 1, available water resources equal the total water resources minus the non-usable flow during floods and environmental flow. This improved concept of available water resources must further consider the water quantity issue by presenting a target function of water service, determined on the basis of a regionalization of river service functions in China. Thus, besides traditional environmental flow consideration, a water quality target is also considered. To reach this target of available water quantity and quality, it is necessary to estimate a required reduction of the wastewater load into a river. This is a new, challenging task for integrated water quality and quantity assessment and water management in China.

The scheme of an integrated water quality and quantity assessment is presented in Figure 2. It includes a definition of water quantities required for sustaining different water quality classes for different targets (e.g. basin or region), different objectives (e.g. water supply or water use, water plan or management), and water resources classification (surface water, groundwater, etc.). The key points are the objective and the water resources classification. Basically, there are three levels of integrated water quality and quantity assessment. In this study, the maximum available water resources assessment was done based on regionalization of river service functions and water quality objectives under the condition of existing water use partners. The details of the integrated water quality and quantity assessment approach developed in this study are presented in the next section.

Maximum Available Water Resources Assessment Approach Based on Water Quality Objective

In the past, water resources assessment in China rarely considered water quality objectives of regionalized river service functions. The main reason was the separate assessment systems for water quantity and quality in different government sectors. Under these circumstances it is difficult to answer a question about water resources available for socio-economic development in accordance with different objectives within the regionalized river service functions. Acceptable wastewater loads into a river system is a water quality problem that can hardly be targeted without assessing water quantity at the same time.

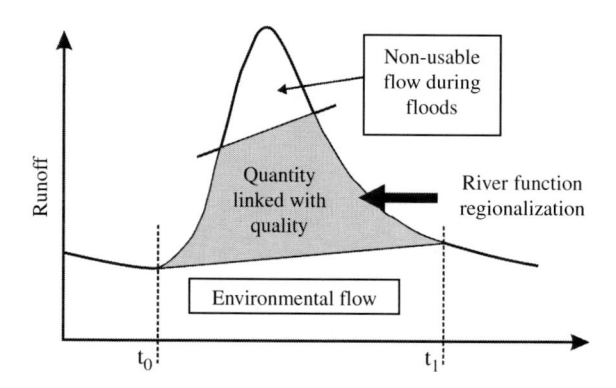

Figure 1. Available water resources linked with water quality issue.

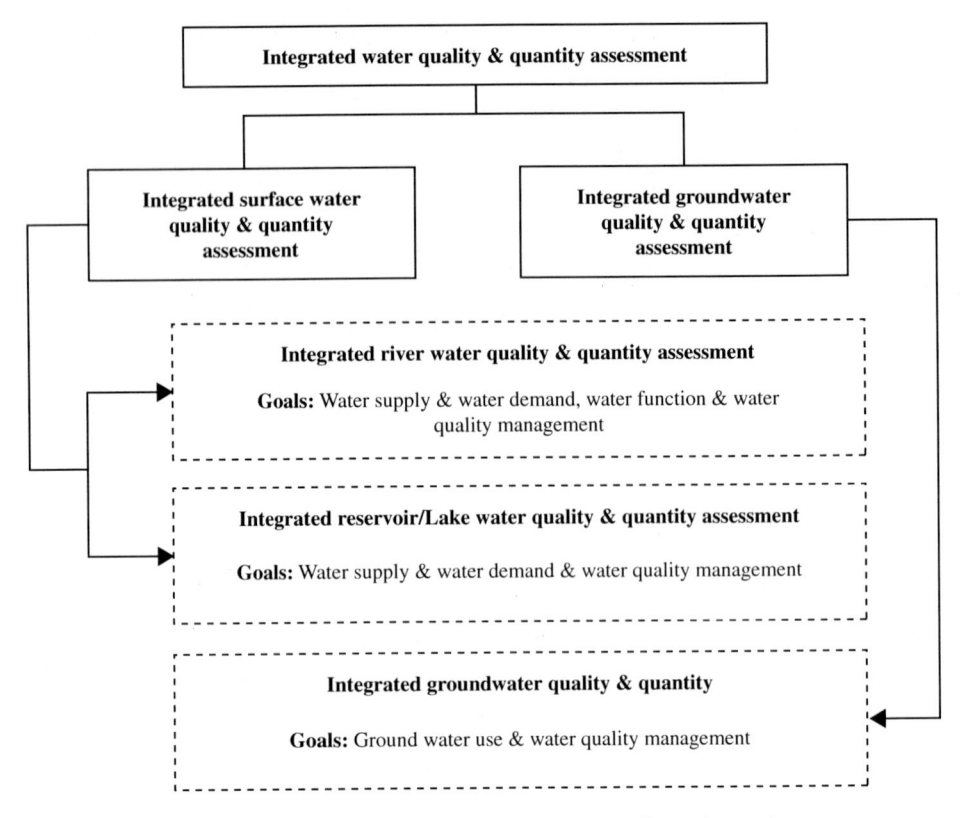

Figure 2. Concept and classification of integrated water quality and quantity assessment.

The idea and the methodology can be introduced as follows. First, a basin or region (i.e. assessed target) is considered as a water system with an interaction of water quality and quantity in storage, transport, wastewater discharge, and so on. Secondly, a workable integrated water quality and quantity model is built based on water balance and load balance components. The model parameters can be estimated using a monitoring data set. Thirdly, a maximum available water resources assessment based on water quality objectives and system constraints on river service functions (related water quality requirement, environmental flow demands, etc.) can be developed. This system approach allows estimating a critical flow with respect to water quantity and quality, as well as wastewater loads that meet the constraints on river service function. This method can be used for integrated water resources assessment and management (see Figure 3) and can be applied to any complex river system and basins. These three major aspects can be implemented by following five steps.

Step 1. Conceptual Model of Integrated Water Quality and Quantity in Unit Sector

Based on water balance and pollutant transport processes of a given water quality standard, that is:

$$\Delta V_i = Q_{i-1} + R_i - q_i - Q_i \tag{1}$$

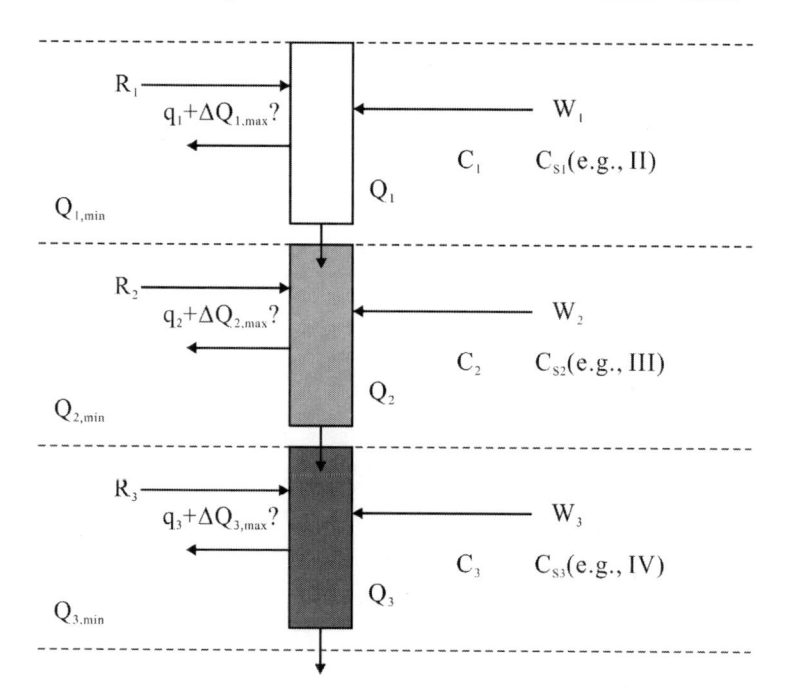

Figure 3. Scheme of integrated water quality and quantity assessment in multiple river sectors. R_i: lateral flow, q_i: water use, Q_i: discharge, C_i: water quality, W_i: wastewater load, C_{Si}: water quality objective, $Q_{i,min}$: critical flow, $\Delta Q_{i,max}$: remaining available water resources.

ΔV_i is the change of water storage in the ith unit sector, Q_{i-1} is discharge into the ith unit sector, R_i is lateral flow, q_i is water use from the ith unit sector.

$$\Delta C_i = \frac{Q_{i-1}C_{i-1} + W_i + R_iC_{Ri}}{V_i} - \left[\frac{q_i + \Delta V_i + Q_i}{V_i} + K_i\right]C_i \qquad (2)$$

where C_i is the water quality of the ith unity sector, ΔC_i is the change of water quality, W_i is the wastewater load of into the ith unity sector, C_{Ri} is water quality of lateral flow of the ith unit sector, V_i is the storage volume of the ith unit sector and K_i is the parameter of water quality model (the index i refers to sections of the river system).

A simple unit model of water quantity and quality could be written as:

$$C_i = \frac{Q_{i-1}C_{i-1} + R_iC_{Ri} + W_i}{q_i + \Delta V_i + Q_i\beta_i} \qquad (3)$$

Where $V_i = \alpha_i Q_i$, $\beta_i = 1 + \alpha_i K_i$, and α is a coefficient of water storage volume and discharge.

Moreover, the above parameters could be estimated using a monitoring data set:

$$\hat{\beta}_i = \frac{Q_{i-1}C_{i-1} + W_i + R_iC_{Ri} - q_iC_i - \Delta V_iC_i}{Q_iC_i} \qquad (4)$$

When $C_{Ri} = C_i$, Equation (4) can be reduced to:

$$\hat{\beta}_i = 1 + \frac{Q_{i-1}(C_{i-1} - C_i) + W_i}{Q_i C_i} \tag{5}$$

Other parameters can be estimated from available data (for details, see Xia *et al.*, 2006).

Step 2. Remaining Available Water Resources

Remaining available water resources (RAWR) in unit river system, $\Delta Q'_{i,\max}$, is defined as water resources available to satisfy both water quality objectives and environmental flow requirements under the present water use pattern and natural conditions. Based on the water balance and water quality relationship and constraints, RAWR can be formulated as:

$$\Delta Q'_{i,\max} = \min \left[\frac{[q_i Cs_i + \Delta V_i Cs_i + \beta_i Q_i Cs_i] - [Q_{i-1} C_{i-1} + R_i C_{Ri} + W_i]}{(\beta_i - 1)Cs_i}, Q_i \right] \tag{6}$$

where $Cs_i = \dfrac{Q_{i-1} C_{i-1} + R_i C_{Ri} + W_i}{q_i + \Delta Q'_{i,\max} + \Delta V_i + (Q_i - \Delta Q'_{i,\max})\beta_i}$ and $(Q_i - \Delta Q'_{i,\max}) \geq 0$.

Step 3. Critical Flow and Maximum Available Water Resources

Based on RAWR, the critical flow $Q_{i,\min}$ and the maximum available water resources (MAWR) can be estimated as:

$$Q_{i,\min} = \max[(Q_i - \Delta Q'_{i,\max}); Q_{i,0}] \tag{7}$$

where $Q_{i,0}$ is environmental flow requirements in the river system, and $Q_i \geq Q_{i,0} \geq 0$. Then, the maximum available water resources (MAWR) can be calculated as:

$$q_{i,\max} = q_i + (Q_i - Q_{i,\min}) - Q_f \tag{8}$$

where Q_f is the non-usable water resources during a flooding period. The percentage of maximum available water resource can be defined as:

$$r\% = q_{i,\max}/(Q_{i-1} + R_i) \times 100\% \tag{9}$$

Step 4. Acceptable Maximum Wastewater Load and Its Reduction

The allowed maximum wastewater load, $W_{i,\max}$, means the system's maximum acceptable wastewater load to satisfy river water quality objectives (Cs) under the conditions of existing water supply and water use. Based on Equation (3), it can be formulated as:

$$W_{i,\max} = [Q_i \beta_i + q_i + \Delta V_i]Cs_i - [Q_{i-1} C_{i-1} + R_i C_{Ri}] \tag{10}$$

The amount of wastewater load DW_i that should be reduced can be calculated as:

$$DW_i = W_i - W_{i,\max} \tag{11}$$

Step 5. Integrated Water Quality and Quantity Assessment in Multiple River Sectors

In multiple sectors of a river system, there are interactions or cascade effects among subsystems of both water quantity and quality. The key issue is how to calculate the maximum available water resources subject to a series of system constraints. The idea is that the unit system method, addressed in Equations (1) to (11), can be extended to a river system with multiple river sectors. For such a situation, the problem of integrated water quality and quantity assessment can be formulated in terms of a multi-objective non-linear programming subject to multiple constraints. The integrated water quality and quantity assessment in multiple river sectors can be considered for two situations: under the existing water use conditions and under the optimal water use conditions.

Available water resources assessment under existing water use conditions. The system objectives can be addressed to calculate the maximum remaining available water resources in a river system under existing water service functions and water uses. This approach can also provide useful decision-making information, that is the amount of wastewater load reduction to satisfy water quality standards in the river system:

$$MAX\ Sum = \sum_{i=1}^{n} \omega_i \Delta Q_i \tag{12}$$

subject to these water quality constrains:

$$C_i = \frac{\left(Q_{i-1} - \sum_{j=1}^{i-1} \Delta Q_j\right) C_{i-1} + R_i C_{Ri} + W_i}{\Delta Q_i + q_i + \Delta V_i + \beta_i \left(Q_i - \sum_{j=1}^{i} \Delta Q_j\right)} \leq C_S \tag{13}$$

$$Q_i - \sum_{j=1}^{i} \Delta Q_j \geq Q_{min,i0} \tag{14}$$

$$\Delta Q_i \geq 0 \tag{15}$$

where ΔQ_i are the increasing available water resources (if water quality does not satisfy water quality standards, $\Delta Q_i = 0$); n is the number of river sectors, ω_i is the weight of the ith reach, and if water use is known, $\omega_i = q_i / \sum_{i=1}^{n} q_i$.

Available water resources assessment under changing water use conditions. For this situation, the objective can be addressed as follows. Based on reasonable water resources allocation, and by changing existing water use partners and controlling pollution, the maximum available water resources satisfying river system water quality standards and environmental flow requirements are calculated. The methodology can be seen in the references (for details, see Xia *et al.*, 2006).

Policy Analysis

As already noted, China has been experiencing new socio-economic, political, and environmental challenges ever since the reform policy of 1979. Water has received more attention than any other issue because of its importance to economic development (e.g. electricity, navigation), daily life (drinking water, sewage discharges), and the risk of natural disasters (such as floods and droughts). Rapid urbanization and industrialization in the reform era has triggered severe pollution in water bodies and has thus increased the difficulty of managing China's water. Integrated water quantity and quality assessment and good water management thus became key issues. To cope with water management challenges, the Chinese central government has constructed a range of water service facilities in major river basins, municipalities, and rural areas.

In addition to these engineering solutions, the government has established a set of laws and regulations, including the Water Law (1988, revised 2002) and the Environmental Protection Law (1979, revised 1989), and has sought to implement policies based on a multi-ministerial system (Shen, 2004; MWR-China Water Conservancy and Hydropower Planning and Design General Institute, 2008; Zhang, 2000; State Council of PR China, 2002a, 2002b). This system, however, has faced a number of problems that caused decades of inefficient water management. The main problems concerned fragmented policy making and implementation, inter-ministerial conflicts, lack of innovative policy tools for water supply and pollution control, and limited means of financing water facilities. The government has also had some policy successes, including the inclusion of sustainable development principles in the 11th and the new 12th Five Year Plan (Ministry of Commerce PR China, 2011), the establishment of integrated water bureaus, and the environmental impact assessment (EIA) projects of the Ministry of Environmental Protection (MEP). For integrated water quantity and quality assessment (IWQQA), a good water governance system including water policy and institutional innovation is needed in China. This will be a new challenge for sustainable water resources integration in China. Fortunately, China's central government has fully recognized the significance of this important issue. Water policy in China is now shifting from traditional water supply management into water demand management, and also from conventional water quantity management into water quality management (see Yan *et al.*, 2006; Edmonds, 2000). These new approaches in water policy will effectively facilitate reaching the target of sustainable utilization of water in 2050. There will also be a good foundation for implementing integrated water quantity and quality assessment in different regions in the country.

Case Study: Luan River, North China

The Luan River is located in the north-eastern part of the Hai River basin in North China (Figure 4). The river's length is 888 km, and the basin's area is 44,880 km^2. Mean annual precipitation in the basin varies from 400 to 800 mm/y. About 80% of the total precipitation is concentrated in the high-water period in June–September.

According to the regionalization of basin's water service functions, the total river system can be divided into 15 zones (Table 1). The data set on hydrology, water use and water quality situation, and socio-economic development were collected and 1988 was taken as a representative year for the basin (due to the baseline year of 2000 for the water resources assessment of the country) (see Table 2).

All parameters in the integrated water quality and quantity model can be identified by monitoring data sets, in which the environmental flow requirement in the Luan River was taken as 10% of the average flow regime. The results of integrated water quality and quantity assessment in multiple river sectors are shown in Figure 5.

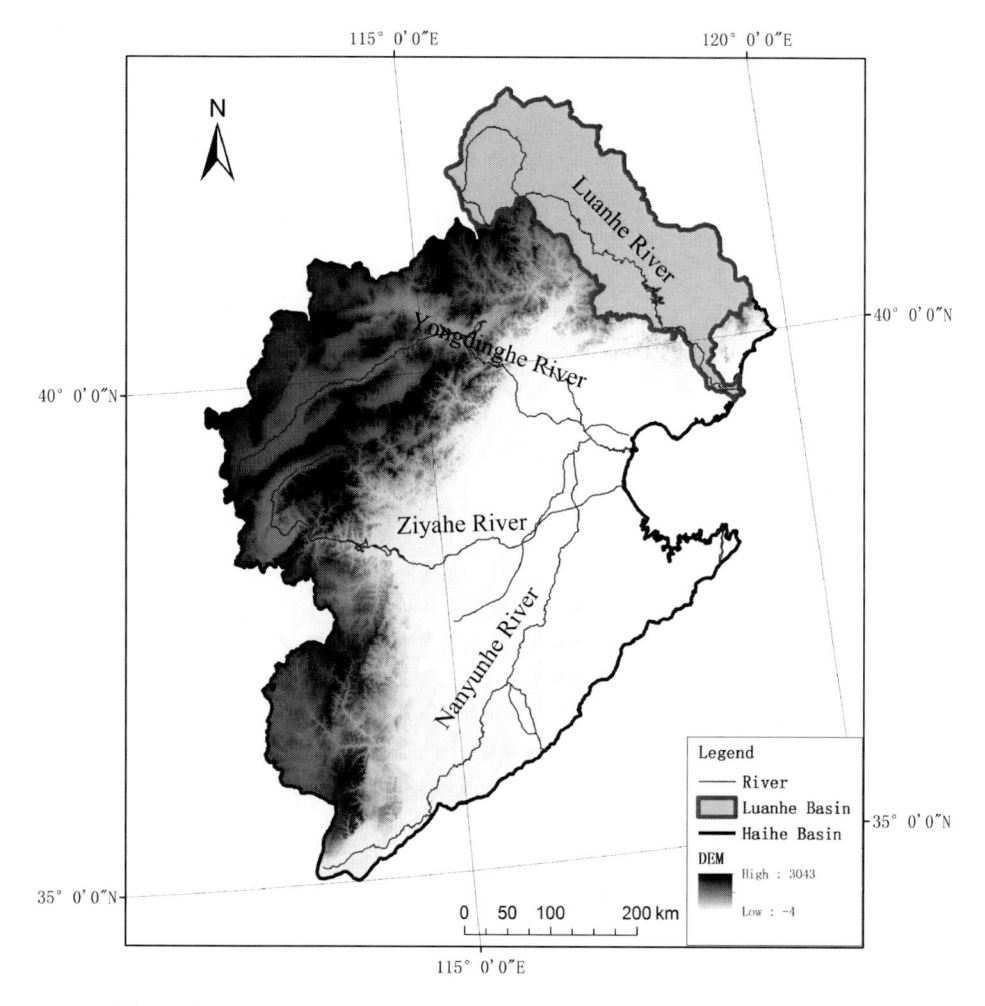

Figure 4. Location of the Luan River and the Hai River basins in North China.

The figure has three columns: (1) the total water resources without subtracting the non-usable water during flood periods, the environment flow, and the bad-quality water, (2) actual water use, and (3) the maximum available water resources calculated by the integrated water quality and quantity assessment approach. The left group of bars shows the calculation result based on currently existing conditions and the right group shows the calculation result based on optimal conditions. For illustrative purposes, the water resources data in 1988 were used as the representative year. The calculation can be performed for any period with data available. The following conclusions can be drawn from Figure 5:

(1) The total water resources, without considering water quality issues and environmental flow requirements in the basin, are 4.02 billion m^3. However, this traditional concept of water resources is not valid for actual water resources management. If water quality, environmental flow, and other factors are considered, the amount of available water resources is changed to a much smaller value.

Table 1. Objectives for water quality and regionalization based on water use in the Luan River basin.

Zone	Interval	Water service function	Objective water quality standards		
			Class	COD_{mn} (mg/L)	Ammonia nitrogen (mg/L)
1	Goutaizi above	Head water protection zone	II	4	0.5
2	Boluoro above	Head water protection zone	II	4	0.5
3	Guotaizi/Waigoumenzi to Guojiatun	Reserved area	III	6	1
4	Boloro/Guojiatun to Sandaohezi	Reserved area	III	6	1
5	Gongmiao Reservoir above	Head water protection zone	II	4	0.5
6	Xiahenana above	Reserved area	III	6	1
7	Xiahenan Gongmiao Reservoir to Hanjiayin	Development and utilization zone	III	6	1
8	Chende above	Reserved area	II	4	0.5
9	Xiabanchen above	Development and utilization zone	III	6	1
10	Sandaohezi/Xiabanchen/ Chengde/Hanjiayin to Wulongji	Development and utilization zone	III	6	1
11	Kuanchen above	Development and utilization zone	III	6	1
12	Liying above	Development and utilization zone	III	6	1
13	Tiaolonkou above	Development and utilization zone	III	6	1
14	Wulongji/Kuanchen/Liyin to Dahedin	Development and utilization zone	III	6	1
15	Taolinkou/Daheidin to Luanxian	Development and utilization zone	III	6	1

(2) Under the currently existing conditions and water use partners, the water quality target of a river system is set to class II in the headwater zones and class III in both the stored area and the development and utilization zone. Water quantity assessments indicate that the maximum available water resource is only 1.73 billion m^3 and the actual total water use is 1.22 billion m^3. This means that the potential increase of the maximum available water use is limited to 0.51 billion m^3. The percentage of the maximum available water resources based on Equation (9) is $1.73/4.02 \times 100\%$, or 43% (see Figure 5). In order to keep this 0.51 billion m^3 available water resources within the required water quality standards, the wastewater load, such as chemical oxygen demand (COD), into the river system should be reduced by 62% during both flood and non-flood periods, based on Equations (10) and (11). Thus, integrated water quality and quantity management should keep the water quality target by means of water

Table 2. Water quality and quantity in the Luan River basin, 1988.

| Zone | Discharge Q (m³/s) | Water quality C | | Water use q (BCM) | Sub-basin runoff R (BCM) | Reservoir storage ΔV (BCM) |
		COD$_{mn}$ (mg/L)	Ammonia nitrogen (mg/L)			
1	0.7429	5.9	0.4	0.0028	0.7457	0
2	1.293	1.4	0.4	0.0872	1.4678	0.0876
3	2.124	17.4	0.18	0.0516	0.5158	0
4	4.9063	42.5	0.16	0.2324	1.7217	0
5	1.211	62.7	5.09	0.0267	1.1512	−0.0865
6	0.7679	3.3	0.76	0.0848	0.8527	0
7	2.3628	22.8	8.23	0.2677	0.6516	0
8	2.0264	51.2	0.34	0.2212	2.2476	0
9	0.5326	2.5	63.36	0.0972	0.6298	0
10	13.5396	23.5	1.77	0.1521	3.8732	0.0096
11	1.0214	2.05	0.34	0.0604	1.0818	0
12	1.4011	4.2	8.79	0.0348	1.4359	0
13	3.3948	1.6	0.04	0.0852	3.8277	0.3477
14	9.0628	3.8	0.42	1.4197	5.9817	11.4613
15	15.3343	7.4	0.235	0.2227	3.0994	0

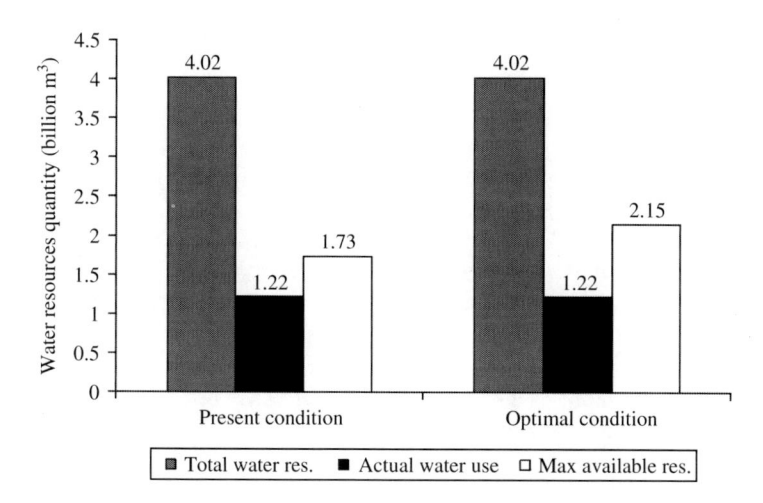

Figure 5. Available water resources in the Luan River, North China.

pollution control, and reasonable water use limited to water resources within 0.51 billion m³. Water saving in agricultural and other sectors will be one of the important solutions in this basin.

(3) Under optimal water allocation conditions, the same water quality target for a river system is kept in both the reserved area and the development and utilization zone. The integrated water quality and quantity assessments indicate that the maximum available water resources increased to 2.15 billion m³. Relative to actual total water use of 1.22 billion m³ in 1988, the potential increase of the maximum available

water is about 0.93 billion m^3 under the optimal water allocation (see Figure 4). With optimal water management, water use efficiency will increase significantly.

It should be noted that for developing countries, such as China, under serious water stress from population growth and environmental issues, integrated water quality and quantity management could be the only way to balance socio-economic development and sustainable water resources utilization.

Concluding Remarks

China is facing big challenges in developing wise management of the limited water resources under great stress from socio-economic development and the need of environmental protection. Integrated water quality and quantity management will be one of the key issues for sustainable water use and, thus, the water policy of the country will play a key role.

China is shifting to a new water strategy based on a triple control principle (the three "red lines" named earlier): control of total water use, control of water use efficiency, and control of total wastewater load. This new water policy also significantly influences China's policy for water quality management.

External assessment of China's water problems and recommendations for policy solutions often fail to recognize interrelated physical, institutional, historical, cultural, and ideologically based contradictions in the water sector, distinctive to the country, that challenge Chinese policy makers in unique ways. Thus, the issue of water quality management will challenge traditional water policy and the governance system with its multiple departments to assess water quantity and quality. Additional challenges include the implementation of integrated water resources management for both water quality and quantity and water resources programmes in a basin as well as the implementation of good water governance practices.

New water policy based on the triple control of total water use, efficiency, and wastewater into a river will bring China's water policy into a new phase. The way to reach these targets by the triple control and solutions represents an urgent problem to solve to achieve more efficient water resources management.

A further development of water accounting and water governance system is also needed in order to efficiently monitor and estimate the total water use in the basins, to quantify efficiency of water uses and to control wastewater. China will have to face these challenges in its way to implement a new water policy. Key issues for implementation are appropriate governance and stronger legislation; dissemination of information on the importance of integrated water resources management; and suitable tools for decision making. Every effort to solve China's water problems will be advantageous for achieving these objectives.

For developing countries, such as China, the conflicts between socio-economic development and environmental protection could become more significant because of the contradiction between limited natural resources and increasing population growth. Along with rapid economic and social development and water pollution, China is facing enormous challenges in water quantity management, particularly in the northern region.

One of the barriers to a proper implementation of water policies is the lack of knowledge as well as instruments at the river basin level. Science and technology can play a key role in understanding the reasons and the mechanisms behind water problems in terms of water quality management, including the impacts of climate change and human activities. Besides water policy and social science, hydrology, environmental sciences, ecology, geography, and their interface can provide a framework for the implementation of integrated water quality and quantity assessment and water management. In this paper, a systematic concept on integrated water resources quantity and quality assessment has been proposed. This innovative approach to the assessment of available water resources is based on a distributed hydrological model, on a water quality model, and on the integrated non-linear programming model that is able to consider environmental flow demand in a river system and also water quality objectives determined by water service functions in the basin. Due to complexity and uncertainties in a basin water system, there are several issues that need to be addressed in future, such as the impact of climate change and adaptive water management. The model developed in this paper needs further tests in other river basins and regions.

In the case study presented in this paper, it is shown that traditional water resources assessment has to shift into integrated water quality and quantity assessment. Available water resources assessment based on water quality objectives of river service function regionalization could be one of the new approaches for China and other regions or countries. Results of the case study revealed that if water quality and environmental flow requirements are considered in integrated water quality and quantity assessment, the amount of available water resources is only 43.0% of the maximum available water resources under present conditions and could increase to 53.4% under an optimal management condition. Thus, the concept of water resources assessment and management should be changed into a new paradigm considering both water quality and environmental flow issues. For developing countries, such as China, with big challenges emerging from social and economic development and environmental problems, water pollution control will be a key issue for sustainable water utilization. The methodology for integrated water quality and quantity assessment can provide a sound scientific and technical decision support tool for water quality management.

Acknowledgements

This study was supported by the National Key Water Project (2009ZX07210-006), National Basic Research Program of China (2010CB428406), and MWR project (Grant Number 200801001). I also very much appreciate the help and contributions to the case study by my colleagues and students, in particular Wang Z. G., Zhang Y. Y., Liu K. Y., and Wang M. L. My thanks also to C. Xu, L. Gottschalk, and I. Krasovskaia for their help in improving the present paper.

References

Boxer, B. (2001) Contradictions and challenges in China's water policy development, *Water International*, 26(3), pp. 335–341.

Chen, Z. K. (2002) The serious impact of the lasting drought and water shortage on eco-environment of the North China Plain, in: *Proceedings of the Sixth Academician Conference of Chinese Academy of Engineering*, Beijing [in Chinese], pp. 90–97.

China State Environmental Protection Administration (2002) *Environmental Quality Standards for Surface Water*, GB 3838-2002 (Beijing: China Environmental Science Press), Beijing [in Chinese].

Edmonds, R. L. (Ed.) (2000) *Managing the Chinese Environment* (Oxford: Oxford University Press).

Ministry of Commerce PR China (2011) Government Report 2011: Main Objectives and Tasks for the Twelfth Five-Year Plan Period. Available at: http:// english.mofcom.gov.cn/aarticle/newsrelease/counselorsoffice/w esternasiaandafricareport/201103/20110307456058.html

MWR–China Water Conservancy and Hydropower Planning and Design General Institute (2008) *Survey & Assessment of China Water Resources and its Development & Utilization*, Beijing: China Water Power Press [in Chinese].

Qian, Z. Y. & Zhang, G. D. (Eds) (2001) *Strategic Studies of Water Resources for Sustainable Development in China*, Vol. 1 (Beijing: Chinese Water Resources and Hydropower Press), [in Chinese].

Shen, D. (2004) The 2002 Water Law: its impacts on river basin management in China, *Water Policy*, 6, pp. 345–364.

State Council of PR China (2002a) Water Act: Water Law of the People's Republic of China. Beijing: China Law Press [in Chinese].

State Council of PR China (2002b) The People's Republic of China Water Pollution Prevention and Control Law. Beijing: China Law Press [in Chinese].

State Council of PR China (2012) Advice on Implementing Most Stringent Institution of Water Resources Management. Document No. 2012-3 [in Chinese].

World Bank (2006) *China Water Quality Management: Policy and Institutional Considerations, Environment and Social Development: East Asia and Pacific Region*, Discussion Paper (Washington, DC: World Bank).

Xia, J., Chen, X. S., Zuo, Q. T., Jiang, Y. S. & Wan, Y. (2009) *The Integrated Carrying Capacity of Water Environment and the Control Countermeasure* (Beijing: China Science Press), [in Chinese].

Xia, J. & Chen, Y. D. (2001) Water problems and opportunities in hydrological sciences in China, *Hydrological Science Journal*, 46(6), pp. 907–921.

Xia, J., Wang, Z. G. & Yang, D. (2006) An integrated assessment method of water quality and quantity related to surface water resources status, *Journal of Natural Resources*, 21(1), pp. 146–153, [in Chinese].

Xia, J., Zhang, L., Liu, C. & Yu, J. J. (2007) Towards better water security in North China, *Water Resources Management*, 21, pp. 233–247.

Xia, J. & Zhang, Y. (2008) Water security in north China and countermeasure to climate change and human activity, *Physics and Chemistry of the Earth*, 33(5), pp. 359–363.

Xia, J., Zhang, Y. & Zhan, C. (2011) Water quality management in China: the case of the Huai River basin, *International Journal of Water Resources Development*, 27(1), pp. 159–172.

Yan, F., Daming, H. & Kinne, B. (2006) Water resources administration institutions in China, *Water Policy*, 8, pp. 291–301.

Zhang, J., Mauzerall, D. L. & Zhu, T. (2010) Environmental health in China: progress towards clean air and safe water, *The Lancet*, 375(9720), pp. 1110–1119.

Zhang, Y. (2000) 21: Ten great challenges facing our nation's water conservancy in the 21st century, *China Water Resources*, 1, pp. 13–15.

Institutional Capacity on Water Pollution Control of the Pearl River in Guangzhou, China

YUAN YU, DIEUDONNÉ-GUY OHANDJA & J. NIGEL B. BELL

Centre for Environmental Policy, Imperial College London, UK

ABSTRACT *This paper analyzes the role of the prevalent formal and informal institutions in Guangzhou in alleviating deteriorating water quality in the Pearl River. In addition to the dominating role of the local government, it examines the influences of other relevant factors such as the role of environmental non-governmental organizations, the media, and the impact of social and cultural norms. It concludes that the current institutional framework is not sufficiently competent to handle water pollution problems and that a multi-dimensional and cross-sectoral approach is necessary for water pollution control in the Pearl River in Guangzhou.*

Introduction

From an environmental protection point of view, institutional capacity focuses on the interactions between "empowerment, social capital, and an enabling environment, as well as the culture, values and power relations that influence us" (Segnestam *et al.*, 2003). In other words, institutional capacity is not just about the capacity of the government; instead it is a collective response combining a range of specific and relevant elements which exert their particular powers to address a particular issue. Nevertheless, it is suggested that in China, the government dominates far more than any other factor (Schwartz, 2003). The world has witnessed China's economic achievement since the beginning of its political reform in 1978, and China is now the world's second largest economy (Bloomberg News, 2010). However, this achievement has arrived at the expense of the environment, and the country is currently encountering a number of serious environmental problems, including water pollution (World Bank, 2001). It has been reported that 70% of the rivers and lakes in China are polluted (Greenpeace, 2009). The Pearl River of southern China is an example.

After 30 years of rapid development, the downstream end of the Pearl River Delta has been transformed into one of the most developed regions in the country, but also one of the most polluted. Each local government within the delta has taken various measures to deal with water pollution, but with mixed results. Some cities in the delta produce more municipal wastewater than they are able to treat, and fail to improve the water quality. Guangzhou, the capital of Guangdong province and the wealthiest city in the delta, is one example where, for many years, water quality has remained poor (Dong & Mei, 2010).

In 1989, the Guangzhou municipal government started to tackle water pollution, with the installation of the first sewage treatment plant. It has progressed intermittently since then, and in 2003, the government published a detailed plan to solve this persistent problem. In 2006, the municipal government launched a campaign in which the mayor and thousands of participants were to swim across the Pearl River in order to demonstrate the improved water quality in the city section, and more importantly, the government's determination to clean the river. When Guangzhou successfully won the bid for the 2010 Asian Games, the municipal government again prioritized water clean-up and restructured the regulatory system. The Water Affairs Bureau of Guangzhou Municipality (WAB) was formed and became the sole department responsible for all water issues within the municipality. At the end of 2008, the municipal government introduced an ambitious plan of projects worth nearly CYN40 billion (US\$6.352 billion), aiming for an improvement in the river quality by the end of June 2010, specifically in terms of dissolved oxygen levels and levels of organic pollutants in the river.

Despite the robust economic development in Guangzhou, the creation of a regulatory framework addressing water pollution, and the massive investment by the municipal government, there is still little improvement in the water quality of the inner-city section of the Pearl River (Song, 2010). Many researchers have assessed the institutional capacity for environmental protection in the delta (Lo & Tang, 1994; Chan *et al.*, 1995). However, many of these studies focused on individual, specific factors such as officials' capabilities and governmental and societal supports (Lo & Fryxell, 2005; Lo *et al.*, 2006; Tong, 2007). This paper aims to present a comprehensive, integrated overview of institutional capacity which includes the relevant factors, and will analyze the overall role of institutional capacity in water pollution control and management in the inner-city section of the Pearl River in Guangzhou.

Study Area

Guangzhou's attempt at water pollution control and management in its section of the Pearl River is a microcosm of China's situation with respect to water management. Economically, it has enjoyed constant growth during the last three decades, with rapid development of the automobile manufacturing industry and an exponential boom in population. These have invariably placed substantial pressures on the Pearl River, whose water quality has been suffering from mounting pollution. A developed city like Guangzhou is a development model that less-developed regions of the country are likely to follow, and therefore the environmental problems associated with this economic development in Guangzhou are likely to be replicated in those other regions in the coming years.

Literature review was the main approach used to identify the potential factors that influence institutional capacity. Relevant information was sourced from academic papers, newspapers, and magazines to identify the link between these factors and water pollution control. Informal interviews were used for data collection to supplement information available in the literature. Various stakeholders were interviewed, including officials in local governmental departments, university professors, and local residents in Guangzhou. Water quality data for the Pearl River section in Guangzhou was collected from the official website of the local Environmental Protection Bureau (EPB). Figure 1 shows the area of discussion in this paper.

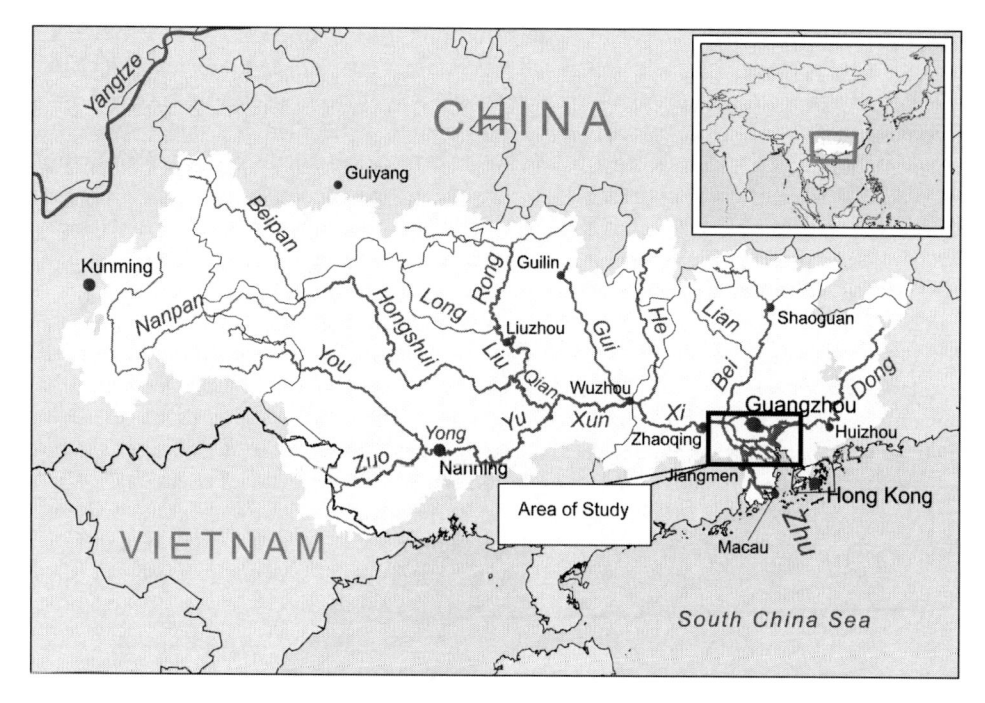

Figure 1. Map of Pearl River.

Government Institutions and Existing Regulatory Framework of Water Pollution Control in Guangzhou

In China, the main governmental bodies responsible for water issues are the Ministry of Environmental Protection (MEP), which is in charge of all environmental protection issues, and the Ministry of Water Resources (MWR), whose focus is on water quality and quantity. At the local level, the EPB represents the MEP, and is able to produce and implement its specific regulations based on the national environmental laws from the MEP. In Guangzhou, the WAB is the local representative of the MWR. The Bureau of Pearl River Water Resources Protection (BPRWRP) is a further local body which also shares some responsibilities in pollution control. Such divided responsibilities over water pollution control demand cooperation to properly address the issue, not only from these local environmental authorities, but also from other local departments that are involved in environmental protection, such as planning commissions, industrial bureaus, and finance bureaus (OECD, 2005). In the current situation, this collaboration is precluded due to a number of factors, including bureaucracy, inconsistencies of approach by individual decision makers, communication difficulties across different authorities, and conflicting policy objectives. Lo *et al.* (2006) argued that the personal perceptions of individual officials responsible for enforcement of environmental decisions also play an important role. These perceptions may be based on their experiences of the environment, but also on their age and their educational level (Tong, 2007; Lo *et al.*, 2006). These various features shape personal values (Lowe *et al.*, 1997; Richards *et al.*, 2002), which can influence the decisions made by these people in their official decision-making capacities, as well as in their negotiation strategies with regulators and polluting industries. Because economic development is perceived as the top priority, collaboration between the officials in charge of economic development and those responsible for environmental protection is very limited (Khator *et al.*, 1992). At the policy-development level, there is a tendency to reject environmental policies in favour of those related to issues such as population control, science, and technology (Tong, 2007). As a result, environmental problems are only ever partially solved, leading progressively to an overall deterioration of environmental quality. In the longer term, the environment further degrades and problems become more entrenched and difficult to solve (Lo *et al.*, 2006; Willems & Baumert, 2003).

The decisive influence of the mayor in Guangzhou gives him the ultimate power to decide on all aspects of the city's development, including environmental protection. The availability of resources to the EPB is at the mayor's discretion; this, in turn, determines the capabilities of the EPB to achieve its targets. The mayor's ambitions to tackle environmental problems are therefore reflected in the quality of the environment in general, and in this case, in the history of water pollution control in Guangzhou. Prior to 2003, when the current mayor took office, little attention was given to environmental protection, because the preceding mayor perceived the economy to be much more important (Lo & Fryxell, 2005), which resulted in limited improvement of the water quality. However, since 2003 there has been more policy focus on improving river quality, because the mayor has been trying to differentiate himself in political achievement from his predecessor; this led to the elaboration of the plan to tackle water pollution in the inner-city part of the Pearl River. In addition, the new mayor considered the Asian Games a unique opportunity to further boost the clean-up of the inner-city section of the Pearl River.

Public Participation in Water Pollution Control in Guangzhou

Good governance, as defined by United Nations Economic & Social Commission for Asia and the Pacific (2005), includes public participation. Further, a meaningful participation, which is underpinned by a deliberate intention to produce competent policies, is most desirable. Plummer and Taylor (2004) adapted Arnstein's concept (1969) into "a ladder of community participation in China", and stated that mere attendance by the public during consultation for policy making is not meaningful participation, but is nevertheless an essential stepping-stone to this in China. However, public participation in decision making is still in its infancy as a result of the lack of transparency and limited knowledge of participants about the specific matters in question (Wang *et al.*, 2002). In 2007, the State Environmental Protection Agency (the precursor to the MEP) issued a specific piece of legislation on environmental information disclosure, entitling the public to obtain information from the environmental authorities. This was regarded as a positive step towards public participation (Chinadialogue.net, 2009). However, its effectiveness is limited: Yuan and Xu (2010) reported that 17 out of 29 EPBs in capital cities across the country ignored or rejected requests for disclosure of the list of companies penalized for breach of environmental legislation. Even in the situations where a response was provided, the information supplied was of poor quality. In this example, Guangzhou EPB did not reject the application but there was no response. As a result, and in the absence of quality information being accessible to the public, it is evident that the policy-making process is still dominated and controlled mostly by government-led groups (Zhao, 2005).

The Impacts of Environmental Non-governmental Organizations (ENGOs) and the Media

The rise of ENGOs in China began as late as the mid-1990s, when the central government recognized its limited capacity to cover all social issues and started engagement with the "third force" (Yang, 2005; Schwartz, 2004). In less than 10 years (1993–2001), the number of ENGOs rose from 2 to more than 70 (Yang, 2005), driven by an overall aim to educate the general public. A number of different approaches, such as online mailing lists and online forums, are used to increase people's environmental awareness (Yang, 2005). ENGOs also have the capacity to facilitate the government's monitoring of polluting industries, and have achieved some success in pressuring some companies to take more stringent pollution-control measures (Johnson, 2009). To many people inside the government, both at national and local level, the rise of ENGOs, especially those with political intentions, is perceived as a threat. Political ENGOs are required to register and to accept censorship, which limits their actions (Yang, 2005; Johnson, 2009; Enserink & Koppenjan, 2007). International ENGOs, such as Greenpeace, form partnerships with local ones to improve the capacity of these grass-roots groups to influence the authorities for better governance (Yang, 2005).

The mass media have gradually become a force that the government cannot ignore (Wen, 1998); they have challenged the authorities by publishing some sensitive environmental issues (Liu & Anbumozhi, 2009). The media become a tool to promote transparency (Johnson, 2009) and to deliver information on environmental issues, which many officials rely on to promote enforcement of environmental regulations. The Internet is another platform, where messages are circulated faster and more widely than in traditional forms of the media. As the number of Internet users continues to grow, the websites of ENGOs clearly can act as gateways for the sharing of more information and to promote discussions with an increasing number of people (Yang, 2005).

Guangzhou's local media are quite robust and environmental issues have received coverage over recent years. The Pearl River in Guangzhou and the inner-city waterways have always been important to the local people, so this is an environmental topic upon which local media regularly report. This media coverage allows local people to keep a close eye on the government's work on water pollution control. The municipal government was, therefore, under a lot of public pressure to address pollution in the river prior to announcing the multi-billion-yuan cleaning plan in 2008. The plan was naturally received as good news by local residents, who hoped for a great change in water quality; a few years on, they are worried about the limited results. With daily reports on poor water quality, people are very concerned (Ni & Liu, 2010).

The Influence of Cultural and Social Norms

Willems and Baumert (2003) suggest that the general public should engage in policy making to ensure good governance. However, the way in which the public engages in policy making will be influenced by cultural and social norms, which shape individual and group behaviour and differ markedly from country to country. As such, in China, environmental governance and institutional efforts to tackle environmental problems, as well as the engagement of the public in shaping environmental policy, are influenced by social and cultural norms.

Guanxi, commonly translated as "connections" or "relationships", is probably the most renowned social norm in China. It is based on China's unique cultural values and socio-politico-economic system. Fan (2002) defines *guanxi* as the process of social interactions that initially involve two individuals. Local government has good *guanxi* with industries located within its jurisdiction, as a result of the favourable policies it offers to businesses which contribute to local revenues. But as far as environmental protection is concerned, such *guanxi* become ambiguous, since curbing pollution often requires industries to adopt costly clean technologies, which reduces profit and therefore the taxes paid to local government (Lo *et al.*, 2006; Tong, 2007). On many occasions, the situation becomes more complex when financial inducement takes place (Chow, 2007). This was corroborated by the informal research interviews undertaken for this paper: as several interviewees (researchers and officials) confirmed, because of such improper practices, some officials tend to help businesses escape inspections, which compromises environmental governance in the long term.

The "rule of man", analogous to the "rule of law" in Western culture, is deeply embedded in the Chinese culture. Under the "rule of man", most matters are handled under the personal discretion of the leaders or other senior personnel, instead of following written regulations. According to Orts (2000), the rule of law has never been at the forefront in the country's legal system. Instead, as advocated by Confucius, the ruler should be of good morals, which he considers already sufficient to result in an orderly society, without a formal legal system. Despite the short period of development of the "rule of law" in China, the legal system is already very complex, with different levels of laws and regulations that are inconsistent with each other. Further, there are a relatively small number of professional people who can fully understand and interpret them. One of the interviewees for this paper, an official at the inspection unit at the EPB in Guangzhou, noticed that, although the national water pollution prevention and control law was revised in 2008 to introduce more stringent measures (such as the compulsory installation of outfall monitoring equipment and uncapped fines for violation), his team hardly ever executed these measures strictly according to the law. This was due to excessive negotiation with business and the limited knowledge of the inspectors to interpret and apply the legislation in real-life situations.

Mianzi is another core concept in Chinese culture, meaning "face" or "dignity". It is earned through time and personal achievements, which determine a person's social status (Ho, 1976). Buckley *et al.* (2006) argued that "saving *mianzi*" is a shortcut to developing more *guanxi* with other parties. This is particularly important for a business, because the more *mianzi* it earns, the better *guanxi* it is able to develop, which creates mutual trust and provides more opportunities for cooperation and trusted relationships for both sides. The environmental bureau actually has more bargaining power when dealing with a company that enjoys distinguished respect among other competitors. As a result, the company will follow the regulations, as a way to give *mianzi* to the government officials and thus maintain good *guanxi* with the government.

Water Quality in the River Pearl in Guangzhou

Classification of water bodies in China is based on the environmental quality standards shown in Table 1. On the basis of these standards, surface water is classified into five grades. Grades I, II, and III represent drinking-water quality, grades IV and V are polluted, and grade V + represents highly polluted waters, not suitable for any use.

Table 2 demonstrates that, even with the increased focus on water improvement by the mayor and the media, there has clearly been no positive, consistent improvement in water quality in the river. From 2001 to 2004, the water was probably of grade III (although many

Table 1. Environmental quality standards for surface water. All are maximum amounts (except pH), in mg/L (except pH and faecal coliform).

Indicators	Grade I	Grade II	Grade III	Grade IV	Grade V
pH	6.5–8.5	6.5–8.5	6.5–8.5	6.5–8.5	6–9
Dissolved O_2	7.5*	6	5	3	2
$KMnO_4^-$	2	4	6	10	15
COD	15	15	20	30	40
BOD_5	3	3	4	6	10
NH_3-N	0.15	0.5	1.0	1.5	2.0
T-P	0.02	0.1	0.2	0.3	0.4
T-N	0.2	0.5	1.0	1.5	2.0
Copper	0.01	1.0	1.0	1.0	1.0
Zinc	0.05	1.0	1.0	2.0	2.0
Fluorinated	1.0	1.0	1.0	1.5	1.5
Selenium	0.01	0.01	0.01	0.02	0.02
Arsenic	0.05	0.05	0.05	0.1	0.1
Mercury	0.00005	0.00005	0.0001	0.001	0.001
Cadmium	0.001	0.005	0.005	0.005	0.01
Chromium VI	0.01	0.05	0.05	0.05	0.1
Lead	0.01	0.01	0.05	0.05	0.1
Cyanide	0.005	0.05	0.2	0.2	0.2
Volatile phenol	0.002	0.002	0.005	0.01	0.1
Petrol	0.05	0.05	0.05	0.5	1.0
Faecal coliform (number/L)	200	2,000	10,000	20,000	40,000

* Approximately 90% saturation
Source: MEP (2002).

parameters were not monitored). Apart from the short-lived improvement in 2006 resulting in grade III, the quality of water in the Pearl River has since worsened, falling back to grade IV. While many factors such as nonpoint sources and upstream pollution can affect the overall water quality in Guangzhou, treatment of local municipal and industrial effluents plays an important role in improving water quality. As shown in Figure 2, from 2003 onwards, nearly all industrial wastewater (96%) received some treatment before being discharged into the river. Although treatment of municipal wastewater also increased, there are still significant quantities of untreated wastewater being discharged into the river.

These data show clearly that the various actors in water management responsible for the river's quality are not yet succeeding in their mission. Despite the fact that municipal and industrial effluents are subject to some form of treatment before discharge, any control measures and discharge standards are not defined—suggesting that the treatment of these effluents may, in fact, be only very basic, and possibly inadequate. These data demonstrate the shortcomings of existing institutional capacity to control water pollution issues in Guangzhou.

Discussion

The institutional capacity to manage pollution in the Pearl River in Guangzhou is still limited, which has resulted in poor water quality. Many institutional barriers hamper effective water pollution control in the river at different levels, including individual capacity, communication within and among government institutions, and the impact of

Table 2. Water quality classification of the Pearl River, Guangzhou section.

Year	Grade	Comments
1999	V +	Concentrations of petrol and organic indicators exceeding guideline[1]
2000	V +	Similar to 1999
2001	III	7 indicators better than 2000
2002	III[2]	8 indicators below guideline
2003	III[2]	5 indicators below guideline
2004	III[2]	5 indicators below guideline[3]
2005	IV	5 indicators below guideline
2006	III	4 indicators below guideline
2007	IV	4 indicators below guideline
2008	IV	4 indicators below guideline
2009	IV	4 indicators below guideline
2010	IV	4 indicators below guideline

[1] Standard of Grade III is used as guideline.
[2] The reports did not state the grade of river quality, but confirmed that most indicators met Grade III standard.
[3] Before 2004, 22 indicators were used; from 2004, 23 indicators were used.
Source: Guangzhou EPB (2011).

social and cultural norms. Addressing such capacity deficits can help in developing strategies for better water governance in the Pearl River.

The Limited Capability of Guangzhou EPB and Incentives for Leaders

The large difference between the percentage of domestic sewage treated and that of industrial wastewater is an example that well illustrates the limited capability of the EPB to control pollution in the Pearl River in Guangzhou. Theoretically, the EPB should collect, treat, and dispose of all municipal wastewaters, but the limited technical and human capacity means that a significant proportion of untreated effluents is discharged into the river, contributing to pollution. In addition, part of the pollution comes from other regions upstream which are beyond the jurisdiction of the EPB. On the other hand, the EPB is able to control industrial discharges, most of which are located in the city. In line with the tight legal requirements, which allow the EPB to fine industries for any illegal or excessive discharge, it is no surprise that there is a nearly 100% treatment rate for industrial wastewater. However, there is concern regarding the appropriateness of the fines set by the under-resourced EPB. In the quest for maximum income, the EPB may set unrealistically high discharge standards, which in turn would reduce polluters' profits and consequently tax revenues to local government (OECD, 2005).

The limited capacity of the EPB to address pollution in the River Pearl in Guangzhou is also partly attributable to the limited autonomy the EPB is granted to design long-term strategies to address pollution issues in the city. Generally, local leaders are pro-economy, because a local leader is assessed largely on the basis of economic development during his administration. Achieving fast economic growth can ensure better promotion prospects for the leader (Chen *et al.*, 2005). Most leaders are promotion-driven and therefore attempt to pursue the maximum economic development during their administration. The relatively brief term of the administration (7 years in Guangzhou) may be too complex and too short a time for officials to fully understand and address all the local environmental problems.

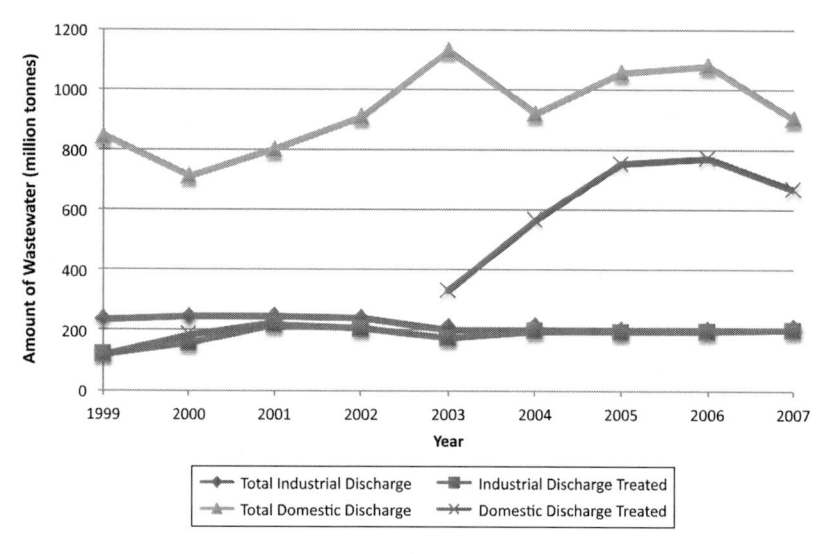

Figure 2. Discharge and treatment levels of domestic and industrial sewage in Guangzhou, 1999–2007. *Source:* Statistics Bureau of Guangzhou Municipality (2010).

As a result, it is difficult for them to suggest an appropriate long-term strategy for environmental protection. Furthermore, as successive leaders always want to be different from their predecessors, they often undertake new initiatives, which can sometimes undermine the programmes of previous administrations or prevent their reaching maturity. Such inconsistency can be detrimental to environmental protection, which needs long-term vision and consistent efforts (Zhang, 2008; Tan, 2007).

Unclear Responsibility among Institutional Structures

Although the EPB is a local representative of the MEP, the Environmental Protection Law (1989) grants power to the local governments for specific environmental protection measures. However, the law does not specify the division of responsibilities between the EPB and the local government to ensure coherence of objectives between the national and local policies. Furthermore, the structure of the local government is similar to that of the central government, where the local government centrally manages all the departments. MEP objectives in terms of pollution control policies may not necessarily bear the same significance at the local level, since the local government may have other priorities. The absence of a framework that delineates the MEP and EPB's separate roles has lead the EPB to depend upon the local government's decisions rather than executing the plans of the MEP (Lo *et al.*, 2006; Tong, 2007). Further, like most local governments that are economy-oriented, the ex-mayor of Guangzhou focused on economic growth, achieving an annual growth of 13.8% from 2001 to 2005, well above the national annual growth of the same period (Mou & Yu, 2011; Zhang, 2011), but with very little improvement of water quality (Table 2). In addition, the three governmental bodies (EPB, BPRWRP and WAB) have each developed some measures for protecting the river, yet work independently. This highlights the limited cross-sectoral capacity of government institutions to address water issues in Guangzhou.

Better Cooperation between Government Departments

The effectiveness of addressing water quality issues in Guangzhou is hampered by the fact that there are several responsible authorities which do not have clear delineation of roles, nor do they coordinate and cooperate to address water pollution. A hundred and fifty years ago, London had a similar problem that saw extensive disputes between the authorities as to who should be responsible for handling water pollution problems on the River Thames (Wood, 1982). Given the current institutional settings in Guangzhou, it is not realistic to expect a single agency in charge of water pollution in the near future. In the meantime, a practical solution is to increase the level and effectiveness of communication between these authorities to improve mutual understanding.

Enabling Incentive Structure for Leaders

Changes to the current incentive structure for leaders might be the key to securing cooperation between various departments. This could mean gradually decoupling economic growth from the assessment system and embedding environmental performance in the incentive structure. This would encourage local leaders to deliver projects that could improve environmental quality. Such an assessment system should be robust and closely monitored in order to ensure transparency.

Systematic Approach to Control Water Pollution

Water pollution control seems to focus on water quality, and in particular on treatment of industrial effluents. While this approach could result in improvement of river quality, pollution originates from many other sources, such as domestic effluents, road and waste management facilities, and storm run-off, in addition to the incoming upstream pollution. Long-term pollution control will need to integrate other sectoral policies, such as town and land planning, and municipal solid waste and wastewater management, to encompass pollution prevention and remedial action. This would require institutional capacity-building at the local level.

Increasing Environmental Information Disclosure and Public Participation

In the EPB's annual report on the state of the environment, the contents could be presented in a consistent way, so that it is easier for interested parties to access data. For water specifically, the report could include the water quality of waterways, in addition to the already available water quality of the Pearl River. There is also a need to educate not only the general public but also officials at the EPB on their responsibilities for environmental quality. Because the public may still have limited influence on decision making, ENGOs may have a crucial role to play in the process of environmental policy making.

Conclusion

Pollution of the Pearl River in Guangzhou is closely linked to the rapid economic development of the city. River water quality in the Guangzhou section of the river has remained relatively poor despite efforts to control pollution. Our analysis has shown a number of issues that impede progress: a bureaucratic structure, unclear roles and responsibilities of different departments, deeply embedded cultural and social norms, ENGOs with limited spheres of influence, and a lack of involvement by and engagement with the general public in policy making. On the other hand, the local media have played an active role in promoting better governance, and have had a positive effect on policy making. Collectively, these factors lead to inadequate configuration of the institutional capacity in water management in Guangzhou at the moment, meaning that there is a need to reform the current institutional capacity to more effectively address river pollution. Effective communication is essential to minimize any potential conflicts and to maximize cooperation between the different governmental bodies responsible for environmental issues. Better communication and clearer delineation of the roles of those bodies will produce a more accountable and comprehensive strategy for pollution control. A greater level of public participation, including a more open application of the existing regulations that allow public access to official environmental information, would further enhance the institutional capacity to address the issue of pollution in the Pearl River. Managed well, the environment of the Pearl River could become a shining example for the less-developed areas of China, demonstrating the successful combination of rapid economic development with water pollution management and control; however, if it is managed poorly, it could become a real-life cautionary tale which could have lasting impact for many years to come.

References

Arnstein, S. (1969) A ladder of public participation, *Journal of American Institute of Planners*, 35(4), pp. 216–224.

Bloomberg News (2010) China overtakes Japan as world's second-largest economy, 16 August, Available at: http://www.bloomberg.com/news/2010-08-16/china-economy-passes-japan-s-in-second-quarter-capping-three-decade-rise.html (accessed 27 August 2010).

Buckley, P. J., Clegg, J. & Tan, H. (2006) Cultural awareness in knowledge transfer in China: the role of *guanxi* and *mianzi*, *Journal of World Business*, 41, pp. 275–288.

Chan, H. S., Wong, K., Cheung, K. C. & Lo, J. M. K. (1995) The implementation gap in environmental management in China: the Case of Guangzhou, Zhengzhou, and Nanjing, *Public Administration Review*, 55, pp. 333–340.

Chen, Y., Li, H. & Zhou, L. (2005) Relative performance evaluation and the turnover of provincial leaders in China, *Economics Letters*, 88(3), pp. 421–425.

Chinadialogue.net (2009) One year of open information, 18 May [in Chinese]. Available at: http://www.china dialogue.net/article/show/single/ch/3015 (accessed 3 September 2010).

Chow, G. (2007) *China's Energy and Environmental Problems and Policies*, Report number 152, Princeton University Centre for Economic Policy Studies.

Dong, Y. J. & Mei, Y. D. (2010) Influence of urbanization on the surface water quality in Guangzhou, *China*, *Wuhan University Journal of Natural Science*, 15(1), pp. 78–84.

Enserink, B. & Koppenjan, J. (2007) Public participation in China: sustainable urbanisation and governance, *Management of Environmental Quality*, 18(4), pp. 459–470.

Fan, Y. (2002) Questioning guanxi: definition, classification and implications, *International Business Review*, 11, pp. 543–561.

Greenpeace (2009) *Poisoning the Pearl: An Investigation into Industrial Pollution in the Pearl River Delta* (Beijing: Greenpeace China).

Guangzhou EPB (2011) *Annual Report on Environmental Quality in Guangzhou* (Guangzhou: Environmental Protection Bureau), [in Chinese]. Available at: http://www.gzepb.gov.cn/zwgk/hjgb/ (accessed 3 August 2010).

Ho, H. F. (1976) On the concept of face, *American Journal of Sociology*, 81(4), pp. 867–884.

Johnson, T. (2009) *Extending Environmental Governance: China's Environmental State and Civil Society*. Ph.D. thesis, University of Glasgow, Scotland, UK.

Khator, R., Ng, K. & Chan, H. S. (1992) Environmental management and street-level regulators: a cultural trap? *Public Administration and Development*, 12, pp. 387–397.

Liu, X. & Anbumozhi, V. (2009) Determinant factors for corporate environmental information disclosure: an empirical study of Chinese listed companies, *Journal of Cleaner Production*, 17(6), pp. 593–600.

Lo, C. & Fryxell, G. E. (2005) Governmental and societal support for environmental enforcement in China: an empirical study in Guangzhou, *Journal of Development Studies*, 41(4), pp. 558–588.

Lo, C., Fryxell, G. E. & Wong, W. (2006) Effective regulations with little effect? The antecedents of the perceptions of environmental officials on enforcement effectiveness in China, *Environmental Management*, 38(3), pp. 388–410.

Lo, C. & Tang, S. Y. (1994) Institutional contexts of environmental management: water pollution control in Guangzhou, China, *Public Administration and Development*, 14(1), pp. 53–64.

Lowe, P., Clark, J., Seymour, S. & Ward, N. (1997) *Moralising the Environment* (London: UCL Press).

Ministry of Environmental Protection (2002) *Standard for Surface Water Environment, GB3838-2002* (Beijing: Ministry of Environmental Protection).

Mou, X. & Yu, Y. (2011) Guangzhou Dingchu Jijiwentuo Mubiao Baowei, *Xin Kuaibao*, 19 January, p. A14.

Ni, M. & Liu, X. (2010) Guangzhou Zhishui Chengjidan Jin Jiexiao, *Guangzhou Daily*, 1 July, p. A24.

OECD (2005) Environment and governance in China, in: *Governance in China*, pp. 487–534 (Paris: OECD Publishing).

Orts, E. W. (2000) The rule of law in China, *Vanderbilt Journal of Transnational Law*, 33, pp. 44–110.

People's Republic of China (1989) *The Law of Environmental Protection in the People's Republic of China* (Beijing: State Council of the People's Republic of China).

Plummer, J. & Taylor, J. G. (2004) The characteristics of community participation in China, in: J. Plummer & J. G. Taylor (Eds) *Community Participation in China: Issues and Processes for Capacity Building*, pp. 36–54, 1st ed. (London: EarthScan).

Richards, J. P., Glegg, G. A., Cullinance, A. & Wallace, H. E. (2002) Policy, principle, and practice in industrial pollution control: views from the regulatory interface, *Environmental Management*, 29(2), pp. 182–194.

Schwartz, J. (2003) The impact of state capacity on enforcement of environmental policies: the case of China, *Journal of Environment Development*, 12(1), pp. 50–81.

Schwartz, J. (2004) Environmental NGOs in China: roles and limits, *Pacific Affairs*, 77(1), pp. 28–49.

Segnestam, L., Persson, Å., Nilsson, M., Arvidsson, A. & Ijjasz, E. (2003) *Country-Level Environmental Analysis: A Review of International Experiences* (Washington, DC: World Bank).

Song, Q. (2010) Guangzhou 500 Yi Zhi Shui, *21st Century Business Herald*, 26 July [in Chinese]. Available at http://www.21cbh.com/HTML/2010-7-27/wMMDAwMDE4ODgwMg.html (accessed 4 September 2010).

Statistics Bureau of Guangzhou Municipality (2010) *Guangzhou Statistical Yearbook 2000–2008* [in Chinese] (Guangzhou: Daguanyuan Media Corporation). Available at: http://data.gzstats.gov.cn/gzStat1/chaxun/njsj.jsp (accessed 25 July 2011).

Tan, W. (2007) Discussion on trust building of the government, *Journal of Yunan Administration College*, 2, 31–34.

Tong, Y. (2007) Bureaucracy meets the environment: elite perceptions in six Chinese cities, *China Quarterly*, 189, pp. 100–121.

United Nations Economic and Social Commission for Asia and the Pacific (2005) *What is Good Governance?* Available at: http://www.unescap.org/pdd/prs/ProjectActivities/Ongoing/gg/governance.asp (accessed 15 August 2010).

Wang, H., Bi, J., Wheeler, D., Wang, J., Cao, D., Lu, G. & Wang, Y. (2002) *Environmental Performance Rating and Disclosure: China's Green-Watch Program*, Report number WPS 2889 (Washington, DC: World Bank).

Wen, B. (1998) Greening the Chinese media, *China Environment Series*, 2, pp. 39–45.

Willems, S. & Baumert, K. (2003) *Institutional Capacity and Climate Actions* (Paris: OECD Publishing).

Wood, L. B. (1982) *The Restoration of the Tidal Thames* (Bristol: Adam Hilger).

World Bank (2001) *China: Air, Land and Water* (Washington, DC: World Bank).

Yang, G. (2005) Environmental NGOs and institutional dynamics in China, *China Quarterly*, 181, pp. 46–66.

Yuan, D. D. & Xu, N. (2010) Huanjing Xinxi Gongkai Za Zhemenan, *infzm.com*, 23 June [in Chinese]. Available at: http://www.infzm.com/content/46698 (accessed 5 September 2010).

Zhang, J. J. (2008) State power, elite relations and the politics of privatization in Chinese rural industry, *Asian Survey*, 18(2), pp. 215–238.

Zhang, M. (2011) "Shier Wu" Shi Zhongguo Jingji Jiegou Zhuanxing De "Zhentong Qi", 5 March [in Chinese] (National People's Congress of the People's Republic of China). Available at: http://www.npc.gov.cn/npc/zt/qt/jj125gh/2011-03/05/content_1633187.htm (accessed 24 January 2012).

Zhao, J. (2005) Defects and improvement of public participation principle in Chinese environment law, *Environmental Science and Technology*, 28, pp. 54–55.

Soil Erosion Control and Sediment Load Reduction in the Loess Plateau: Policy Perspectives

ZHONGBAO XIN*, LISHAN RAN** & X. X. LU**

*College of Soil and Water Conservation, Beijing Forestry University, Beijing, China; **Department of Geography, National University of Singapore, Singapore

ABSTRACT   *The sediment load of the Loess Plateau has shown a sharp decreasing trend in the past decades. This paper gives a comprehensive review of the driving factors of the sediment decrease with respect to human activities, including soil and water conservation, dam construction, and vegetation restoration. Also presented is an overview of the main achievements of soil and water conservation and the main soil erosion control programmes implemented in the Loess Plateau. The paper concludes with suggestions for further policy modifications that could move management towards ecological sustainability and will be greatly beneficial to the regional water resources management and restoration of an eco-environmental system in the Loess Plateau.*

Introduction

The sediment load of the Yellow River contributes approximately 10% of the world's sediment load to the sea, and approximately 90% of the sediment in the Yellow River originated in the Loess Plateau (Tang, 2004). Soil erosion, an important eco-environmental index of the Loess Plateau, is closely related to sediment concentration, which is an important index of water quality because it is correlated with the transportation, adsorption, and degradation of contamination. The Loess Plateau has been suffering from serious soil erosion, which results in eco-environmental deterioration, slow economic development, and poverty, and is the fundamental cause of flood disasters in the lower Yellow River. Therefore, the trend and driving factors of the sediment load from the Loess Plateau have attracted attention from the public, the government, and scholars of hydrology, environment, and management.

Many scholars have analyzed the direct driving factors: precipitation, soil erosion, soil and water conservation practices, agricultural practices, deforestation, check-dams, reservoirs, and so on (Wang *et al.*, 2007; Wang *et al.*, 2010). It is clear that the policies related to agricultural practices, deforestation, soil erosion control, and sediment load reduction have not been given proper consideration.

The objective of this paper is thus to analyze the eco-environmental policies of soil and water conservation over the past decades and to enhance the understanding of soil erosion and sediment load, thus helping improve the policies of eco-environmental management in the Loess Plateau.

The Loess Plateau

The Loess Plateau of China is located in the middle reaches of the Yellow River, and encircled by the Ela Mountains to the west, the Taihang Mountains to the east, the Yin Mountains to the north, and the Qingling and Funiu Mountains to the south (Figure 1). The Loess Plateau is the region with most severe soil erosion and yield of sediments in China because of its very erodable loess cover. The Loess Plateau has an elevation of 1,200 to 1,600 m above sea level, and is predominantly covered by loess deposits ranging from 30 to 80 m in thickness (Chen *et al.*, 2007).

The annual mean temperature ranges from 6 to 14°C. The mean temperature in the coldest month (January) ranges between -22 and 6°C, and in the hottest (July) between 14 and 34°C, with an increasing trend from northeast to southwest. Annual mean precipitation in the Loess Plateau ranges from 200 mm in the north to 700 mm in the south, while the centralized and intense rainfall of June, July, and August accounts for about half the total annual precipitation (Shi & Shao, 2001; Tang, 2004; Chen *et al.*, 2007). In addition, summer rainfall, especially in the central Loess areas, often comes in quick cloudbursts which overcome the infiltration capacity of the soil and carry massive quantities of sediment into the Yellow River and its tributaries. In terms of population in the Loess Plateau, as of 2008 it was 108.17 million, of whom 67.8% were rural residents. Among the total cultivated farmland of 14.58 km^2, 46.5% was cultivated on slopes (NDRC, 2010).

Soil erosion on the Loess Plateau affects an area of 450,000 km^2. Ninety per cent of the sediment in the Yellow River originated from soil erosion on the Loess Plateau (Tang *et al.*, 2004; Chen *et al.*, 2007). As an area with the most severe soil and water losses in the world, the average erosion reaches 5,000–10,000 t km^{-2} per year, sometimes even up to 20,000–30,000 t km^{-2} per year; extremely high rates of up to 59,700 t km^{-2} per year have also been recorded (Shi & Shao, 2000). As a result, the lower reaches have risen at an annual rate of 8–10 cm, resulting in a so-called 'river above ground' of 800 km in length and creating enormous sedimentation problems and flood risks in the downstream of the Yellow River (Shi & Shao, 2000; Tang, 2000).

Decline of Sediment Loads in the Loess Plateau

The annual mainstream sediment load of the Yellow River showed a significant decreasing trend from 1950 to 2009 (Table 1). The annual sediment load at Toudaoguai station decreased by 60.9% and 62.2% in the 1990s and the 2000s, respectively, compared to the averaged sediment load during 1950–2009. The annual sediment load at Huayuankou station, representing the sediment export from the Loess Plateau, decreased by 88.7% during 2000–2009, compared to the average sediment discharge of the period 1950–2009 (Table 1). Both the water discharge and the sediment load in the Loess Plateau, as indicated by the difference between the Huayuankou and the Toudaoguai stations, had a significant decreasing trend over the past six decades, especially during 2000–2009 (Figure 2).

Such a decreasing trend is also common for the main tributaries of the Yellow River (Table 1). The annual sediment load of Fenhe River decreased by 79.4% in the 1980s. The tributaries of the Fenhe, Yiluohe, and Qinhe decreased by 85.6%, 92.3%, and 81.3% in the 1990s, respectively. Other tributaries of the middle Yellow River have also decreased in the period 2000–2009;for example, the Kuyehe, Fenhe and Yiluohe Rivers have

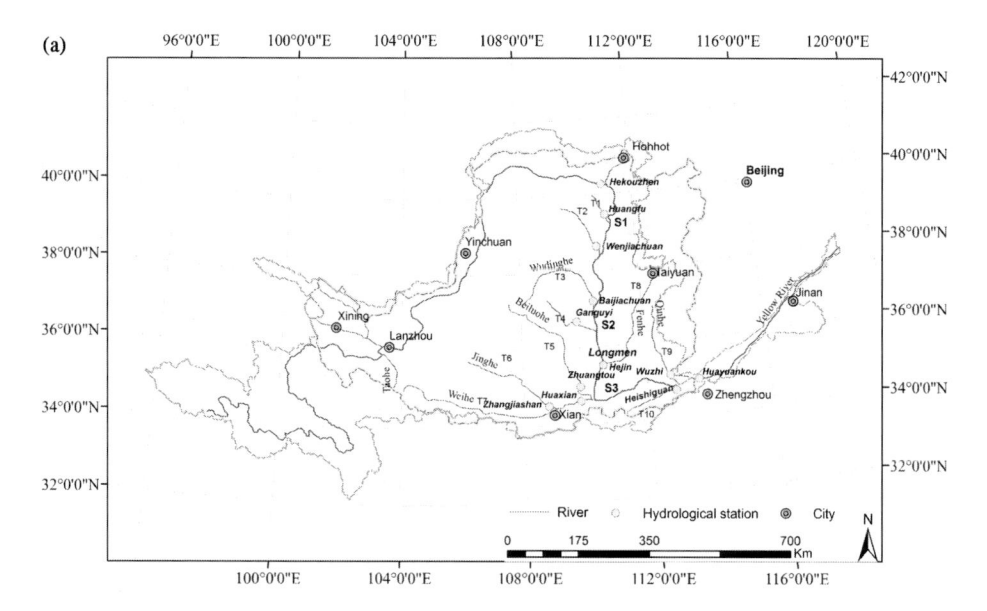

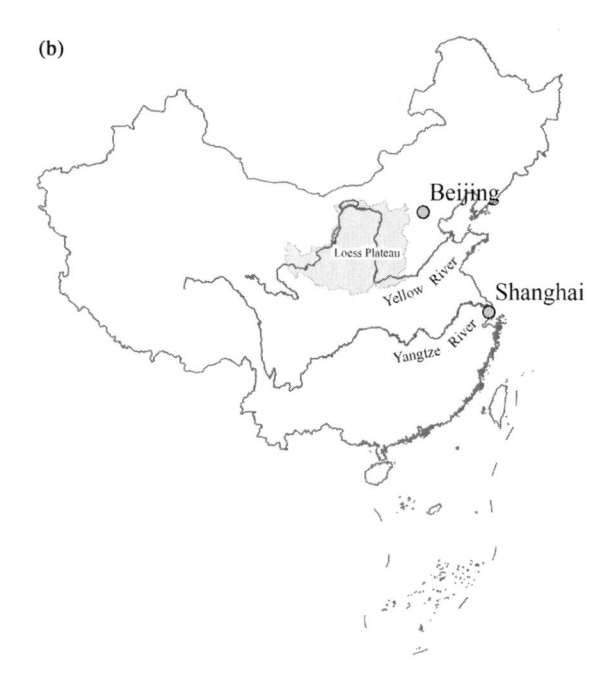

Figure 1. The Loess Plateau and Yellow River, China.

Table 1. Inter annual variability of sediment load of the main rivers in the Loess Plateau, 1950–2009.

River	Hydrological station	Controlled area (km^2)	Sediment load 1950–2009 (10^8 t)	Abnormal percentage to averaged sediment load of 1950–2009 (%)					Correlation coefficient	Observed period
				Before 1970	1970s	1980s	1990s	2000s		
Yellow River	Toudaoguai	367,898	1.05	60.0	9.9	− 6.7	− 60.9	− 62.2	− 0.63***	1950–2009
Yellow River	Huayuankou	730,036	9.12	46.6	35.6	− 15.1	− 25.0	− 88.7	− 0.66***	1950–2009
Huangfuchuan	Huangfu	3,175	0.42	43.2	47.3	0.9	− 39.9	− 77.3	− 0.46***	1954–2009
Kuyehe	Wenjiachuan	8,515	0.85	46.7	64.3	− 21.2	− 23.9	− 93.9	− 0.50***	1954–2009
Wudinghe	Baijiachuan	29,662	1.10	98.3	5.3	− 52.1	− 23.6	− 67.1	− 0.61***	1956–2009
Yanshui	Ganguyi	5,891	0.42	39.3	11.3	− 24.1	1.9	− 59.7	− 0.33**	1952–2009
Jinghe	Zhangjiachuan	43,216	2.23	21.6	16.5	− 16.3	6.5	− 49.8	− 0.31*	1950–2009
Beiluohe	Zhuangtou	25,645	0.75	37.5	18.1	− 33.2	18.1	− 70.5	− 0.38**	1950–2009
Weihe	Huaxian	106,498	3.23	33.8	18.9	− 14.7	− 14.5	− 57.3	− 0.44***	1950–2009
Fenhe	Hejin	38,728	0.22	138.2	− 12.8	− 79.4	− 85.6	− 98.6	− 0.62***	1950–2009
Yiluohe	Heishiguan	18,563	0.12	127.0	− 42.2	− 25.6	− 92.3	− 93.9	− 0.60***	1950–2009
Qinhe	Wushe	12,880	0.05	112.8	− 15.8	− 48.2	− 81.3	− 80.4	− 0.62***	1950–2009

*** significant at 0.001; ** significant at 0.01; * significant at 0.05

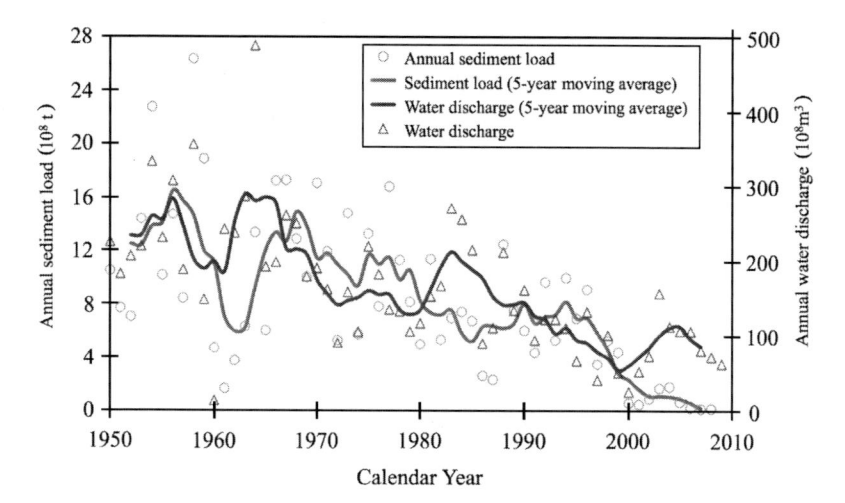

Figure 2. Inter annual variability of water discharge and sediment load from the Loess Plateau (section from Toudaoguai to Huayuankou), 1950–2009.

decreased by 93.9%, 98.6%, and 93.9%, respectively. Liu *et al.* (2008) reported that the annual suspended sediment load of the Yellow River decreased from 12×10^8 t in the 1950 and 1960s to 1.6×10^8 t in recent decades.

The spatiotemporal variation of sediment yield in the Loess Plateaus has been presented in several studies (Hassan *et al.*, 2008; Xin *et al.*, 2009; Xin *et al.*, 2011). Xin *et al.* (2009) investigated the spatiotemporal variation of sediment yield in the Loess Plateau from 1950–1989 at 115 hydrological stations. Comparing the periods prior to (1956–1969) and after (1970–1989) the implementation of soil conservation measures, the most significant decrease in the Loess Plateau was observed in the Middle and Lower Wudinghe River and north central Shanxi province, where sediment yield decreased by more than 40% (Figure 3). The results are similar to those of Hassan *et al.* (2008), who presented the spatial and temporal variations of sediment yield in the Yellow River basin.

Reduction of Soil Erosion in the Loess Plateau

In the past six decades, soil erosion control on the Loess Plateau was always an important goal for China's government. Soil and water conservation was always considered an important measure to solve the problems of soil erosion in the Loess Plateau and siltation in the lower Yellow River, and great achievements have been accomplished. According to the *2010 Water and Soil Conservation Bulletin of the Yellow River*, the preliminary control soil erosion area reached 22.6×10^4 km^2, accounting for 28.4% of the total basin area and 52.0% of the soil and water loess area of the plateau. It includes 5.55×10^4 km^2 of basic farmland, 11.92×10^4 km^2 of planted forest, 3.67×10^4 km^2 of planted grass, 1.42×10^4 km^2 of natural restoration, 1.84 million small water-conservation projects and 91,000 check-dams (YRCC, 2011).

These large-scale soil conservation measures have successfully reduced sediment export from the Loess Plateau (Chen *et al.*, 2007; Miao *et al.*, 2011). According to the *2000 Yellow River Sediment Bulletin* (MWR, 2001), 3 billion t of sediment were intercepted in

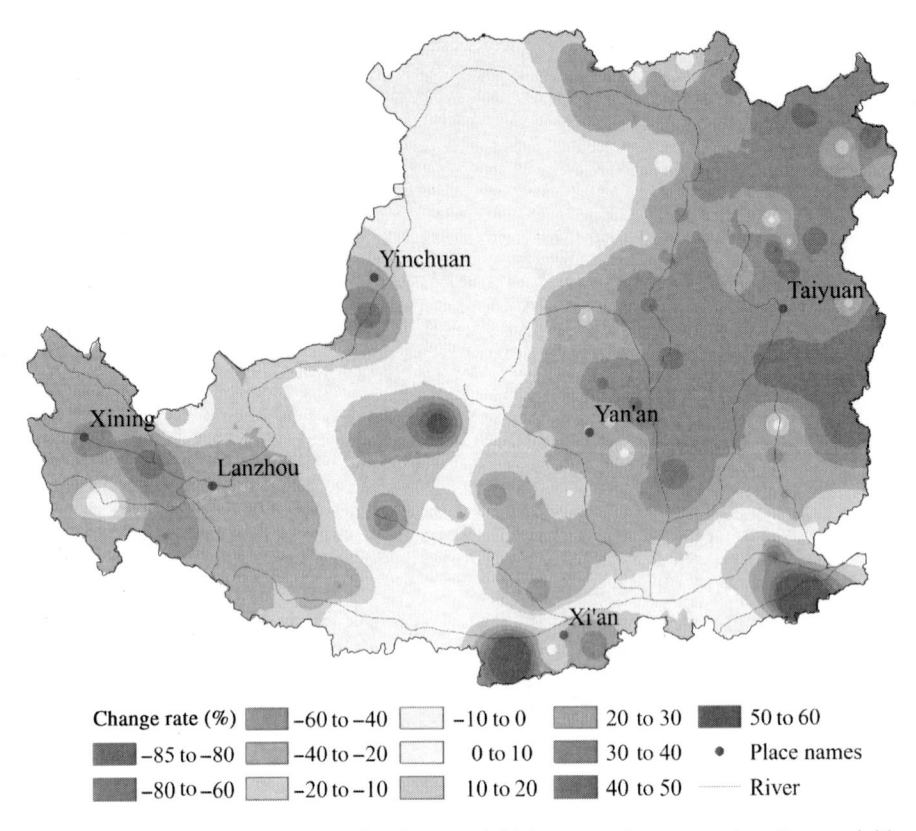

Change rate (%)   ■ –60 to –40   □ –10 to 0   ■ 20 to 30   ■ 50 to 60
                  ■ –85 to –80   ■ –40 to –20   □ 0 to 10   ■ 30 to 40   • Place names
                  ■ –80 to –60   □ –20 to –10   □ 10 to 20   ■ 40 to 50   — River

Figure 3. Spatiotemporal variation of sediment yield between the averaged sediment yields of 1950–1969 and 1970–1989. *Source:* Xin *et al.* (2009).

Loess Plateau between the 1970s and 1998. According to Wang and Fan (2002), sediment reductions by soil and water conservation have increased from 0.11×10^8 t/y in the 1950s to 4.06×10^8 t/y in the early and mid-1990s. Some 4.1–4.5 billion t of sediment were intercepted due to soil and water conservation practices in the Loess Plateau by the end of 2005, which accounts for 50% of the sediment decline in the Yellow River (MWR *et al.*, 2010a). The ability to trap sediments through soil and water conservation practices has been enhanced in the past decades. On the average, about 3.5–4.5 billion t per year have been trapped in the Yellow River Basin (YRCC, 2011).

The effects of soil and water conservation practices vary according to spatial and temporal scales. In the most severely eroded area of the central Loess Plateau, soil conservation practices reduced the mobilization of sediment, typically accounting for approximately 75% of the observed reductions in annual sediment yields (Rustomji *et al.*, 2008). It is estimated that soil conservation practices, which are the main reason for the decrease insediment load at Huayuankou, account for 40% of the total reduction from the 1950s to 2000–2005 (Wang *et al.*, 2007; Peng *et al.*, 2010). The practices of six decades show that soil and water conservation practices were a fundamental measure to reduce the sediment of the Yellow River, which has alleviated the deposit problem in the lower Yellow River and reduced the possibility of flood disasters. It has also been an effective way to improve the ecological, environmental, and living conditions in the Loess Plateau.

Measures of Soil and Water Control in the Loess Plateau

Check-Dams and Reservoirs

In the Loess Plateau, most of the sediment is produced by gully erosion in developed gully systems, with the erosion being nearly equivalent to the river sediment load of the Yellow River (Mu & Meng, 1982). Many years' experience in soil and water conservation in the Loess Plateau have demonstrated that check-dams and reservoirs are effective measures to control gully erosion; this is the reason they have been widely constructed in the past decades.

Since the late 1960s, check-dam construction has become a core method of soil control in the Loess Plateau, and an important component of the water resource and sediment regulation system in the Yellow River. At present, about 100,000 check-dams have been constructed in the Loess Plateau and more than 210×10^8 t of sediment have been trapped by them (UMYRB, 2007). Under the guidance of the *Plan of the Soil and Water Conservation and Check-Dam* issued in 2003, numerous check dams will be constructed with the objective to further reduce the amount of sediments (Liu, 2003; MWRC, 2003).

Although not built for sediment control in many cases, dams play an important role in controlling floods, with the result that large amounts of sediments have been impounded. Since the 1950s, more than 3,147 reservoirs have been built in the Yellow River basin, which has become a highly fragmented and regulated river system (Wang *et al.*, 2007). The water storage capacity has been estimated to be 66.71 km^3, and the residence time has increased to 3.97 years in recent years, ranking the Yellow River in the world's top three in terms of regulation among large river systems (Ran & Lu, 2011).

The Sanmenxia Reservoir was constructed in 1960. From 1960 to 1964, it was used for water storage and about 62.19×10^8 t of sediment was trapped by the reservoir. As of the end of 2007, the Sanmenxia dam had trapped 95.54×10^8 t of sediment. Xiaolangdi reservoir, located between the Sanmenxia reservoir and Huayuankou gauging station, started to store water in 1999 with a capacity of 127×10^8 m^3. There was considerable siltation in the reservoir after its commissioning, trapping a total of 32.47×10^8 t of sediments from 1997 to 2007. The sediment trapped by Sanmenxia and Xiaolangdi reservoirs accounted for 30% of the total amount of reduction for the Yellow River (Peng *et al.*, 2010).

Terraces

Excessive reclamation of sloping land has substantially exacerbated soil erosion in the Loess Plateau. Terracing, an effective practice for mitigating soil erosion and retaining the eroded sediment, has been widely used in the Loess region. In 1952, massive terrace construction was started on the Loess Plateau. Before 1958, sloping terraces were the mainstream element of such terracing strategy, but it had to stop due to the "sloping land conversion to terraces" policy issued by the government in September 1958. The conversion of sloping land to terraces reached its peak in December 1961, when a policy promoted that soil conservation should focus more on sloping land. In 1973, the State issued an initiative where each farmer was to have at least 67 m^2 of terraces, which further promoted the development of terraces in the Loess Plateau.

Although the support of terracing was mostly suspended and corresponding financial investment was cut during the earlier years of reform and opening-up, massive terrace construction started once again in 1984 due to the promotion of the government's agricultural policies. A total of 4.6×10^4 km^2 of sloping land had been converted into terraces on the Loess Plateau by 1998 (MWR, 2001). In recent years, with the rapid development of agricultural mechanization, a large tract of machine-built terraces has been completed in the Loess Plateau.

As an important soil conservation measure, terracing has played a significant role in controlling soil erosion in the Loess Plateau. For example, the constructed terraces in the Weihe and Jinghe River basins as the largest tributaries have reduced sediments by $1,265 \times 10^4$ t and $1,200 \times 10^4$ t, respectively, which accounted for 58.0% and 32.6% of the total soil erosion reduction by soil and water conservation measures (Wang & Fan, 2002). In addition to their effects on retaining soil particles, terraces can also greatly increase grain yield and help ensure food security for the local farmers. Therefore, terracing practices can help to ensure the implementation of returning cropland to forests.

Vegetation Restoration

Planting vegetation is one of the best ways to stabilize soils and minimize erosion (Farley *et al.*, 2005; Peel *et al.*, 2010). China has been trying to increase the forest-covered areas through six different forestry programmes (Ran *et al.*, Forthcoming). With the implementation of large-scale initiatives, the vegetation cover of the Loess Plateau increased rapidly during 2002–2006 (Xin *et al.*, 2008), especially in gullied and hilly areas (Figure 4). Yan'an, situated in the hilly and gullied area, is the most typical area with severe soil erosion in the Loess Plateau. By the end of 2010, the conversion of cropland to forest or grasslands, driven by the implementation of the Grain for Green project, has been

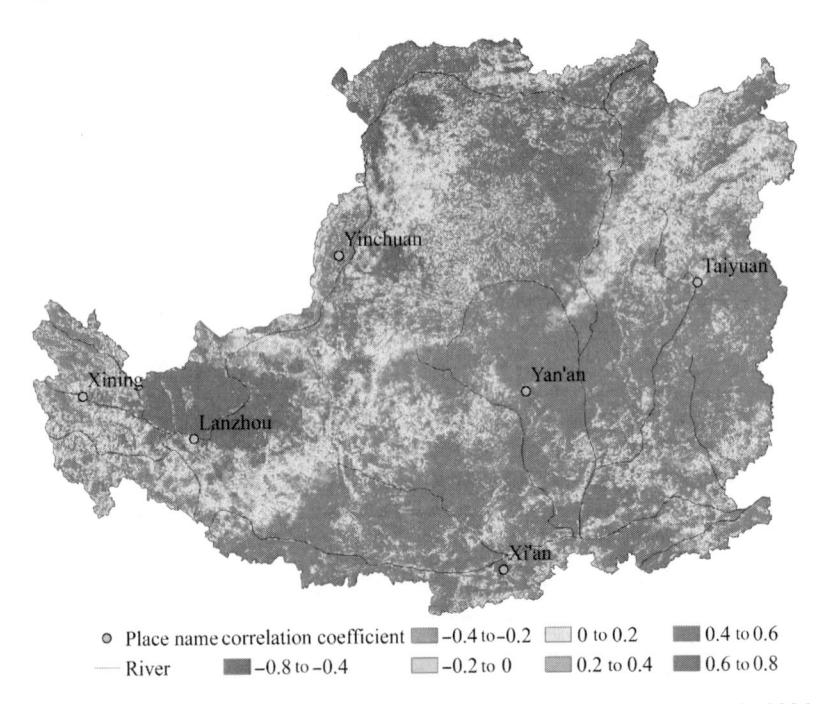

Figure 4. Spatiotemporal variation of vegetation covers in Loess Plateau during 1999–2006 driving by Grain for Green project. Green colour indicates increasing vegetation cover, and red decreasing, during this period. *Source:* Xin *et al.* (2008).

completed in an area of $6.5 \times 10^3 \text{ km}^2$, which accounts for 16.7% of the total area of Yan'an city; vegetation cover increased from 45.4% to 67.4%, and the degree of control of soil and water comprehensive management has increased by 25% since 1999 (Liu & Duan, 2010). In the Loess Plateau, Fu *et al.* (2011) found that the average soil retention rate by vegetation cover was up to 63.3% as a result of vegetation restoration during 2000–2008 and the rate of soil loss decreased in 34% of the entire plateau, meaning that areas suffering from intense erosion have shrunk and lightly eroded areas have expanded.

Recent Programmes of Soil and Water Control in the Loess Plateau

In the last 30 years, many soil erosion control programmes have been implemented in the Loess Plateau. With the completion of these programmes, the soil erosion problems in the region has been greatly reduced. These programmes were conducted as part of the central government's policies.

National Key Projects of Soil and Water Conservation

The National Key Projects of Soil and Water Conservation, which started in 1983, is the first series of projects financially supported by the government to carry out large-scale soil erosion control measures within the country. The planned four phases have been completed, including phase I from 1983 to 1992, phase II from 1993 to 2002, phase III from 2003 to 2007, and phrase IV from 2008 to 2012. A total of CNY4.896 billion have been invested up to 2010, of which CNY1.61 billion came from the central government. The area where soil erosion measures have been implemented has reached $4.79 \times 10^4 \text{ km}^2$.

In 1982, the Wudinghe, Sanchuanhe (Jiaoshuihe after 1988), and Huangfuchuan rivers and Dingxi county were listed by the State Council as the main soil-eroded areas to be targeted. A reduction of about 30×10^6 t of sediment into the Yellow River mainstream channel was seen as the four areas were treated. Specifically, the annual sediment load for the Wudinghe River has declined by 59.1%, while the annual sediment load for the Sanchuanhe River has decreased by 52.2% (Duan, 1996). By 2003, the total soil erosion control area had increased to $1,229 \text{ km}^2$, of which cropland and afforestation account for 67 km^2 and 570 km^2, respectively. In addition, 4,223 small silt check-dams have been constructed. Financially, CNY94.89 million have been successfully invested, of which CNY65.88 million came from the central government and the rest from local government (MWR *et al.*, 2010a).

Grain for Green Project in the Loess Plateau

In the past decades, restoration projects were implemented to improve soil erosion control in the Loess Plateau. The Grain for Green project (GGP), converting sloping croplands with slope gradients over 25° into forest or grasslands, was launched in 1999 and is one of the world's most ambitious ecological restoration programmes (Xu *et al.*, 2006). The Grain for Green project promotes recovery of vegetation cover, watershed management, and poverty alleviation through a grain and cash subsidy scheme. The project now covers 25 provinces in over 1,600 counties and involves 15 million households and 60 million farmers. The Chinese government will invest more than CNY430 billion (US$63 billion) to implement the GGP, including compensation to farmers, seedling purchase, and stand management, to reduce soil erosion and improve land quality in the Loess Plateau (SFA, 2008). The project aims to increase the area of forest and grassland to 32×10^4 km^2 by 2010, including 14.67×10^4 km^2 former croplands and 17.33×10^4 km^2 former barren lands. The Loess Plateau is a key implementing and initial experimental area for the GGP in 1998 due to its severe soil erosion. Depending on the natural vegetation restoration, significant increases in vegetation cover have been observed in the Loess Plateau, which is believed to promote rural economic development and thus increase farmers' income as quite large portions of the restored soil-eroded areas were planted with fruit trees.

The Ecological Programme of Soil and Water Conservation in the Yellow River

This programme was officially proposed in March 2001 by the Yellow River Conversancy Committee, which aimed to conduct ecological construction in the Yellow River Basin. With coverage of 36 counties in 8 provinces and 11 tributaries, the programme includes 17 projects, including key control areas, demonstration areas, check-dam construction areas in small watersheds, dam construction areas, and ecological restoration areas. By 2005, 6,600 km^2 had been ecologically restored, and 2,333 check-dams, including 650 key dams, had been completed (MWR et al., 2010a). These measures have already played a very important role in addressing soil erosion in the region. Meanwhile, the programme set an excellent example for other soil erosion areas, which will promote ecological restoration and soil conservation.

Soil and Water Conservation Plan

Gully erosion accounts for 60–90% of the soil erosion in the Loess Plateau. Constructing check-dams in the gullies is an effective strategy for reducing sediment loss (Xu et al., 2004; Wang et al., 2011). About 100,000 check-dams were built in the Loess Plateau in the late 1960s to 1970s. With these check-dams, about 21 billion t of sediment have been trapped, resulting in a net sediment reduction of 3×10^8 t for the Yellow River. In particular, those check-dams have contributed 80% to the total sediment reduction by soil conservation measures since the 1970s (UMYRB, 2007).

Compared to the 100,000 check-dams in the 1960s and 1970s, only 1,118 check-dams were constructed from 1986 to 1999 in the Loess Plateau (Xu et al., 2004). In 2003, the 2003 Plan of the Soil and Water Conservation and Check-Dam in the Loess Plateau (Liu, 2003) was issued by the State Council, in which check-dams were recommended as one of the three main projects of the MWR. Large-scale check-dam construction has been conducted across the Loess Plateau. According to the plan, about 16.3×10^4 check-dams are to be constructed in the soil-eroded regions, covering an area of about 27.2×10^4 km^2, of which 30,000 are large dams and the others small or medium. Total investment is for up to CNY 83.06 billion, of which CNY48.12 billion comes from the central government and the rest from the local government.

It is expected that check-dams will be built in most of the large valleys entering the Yellow River, and 80% of the soil erosion area will be treated by check-dams in the Loess Plateau by 2020. Also, cropland formed by check-dams is expected to increase, which is expected to enhance rural economic sustainability. For the Yellow River sediment transport, more than 4×10^8 t/y of sediment is expected to be reduced with the operation of these dams. That will be a great benefit not only for the Yellow River itself to maintain a healthy fluvial system, but also for the riparian residents to develop their economies and improve their overall quality of life. For the sloping lands, more than 400×10^8 t of soil material will be impounded behind the dams, which indicates that the area of newly increased cropland and afforestation could be up to $5,000 \, km^2$ and $6.2 \times 10^4 \, km^2$, respectively (MWR et al., 2010b).

Policies and Legislation on Soil Erosion Control in the Loess Plateau

The implementation of soil erosion control measures has been due to the effort of farmers and agricultural practices, but also to the government, which has developed overall policies and regulations and has funded soil conservation projects.

In 1952, the middle reach of the Yellow River was listed by the newly founded Chinese government as a region which required soil erosion control. In particular, the Resolutions on Planning to Solve the Yellow River Water Disasters and Water Resources Development were passed in July 1955, which indicates that soil conservation work in the region was included in the national economic development plans. In the same year, the National Soil and Water Conservation Committee was established and the Interim Plan of Soil and Water Conservation was issued, promoting the region's soil erosion control.

In 1958, the notorious "Great Leap Forward" happened across the country. These radical economic policies resulted in massive deforestation and severe soil erosion— a huge ecological disaster. Three years later, the central economic policies were modified for protection of the environment. On 28 April 1963, the Decisions on Soil and Water Conservation in the Middle Reaches of the Yellow River Basin were issued by the State Council. Since then, soil conservation has been on the national agenda, and some key areas have been identified for immediate action. Most importantly, a guideline was elaborated that soil erosion control should depend more on the local population with the support of the government. Between 1966 and 1976, during the so-called Cultural Revolution, most of the soil conservation work was disrupted, but construction of silt check-dams and terraces was greatly encouraged by the government to increase grain output.

Starting from 1978, China entered a new period of reform and opening up; previous unsuitable soil conservation policies were modified and some new policies were gradually developed. In the 1980s, many small watersheds were included in the National Guidance for Small Watershed Management. In the 1990s, soil conservation work focused more on the formulation of laws and policy formulation for sediment control. For example, in August 1997, General Secretary Jiang Zemin (1997) issued a call "to treat soil erosion to improve the ecological environment" and "to rebuild a beautiful landscape of the northwest region". In 2000, the State upgraded the Ecological Recovery Strategy to a new strategic level of ecological awareness. The concept of natural recovery was acknowledged, and soil erosion control work entered a new era. From the perspective of policy development, it is clear that the soil conservation work in the Loess Plateau has moved from a previous strategy of solving water disasters and promoting agricultural production to one of protecting the overall ecological environment and enhancing ecological security.

Prior to 1982, there were only some preliminary rules on soil erosion control, such as the Interim Outline of Soil and Water Conservation issued by the State Council in 1955. The Work Regulation of Soil and Water Conservation, issued in 1982, is the first real regulation on soil erosion control which provided detailed directions. However, as it was not legally binding, many soil erosion–related problems could not be addressed completely. To fight the serious soil erosion in the Shanxi–Shaanxi–Inner Mongolia region caused by unreasonable coal and petroleum exploitation, a specific provision named Regulation on Soil and Water Conservation in the Shanxi–Shaanxi–Inner Mongolia Region was published by the State Council in October 1988 (SPC & MWR, 1988).

The 1990s was a very important period for soil conservation laws and regulations. The Law of the People's Republic of China on Water and Soil Conservation, issued by the central government on 29 June 1991, represents a milestone. It provides detailed guidance, focusing on activities, safety measures, surveillance, and responsibilities for soil erosion control measures. The Enforcement Regulation on Water and Soil Conservation was issued in 1993 (State Council, 1993a) as a supplement to the Law of the People's Republic of China on Water and Soil Conservation. Since then, a series of other measures, such as the Regulation Methods on the Construction of Water and Soil Conservation Projects, have been issued.

In March 2011, the 1991 version of the Water and Soil Conservation Law was amended, with the liability of the government being enhanced (State Council, 2011).

In addition to the direct laws related to soil conservation, there are also many other regulations and rules, including the Water Law of the People's Republic of China (State Council, 2002), the Law of the People's Republic of China on Prevention and Control of Water Pollution (issued 1984, amended 2008 (State Council, 2008)), the Flood Control Act of the People's Republic of China (State Council, 1998), the Regulations for the Yellow River Water (State Council, 1993b), and the Regulations for River Management (State Council 1988).

After 30 years, a relatively comprehensive legal system concerning soil erosion control has been successfully established in China. The implementation of these laws and regulations has greatly mitigated human-made soil erosion, alleviating soil erosion intensity and helping the local people develop their economy.

Policies Recommended for Future Soil Erosion Control in the Loess Plateau

Enhancing Supervision Policies

Recently, the Loess Plateau has become China's most famous coal and petroleum base. These two resources account for more than 50% of the total output of China (MWR *et al.*, 2010a). As a large amount of coal cinder is dumped into sloping lands and stream channels, the effects of various soil conservation measures on soil erosion are considerably reduced. To implement the Law of the People's Republic of China on Water and Soil Conservation, a monitoring system covering the whole basin should be established for better soil conservation management and assessment.

Expanding Soil Erosion Control Investment Sources

Insufficient financial investment is the main limiting factor for soil erosion control work in the Loess Plateau. How to increase financial sources has been a pressing problem for current soil conservation efforts. In Western countries, soil conservation projects are mostly supported by the government, while the private sectors and soil conservation beneficiaries do not contribute much. In contrast, in China, the soil conservation work carried out during 1950–2005 was usually guided by the government, while the local people provided the labour force and funds. Financially, the government only supported 9% of such activities; the rest came from the local people, which is a striking contrast to the mode adopted in the US, where about 55% of the funding comes from the government (MWR *et al.*, 2010c). Therefore, expanding government investment is quite necessary for present soil conservation.

Reassessing the Vegetation Rehabilitation Policy

When the president of China, Hu Jintao, gavehis speech about climate change at the UN Climate Summit in New York in 2009, he emphasized China's plan to increase the forest cover to 40×10^4 km^2 by 2020 (*New York Times*, 2009). It is believed that vegetation restoration will be part of a long-term strategy to combat soil erosion in the Loess Plateau.

Although the vegetation cover has been greatly improved in the past decade as a result of various projects, the effects of large-scale afforestation on environmental restoration in semi-arid regions of northern China require further investigation. China's huge investment in increasing forest cover seems likely to exacerbate environmental degradation if the local site conditions are ignored (Cao, 2008; Cao *et al.*, 2011).

Given that water resources are currently over-depleted in the Yellow River basin, the hydrological impacts from current and planned re-vegetation activities need to be taken into account by natural resources managers and policy makers (McVicar *et al.*, 2007). In the future, water-bearing capacity needs to be considered in vegetation restoration initiatives, and relevant evaluations on its sustainability and effects on soil erosion should also be conducted. For instance, current financial support encouraging vegetation restoration is far from enough and the corresponding policies lack consistency, which leads the local farmer to focus on short-term benefits. In addition, overemphasis on economic benefits has resulted in excessive plantation of the tree species that can quickly bring economic benefits; as a result, the soil erosion control benefits are not as strong as expected.

Reassessing Check-Dam Construction Policy

Currently, the annual sediment load from the middle Yellow River accounts for only about 1/10th of the inter-decadal average; that is, the sediment load has been reduced by an order of magnitude. It is expected that the sediment load of the Loess Plateau will be further reduced as the ecological system improves and more silt check-dams are constructed. According to the Guidance on the Construction of Silt Check-dams in the Loess Plateau, issued in 2003, a number of high silt check-dams are to be built in the region. However, as the construction of these dams, in particular high dams, is closely related to the local governments in terms of economic benefit, the scale of many silt check-dams is intentionally increased, resulting in an enormous waste of soil erosion control funds.

Environmental Policies and Poverty Alleviation

The soil loss areas are usually the regions with degraded ecological systems and poverty, which in turn severely affect the local people's overall quality of life. More importantly, the soil loss becomes more serious through land over-reclamation and wood harvesting, causing a vicious cycle. During a national project called the 1987 Poverty Alleviation Plan (State Council, 1994), there were about 80 million people in 592 counties in China who needed support, among which were 126 counties, with 23 million people, in the Loess Plateau. For the ecological compensation mechanism adopted in recent ecological restoration projects, the vicious cycle between local people and the deteriorated environment has been greatly ameliorated as certain economic benefits have been given to the farmers. This has helped to promote local economic development. However, it should be pointed out that as these ecological restoration projects come to the end, the environment is again vulnerable to degradation as the ecological compensation is suspended. Therefore, a long-term and continuous ecological compensation system is strongly needed to maintain the restored environment and improve the local people's quality of life. At present, because the model being used in the Loess Plateau can effectively improve the ecological environment *and* increase the farmers' income, it should be explored and thus applied to other regions.

Conclusions

As a well-known soil-eroded region in the world, the Loess Plateau has been a key area in China where soil erosion measures have been implemented during the past 60 years. Although they have encountered various difficulties, control efforts have never stopped. Particularly in the last 30 years, the State-led Loess Plateau management strategy has greatly reduced soil erosion and improved ecological environment.

Under the natural recovery guidance, the ecological cover in the Loess Plateau has remarkably increased and the magnitude of soil erosion has been sharply reduced as a result. However, there is an urgent need to build an evaluation system towards ecological sustainability based on water-bearing capacity, so as to avoid exacerbated soil drought resulting from increased ecological water consumption and thus further ecological degradation. Over the past 60 years, about 100,000 silt check-dams have been constructed in the Loess Plateau, which has significantly controlled the once serious soil erosion regions, especially for gravitational erosion. In addition, with the operation of the cascade of reservoirs, such as the Xiaolangdi Dam located on the mainstream of the lower Yellow River, sediments from the Loess Plateau have been mostly trapped. Currently, linked to the reduced soil erosion and ecological recovery, it is strongly needed to reassess the ongoing silt check-dam construction policies to avoid unnecessary construction and waste of funds.

In addition, because of the accelerated development of coal and petroleum resources, human-induced soil erosion has become much more severe than before, for which an enhanced monitoring system is also needed to maintain the attained soil conservation achievements.

Lack of funds, poverty, and discontinuous ecological policies are the major external factors affecting current ecological recovery in the Loess Plateau. Therefore, in addition to the enhanced ecological restoration activities by the government, an innovative management system which includes the government, private enterprises, and individuals should be established to better conduct soil conservation projects. Most importantly, the management system should consider both ecological restoration and the quality of life of the local population. That is, the restored ecological environment should also help improve the local farmers' living standards and increase their overall income. The local farmers can benefit from the ecological restoration projects only if the soil conservation projects are sustainable and supported by them.

As the economy and the local people's living standards have both been significantly improved, and with the unprecedented emphasis on soil erosion control by the central government, it can be concluded that soil erosion in the Loess Plateau has been substantially reduced. However, given the fragility of its ecological system and the complexity of soil erosion control, future soil conservation efforts in the Loess Plateau should be based more on water resources and ecological security. Therefore, adjustments of ongoing policies or new policies are necessary to meet the emerging challenges to achieve environmental management and alleviate poverty.

Acknowledgements

Financial support is acknowledged from the Fundamental Research Funds for the Central Universities (Nos.YX2011-35 and TD2011-2), the National Natural Science Foundation of China (Grant Nos. 41001362 and 30972419), and the Special Fund of Forestry Industrial Research for Public Welfare of China (201104005-01-C and A). The authors would also like to thank Prof. Asit K. Biswas and Dr. Cecilia Tortajada of the Third Word Centre for Water Management for their insightful comments and editing.

References

Cao, S. X. (2008) Why large-scale afforestation efforts in China have failed to solve the desertification problem, *Environmental Science and Technology*, 42(5), pp. 1826–1831.

Cao, S. X., Chen, L., Shankman, D., Wang, C. M., Wang, X. B & Zhang, H. (2011) Excessive reliance on afforestation in China's arid and semi-arid regions: lessons in ecological restoration, *Earth-Science Reviews*, 104, pp. 240–245.

Chen, L. D., Wei, W., Fu, B. J. & Lü, Y. H. (2007) Soil and water conservation on the Loess Plateau in China: review and perspective, *Progress in Physical Geography*, 31(4), pp. 389–403.

Duan, Q. F. (1996) Great achievements of soil and water conservation have obtained in the Yellow River, *Soil and Water Conservation in China*, 10, pp. 3–6 [in Chinese].

Farley, K. A., Jobbágy, E. G. & Jackson, R. B. (2005) Effects of afforestation on water yield: a global synthesis with implications for policy, *Global Change Biology*, 11, pp. 1565–1576.

Fu, B. J., Liu, Y., Lü, Y. H., He, C. S., Zeng, Y. & Wu, B. F. (2011) Assessing the soil erosion control service of ecosystems change in the Loess Plateau of China, *Ecological Complexity*, 8(4), pp. 284–293.

Hassan, M. A., Church, M., Xu, J. & Yan, Y. X. (2008) Spatial and temporal variation of sediment yield in the landscape: example of Huanghe (Yellow River), *Geophysical Research Letters*, 35, L06401.

Jiang, Z. (1997) Rebuild a beautiful landscape of the northwest region of China (issued 5 August 1997). Available at: http://cpc.people.com.cn/GB/64184/64185/180137/10818748.html [in Chinese].

Liu (2003) A summary of the Plan of the Soil and Water Conservation and Check-Dam, *Soil and Water Conservation of China*, 24(12), pp. 8–10 [In Chinese].

Liu, C., Sui, J. & Wang, Z. Y. (2008) Changes in runoff and sediment yield along the Yellow River during the period from 1950 to 2006, *Journal of Environmental Informatics*, 12(2), pp. 129–139.

Liu, F. & Duan, B. (2010) The area of Grain for Green project in Yan'an was counted for about 1/3 area to the total area of Shanxi province, *Xinhua Net*. Available at http://www.sn.xinhuanet.com/2010-09/04/content_20812731.htm [in Chinese] [accessed 4 September 2010].

McVicar, T. R., Li, L. T., Van Niel, T. G., Zhang, L., Li, R., Yang, Q. K., Zhang, X. P., Mu, X. M., Wen, Z. M., Liu, W. Z., Zhao, Y. A., Liu, Z. H. & Gao, P. (2007) Developing a decision support tool for China's re-vegetation program: simulating regional impacts of afforestation on average annual streamflow in the Loess Plateau, *Forest Ecology and Management*, 251, pp. 65–81.

Miao, C. Y., Ni, J. R. & Borthwick, A. G. L. A. (2011) Preliminary estimate of human and natural contributions to the changes in water discharge and sediment load in the Yellow River, *Global and Planetary Change*, 76(3–4), pp. 196–205.

Ministry of Water Resources [MWR], People's Republic of China (2001) *Chinese River Sediment Bulletin of 2000 (Yangtze and Yellow River)* (Beijing: China Water Power Press) [in Chinese].

Ministry of Water Resources of China (MWRC) (2003) Guidance on the Construction of Silt Check-dams in the Loess Plateau (issued 10 November, 2003). Available at: http://www.people.com.cn/GB/jingji/1038/2179265.html [in Chinese].

Ministry of Water Resources [MWR], Chinese Academy of Sciences & Chinese Academy of Engineering (2010a) *Control Soil and Water Loss and Ecological Security in China: Loess Plateau of the Northwestern China* (Beijing: Science Press) [in Chinese].

Ministry of Water Resources [MWR], Chinese Academy of Sciences & Chinese Academy of Engineering (2010b) *Control Soil and Water Loss and Ecological Security in China: Policy of Soil and Water Loss* (Beijing: Science Press).

Ministry of Water Resources [MWR], Chinese Academy of Sciences & Chinese Academy of Engineering (2010c) *Control Soil and Water Loss and Ecological Security in China: Effect of Soil and Water Loss* (Beijing: Science Press).

Mu, J. Z. & Meng, Q. M. (1982) Sediment delivery ratio as used in the computation of the watershed sediment yield, *Journal of Sediment Research*, 2, pp. 60–65 [in Chinese].

National Development and Reform Commission (NDRC) (2010) *Outline of the Plan for Integrated Management Plan of the Loess Plateau Region (2010–2030)* (Ministry of Water Resources, Ministry of Agriculture, State Forestry Administration) [in Chinese].

New York Times (2009) *Hu Jintao's speech on climate change*, 22 September. Available at http://www.nytimes.com/2009/09/23/world/asia/23hu.text.html (accessed 18 May 2010).

Peel, M. C., McMahon, T. A. & Finlayson, B. L. (2010) Vegetation impact on mean annual evapotranspiration at a global catchment scale, *Water Resources Research*, 46, W09508.

Peng, J., Chen, S. L. & Dong, P. (2010) Temporal variation of sediment load in the Yellow River Basin, China, and its impacts on the lower reaches and the river delta, *Catena*, 83(2–3), pp. 135–147.

Ran, L. S. & Lu, X. X. (2011) Delineation of reservoirs using remote sensing and their storage estimate: an example of the Yellow River Basin, China, *Hydrological Processes*, published online 22 July. DOI: 10.1002/hyp.8224.

Ran, L. S., Lu, X. X. & Xu, J. C. (Forthcoming) The effects of vegetation restoration on soil erosion and sediment yield in China: a critical review, *Critical Review of Environment Science and Technology*.

Rustomji, P., Zhang, X. P., Hairsine, P. B., Zhang, L. & Zhao, J. (2008) River sediment load and concentration responses to changes in hydrology and catchment management in the Loess Plateau region of China, *Water Resources Researches*, 44, W00A04. DOI:10.1029 /2007WR006656.

Shi, H. & Shao, M. (2000) Soil and water loss from the Loess Plateau in China, *Journal of Arid Environments*, 45, pp. 9–20.

State Council (1988) The Regulations for River Management (issued 10 June 1988 and implemented 10 June 1988). Available at http://www.mwr.gov.cn/zwzc/zcfg/xzfghfgxwj/198806/t19880610_155906.html [in Chinese].

State Council (1993a) Enforcement Regulation on Water and Soil Conservation (issued 1 August 1993 and implemented August 1993). Available at http://www.mwr.gov.cn/zwzc/zcfg/xzfghfgxwj/199308/t19930801_155912.html [in Chinese].

State Council (1993b) The Regulations for the Yellow River Water (issued 5 July 2006 and implemented 1 August 2006). Available at http://www.gov.cn/ziliao/flfg/on 2006-07/28/content_367584.htm.

State Council (1994) National Eight-Seven Poverty Alleviation Plan (issued 15 April 1994). Available at http://news.xinhuanet.com/ziliao/2005-03/17/content_2708857.htm [in Chinese].

State Council (1998) The Flood Control Law of the People's Republic of China (issued 1 January 1998 and implemented 1 January, 1998). Available at http://www.mwr.gov.cn/zwzc/zcfg/fl/199801/t19980101_155903.html [in Chinese].

State Council (2002) The Water Law of the People's Republic of China (issued 29 August 2002 and implemented 1 October 2002). Available at http://www.mwr.gov.cn/zwzc/zcfg/fl/200210/t20021001_155904.html [in Chinese].

State Council (2008) The Law of the People's Republic of China on Prevention and Control of Water Pollution (issued 28 February 2008 and implemented 1 June 2008). Available at http://www.mwr.gov.cn/zwzc/zcfg/fl/200802/t20080228_155905.html [in Chinese].

State Council (2011) The Water and Soil Conservation Law (First issued 29 June 1991, and in modified version 25 December, 2010 and implemented 1 March 2011). Available at http://www.mwr.gov.cn/zwzc/zcfg/fl/199106/t19910629_155902.html [in Chinese].

State Forestry Administration [SFA] (2008) *Forestry and Ecological Construction Bulletin of China* (official document) [in Chinese].

State Planning Commission (SPC) and Ministry of Water Resources (MWR) (1988) Regulation on Soil and Water Conservation in the Shanxi–Shaanxi–Inner Mongolia Region (issued 1 October 1988 and implemented 1 October 1988). Available at http://www.mwr.gov.cn/zwzc/zcfg/xzfghfgxwj/198810/ t19881001_155907.html [in Chinese].

Tang, K. L. (2004) *Soil and Conservation in China* (Beijing: Science Press) [in Chinese].

Upper and Middle Yellow River Bureau [UMYRB] (2007) 21 billion tons sediment has been trapped by the check-dams in the Loess Plateau, *Xinhuanet*, 7 September [in Chinese]. Available at http://news.xinhuanet. com/newscenter/2007-09/07/content_6682085.htm. [accessed 7 September 2007].

Wang, G. & Fan, Z. (2002) *Research on Runoff and Sediment Change of the Yellow River*, Vol.2 (Zhengzhou: Yellow River Water Conservancy Press) [in Chinese].

Wang, H., Bi, N., Saito, Y., Wang, Y., Sun, X., Zhang, J. & Yang, Z. (2010) Recent changes in sediment delivery by the Huanghe (Yellow River) to the sea: causes and environmental implications in its estuary, *Journal of Hydrology*, 391(3–4), pp. 302–313.

Wang, H., Yang, Z., Saito, Y., Liu, J. P., Sun, X. X. & Wang, Y. (2007) Stepwise decreases of the Huanghe (Yellow River) sediment load (1950–2005): impacts of climate change and human activities, *Global and Planetary Change*, 57, pp. 331–354.

Wang, Y. F., Fu, B. J., Chen, L. D., Lu, Y. H. & Gao, Y. (2011) Check dam in the Loess Plateau of China: engineering for environmental services and food security, *Environmental Science & Technology*, 45, pp. 10298–10299.

Xin, Z. B., Xu, J. X. & Yu, X. X. (2009) Temporal and spatial variability of sediment yield on the Loess Plateau in the past 50 years, *ActaEcologicaSinica*, 29(3), pp. 1129–1139 [in Chinese].

Xin, Z. B., Xu, J. X. & Zheng, W. (2008) Spatiotemporal variations of vegetation cover on the Chinese Loess Plateau (1981–2006): impacts of climate changes and human activities, *Science in China, Series D: Earth Sciences*, 51(1), pp. 67–78.

Xin, Z. B., Yu, X. X. & Lu, X. X. (2011) Factors controlling sediment yield in China's Loess Plateau, *Earth Surface Processes and Landforms*, 36, pp. 816–826.

Xu, J. T., Yin, R. S., Li, Z. & Liu, C. (2006) China's ecological rehabilitation: unprecedented efforts, dramatic impacts, and requisite policies, *Ecological Economics*, 57, pp. 595–607.

Xu, X. Z., Zhang, H. W. & Zhang, O. Y. (2004) Development of check-dam systems in gullies on the Loess Plateau, China, *Environmental Science & Policy*, 7, pp. 79–86.

Yellow River Conservancy Commission [YRCC] of the Ministry of Water Resources (2011) *2010 Soil and Soil Conservation Bulletin of the Yellow River Basin* [in Chinese].

Managing Urban Rivers and Water Quality in Malaysia for Sustainable Water Resources

NGAI WENG CHAN

School of Humanities, Universiti Sains Malaysia, Penang

ABSTRACT *Rivers are rich ecosystems and sources of life, providing many functions for the survival of natural and human systems. In Malaysia, due to poor management and public apathy, they are severely degraded. Rapid development and urbanization have also overstressed and polluted them, and governance practices are mostly focused on managing water shortages, floods, and pollution. Limitations include low priority in the political agenda, inadequate economic, managerial, and human resources, poor enforcement of laws and regulations, poor public involvement, and inadequate use of non-structural measures. Recent government, private sector, and NGO partnerships, however, have shown great potential for improved management of rivers.*

Introduction

Globally, the world appears besieged by water stress. However, experts have concluded that the main issue is not water scarcity but poor management which is precipitating a crisis (Biswas & Tortajada, 2011). Corresponding to the continual deterioration of water quality on a global basis is the degradation at the country level, most notably in developing countries.

In Malaysia, rivers are vital for nature and human society. Major cities have been established and flourished along rivers. Rivers are rich ecosystems and sources of life, providing water supply, irrigation for agriculture, a means of transportation, a source of food in fisheries, hydro-electric power, and water use for industries (Chan, 2002a). They are also the habitats for riverine and aquatic flora and fauna and the riparian environment supports a rich biodiversity of life forms (Naiman & Bilby, 1998). However, over the years, a combination of low priority on the government agenda, public apathy, neglect, and poor management have resulted in severely degraded rivers including their water quality.

In the last three or four decades, the country has developed very rapidly, with urbanization increasing dramatically in all the major cities and towns (Chan, 2005). Coupled with this, agriculture expansion and industrialization have severely negatively impacted rivers. The cost of degradation has been high, negatively affecting water supply in terms of quantity and quality for irrigation, navigation, recreation, and tourism, and resulting in floods and pollution (Chan, 2002b).

Major Issues in River Management in Malaysia

In Malaysia, the major river management issues are all linked to water quality. Since 97% of Malaysia's water supply comes from rivers, poor river water quality will severely affect water supply. A combination of mismanagement, apathy, low priority on government agendas, lack of funds, poor public involvement, and poor enforcement has severely degraded river water quality. Today, many Malaysian rivers (especially in urban areas) are in an appalling state, with many resembling open sewers (Hj Keizrul bin Abdullah, 2002). Hence, major management issues are all closely related to water quality and have been identified as pollution, deforestation, water catchment deterioration, water shortages and floods, and weaknesses in institutions and legislation.

The percentage of polluted rivers increased significantly between 1987 and 2009, resulting in poor water quality that has affected water supply (Table 1). In fact, river pollution is one of the most serious issues in Malaysia, with more than half the rivers polluted (Netto, 2006). Sources of pollution are agriculture, livestock farming, and urban areas and industries (Chan & Kung, 2001). Pollution of water from both point and nonpoint sources has resulted in environmental problems and adversely affected river water quality and the habitats of aquatic flora and fauna. In the Kelang River basin, water quality has declined due to high sediment loads from construction and deforestation, large quantities of litter and rubbish, untreated sewage, and industrial and commercial effluents (Asian Development Bank, 2007).

Squatters are another major source of river pollution since rubbish is dumped into the rivers. Toilets are also constructed on top of the rivers. For example, the Department of Environment (DOE) noted in 2009 that industrial waste is no longer a pollution threat to

Table 1. River water quality in Malaysia, 1987–2009.

Year	No. of rivers monitored	Clean	Slightly polluted	Very polluted
1987	91	43	45	3
1988	91	48	40	3
1989	91	45	43	3
1990	90	48	35	7
1991	87	37	44	6
1992	87	25	55	7
1993	116	30	75	11
1994	116	38	64	14
1995	115	48	53	14
1996	116	42	61	13
1997	117	24	68	25
1998	117	33	68	13
2002	120	30	68	22
2004	120	58	53	5
2005	146	80	51	15
2006	146	80	59	7
2007	143	91	45	7
2008*	382	334	48	(Classified as polluted)
2009	360	306	54	(Classified as polluted)

*From 2008 on, river classification is based on river basins. (*Sources:* Ariff, 2011; Department of Environment Malaysia, 2010b)

rivers in Penang state, but garbage thrown by the public is the main cause (Environmental Development in Malaysia, 2009).

Deforestation and water catchment deterioration is another serious issue. Before the British came in the late 1870s, the amount of forest cover was close to 90%. It probably dropped to about 80% during British rule. Between independence (in 1957) and the 1970s, it hovered around 70%. As of 2010, according to the UN Food and Agriculture Organization, 62.3% or about 20,456,000 ha of Malaysia is forested, of which only 8.8% (1,807,000 ha) is classified as primary forest (Mongabay.com, 2011). As a result, a large number of water catchments have deteriorated, leading to high concentrations of sediment in the rivers. A case in point is the Ulu Muda Forest Reserve, which acts as a water catchment for Kedah, Penang and Perlis states (Friends of Ulu Muda II, 2008).

Institutional and legal issues related to governance also affect river management (Chan, 2009). The most serious institutional issue is poor cooperation and integration between federal and state governments, between different state governments, and between state and local governments. There are few formal mechanisms to integrate and co-ordinate activities within a river basin, though Selangor (through the Selangor Waters Management Authority Enactment [*Enakmen Lembaga Urus Air Selangor*, LUAS], approved by the Selangor State Legislative Assembly on 9 April 1999) and the Sarawak Rivers Board (SRB) have taken a lead in setting up one-stop agencies to manage rivers. The success of Selangor and Sarawak, however, is still limited to the state level. There is no single federal ministry or government agency that is entrusted with the sole function of managing rivers but many ministries, departments, and agencies are involved. This has led to overlap of responsibilities, competition, and disputes related to rivers.

In terms of laws, Malaysia probably has an overabundance of sector-based water laws at both the federal and state levels. What it lacks is a comprehensive water law or river law. Currently, related to rivers, water legislation is contained within the laws which are enforced by various water-related government agencies at all levels of government. Many of these laws are now outdated. More significantly, this outdated water legislation is sector based, focuses on limited aspects of specific water sectors, and provides for resource utilization rather than conservation (Hj Keizrul bin Abdullah, 2002).

Management of Urban Rivers and Water Quality

In Malaysia, all three levels of government (federal, state, and local) play a role in managing rivers. Urban rivers are largely managed by local governments such as municipalities or city halls since the rivers flow within cities or towns.

From the federal level to local government, there are many policies that promote river water quality improvements. While state governments have jurisdiction over rivers and water, it is the federal government of Malaysia that outlines the policies and strategies in the national plans to ensure rivers are effectively managed so that they provide access to safe and clean drinking water supply. Federal policies and strategies generally promote water quality improvement as well as collaboration between relevant agencies (federal and state) in the prevention and control of contamination of rivers and raw water sources that are abstracted for consumption (bin Mokhtar, 2010). There are also policies for the continuous monitoring and surveillance of drinking water quality.

Despite the absence of a comprehensive water and river law, the country has formulated several acts that serve to protect water sources from contamination. For example, the

Ministry of Health established the National Drinking Water Quality Standards in 1983 (Ministry of Health Malaysia, 2002), stipulating limits for physical, chemical, microbiological, and radiological parameters. Compliance with these standards is mandatory for all private water suppliers.

To effectively manage rivers, Malaysia has, on paper, supported and implemented integrated water resources management (IWRM) and integrated river basin management (IRBM) approaches to improving river and groundwater quality (bin Moktar *et al.*, 2001; Economic Planning Unit, 2006). According to bin Mokhtar (2010), to ensure river water is not polluted by sewer effluent, public sewer systems have been upgraded and additional centralized sewage treatment plants have been constructed. The federal government put a national policy in place during the 8th Malaysia Plan (2001–2005) to improve river quality. For example, under the pollution prevention and water quality improvement programme of the 8th Malaysia Plan, 26 rivers have been identified for general improvement, starting with 6 rivers in 2001 (the Langat, Skudai, Segget, Tebrau, Melaka, and Miri). Under the 8th Malaysian Plan (Government of Malaysia, 2001a) and the 3rd Outline Perspectives Plan (2001–2010) (Government of Malaysia, 2001b), 24 rivers have been identified specifically for water quality improvement (Rahman, N.d.)

The Department of Drainage and Irrigation Malaysia (DID) is a federal agency responsible for managing rivers. Via the DID, the federal government also launched the One State One River programme in 2005. Under this programme, state DID offices were selected to carry out restoration and water quality improvement works for one major river in their state (Global Environment Centre, N.d.b). This programme aims to involve all stakeholders in the management of the river so that all resources can be focused on the rehabilitation and protection of that river. This would act as a best management practice that can then be replicated to other rivers nation-wide. The many objectives in this programme are: to ensure clean, living, and valuable rivers with a minimum water quality of Class II (WQI = 76.5–92.7) by the year 2015; to make rivers and their surrounding areas natural recreation areas; to ensure rivers are free of rubbish and do not flood; to successfully implement an integrated river basin management system; and to expand the success of this river management programme to other rivers through a "one district one river" programme (Kaur, 2011).

The Department of Environment Malaysia (DOE) is responsible for monitoring water quality in the rivers (Department of Environment Malaysia, 2010b). The DOE has been monitoring river water quality since 1978. The main purposes have been to establish baselines and to detect water quality changes. However, the DOE's functions have since been extended to the identification of pollution sources. Currently, the DOE monitors a total of 1,064 manual stations in 143 river basins throughout the country. There are also 15 automatic water quality monitoring stations installed to monitor changes on a continuous basis at some of the major rivers in the country.

Based on data collected at these stations, the water quality is classified into three categories: clean, slightly polluted, and polluted. The data is then used to further classify rivers into Class I, II, III, IV, or V based on the water quality index (WQI) and the Interim National Water Quality Standards for Malaysia (Department of Environment Malaysia, 2008). Class I is the best and Class V is the worst. Class I and II can be used for drinking water after treatment; Class V is only suitable for navigation. The WQI is based on six main parameters: biochemical oxygen demand (BOD), chemical oxygen demand (COD), ammoniacal nitrogen (NH_3N), pH, dissolved oxygen (DO), and suspended solids (SS)

WATER QUALITY POLICY AND MANAGEMENT IN ASIA

(Rahman, N.d.) In 2006, the DOE registered 18,956 water pollution sources comprising 9,060 sewage treatment plants (47.79%), 8,543 manufacturing industries (45.07%), 869 animal farms (4.58%), and 484 agro-based industries (2.56%) (Department of Environment Malaysia, 2010a). At present, the most developed states, such as Selangor, Penang, Perak, and Johor, have the highest number of pollution sources (see Table 2).

In Malaysia, biological oxygen demand (BOD) pollution from domestic sewage discharge is the largest contributor of river pollution (an estimated BOD load of some 883,391 kg/day). Hence, the role of Indah Water Konsortium (IWK), the agency responsible for sewage treatment, is vital. This agency has a big role to play in managing river water quality. According to Din (2010), the IWK, now wholly owned by the Malaysian government, is responsible for providing sewage services, operating and maintaining over 5,567 public sewage treatment plants and a 14,190 km network of sewage pipelines, and desludging and septage management for one million individual septic tanks. The IWK covers most parts of Malaysia for operation and maintenance whilst providing technical expertise to the remaining unserviced area. Based on its improving performance, it was shown that the number of clean rivers increased from 28% in 1993 to 64% in 2007 while the number of slightly polluted rivers dropped in the last few years. There have been significant improvements since 1997 when the IWK became fully operational as almost all river basins with its presence are categorized by the DOE as having improved in terms of water quality.

River management is also carried out at the level of state government. For example, the DID's Penang state branch has an aggressive programme to rehabilitate polluted rivers. Two rivers classified as "dead rivers", Sungai Pinang and Sungai Juru, were targeted to be rehabilitated from Class V to Class II by 2015. Class V rivers are the most polluted, with no marine life and suitable only for navigation. Class II rivers are clean enough for water supply after treatment and for contact water sports like swimming.

Another example of a government-led top-down river restoration programme in terms of water quality is the Klang River Cleanup Programme (Chan, 2005). This programme,

Table 2. Total BOD load (kg/day) from sewage treatment plants (STP) in Malaysia in 2006.

State	No. of STP	Total population equivalent (PE)	Flow (m³/day)	BOD load (kg/day)
Selangor	2,563	5,908,450	1,329,401	332,350.31
Perak	1,343	1,300,430	292,597	73,149.19
Johor	1010	1,198,417	269,644	67,410.96
Negeri Sembilan	928	931,458	209,578	52,394.51
Kedah	755	556,637	125,243	31,310.83
Melaka	725	570,192	128,293	32,073.30
Pulau Pinang	650	2,149,001	483,525	120,881.31
Pahang	486	314,830	70,837	17,709.19
Federal Territory of Kuala Lumpur	299	2,571,877	578,672	144,668.08
Terengganu	224	75,184	16,916	4,229.10
Perlis	36	16,156	3,635	908.78
Federal Territory of Labuan	32	39,265	8,835	2,208.66
Federal Territory of Putrajaya	9	72,833	16,387	4,096.86
Total	9,060	15,704,730	3,533,563	883,391.08

Source: Department of Environment Malaysia, 2010a.

161

located in one of the most densely developed areas of the country with 3.6 million people, has had mixed results (Chop & Jusoh, 2002). The Klang is an urban river, passing through the major urban centers of Ampang, Kuala Lumpur, Klang, Shah Alam, Subang Jaya, Petaling Jaya, Kajang, Ampang Jaya, and Selayang. The river is classified as one of the most severely polluted rivers in the country (Chop & Jusoh, 2002). This programme was not formalized until 1992. Its objectives were: (a) to clean up the Klang River and its major tributaries from rubbish and silt; (b) to improve the water quality of the Klang River and its major tributaries to a minimum of Class III standards (WQI = 60); and (c) to improve the river for recreation purposes. However, when funds ran out, the programme came to an end and the river became degraded once more.

The role of local governments is equally important in river management and conservation. In Penang, the Seberang Prai Municipal Council actively involves residents' associations, *rukun tetangga* (community vigilance groups), and community development and security committees. These groups have been brought together to work closely with local authorities to keep the rivers in their areas clean. Council president Maimunah Mohd Sharif envisioned a more concerted effort between community-based organizations and government bodies to further improve the water quality in Seberang Prai rivers. The Penang state DOE and the council's Local Agenda 21 started a programme to periodically monitor rivers in residential and commercial areas (Majlis Perbandaran Seberang Perai, N.d.).

The council also works closely with NGOs and local communities in managing river water quality via awareness and education efforts (Majlis Perbandaran Seberang Perai, N.d.) Kuala Lumpur City Hall is also actively involved in the Kelang River Cleanup Programme as one of the key partners. Its Local Agenda 21 (LA21) programme, with the theme "Safe City", was launched on 14 April 2011. During the launch, a memorandum of understanding was signed between the city hall and 22 partners, which include NGOs and private sector and community-based organizations, to ensure the success of the programme (Kuala Lumpur City Hall, N.d.) Melaka City Hall has also been actively involved in rehabilitating the Melaka River until it became a major tourist attraction. The river was once the heart of trade of the Melaka Empire during historical times. It is now restored to allow tourists to experience the Melaka River Cruise (Majlis Bandaraya Melaka Bersejarah, N.d.)

The role of NGOs is also very important in the management, conservation, and improvement of water quality in the rivers. In the Pinang River, the role of NGOs and citizens is becoming increasingly important. The work of Water Watch Penang is a good example of NGO work in managing urban rivers (Water Watch Penang, N.d.) Some of its river conservation activities include the Pinang River Walk, the Caring for Our Rivers campaign, river monitoring training, and river mapping. Their objectives include instilling awareness and love for our rivers as well as to sensitize the public towards the importance of rivers. Another NGO, the Global Environment Centre, has successfully implemented the Nenggiri River Conservation Programme since 2004 (Global Environment Centre, N.d.a).

Obstacles to Effective Management of Urban Rivers and Water Quality

Arguably, federal-state-local government disputation over rivers and their associated water and land is one of the major obstacles that need to be addressed if Malaysia is to realize its dream of rehabilitating its rivers to pristine conditions. After years of research, Ujang (2010) has concluded that in Malaysia, politics play a vital role in river management. In recent years, this issue has been further exacerbated by politics whereby some state governments have been won by opposition parties, while the federal government remains in the hands of the National Front. When the federal and state governments are from different political parties, it is inevitable that some development programmes will not run as smoothly as they ought to, including river management programmes. It is also alleged that federal funds have been held back or dispensed very slowly to opposition-led states (Chi, 2011). State governments, both from the National Front as well as from opposition parties, are also alleged to have not adopted federal laws and regulations (The Nut Graph, 2008). Federal-state government disputes also surfaced in the inter-state water transfer project between Selangor and Pahang states and remain unresolved.

River pollution represents another serious obstacle to overcome in Malaysia's quest for clean rivers. Although Indah Water Konsortium, one of the identified main polluters, has improved its operations, much remains to be done. Also, there are many sectors that continue to pollute, including the agricultural, industrial, and domestic sectors. While many factories and industries have adopted ISO 14001 and coporate social responsibility (CSR) programmes that have reduced their polluting impacts (CSR examples include Indah Water Konsortium's sewage education programme for secondary schools and local communities, Royal Bank of Scotland's river education programme with Water Watch Penang, and Coca Cola's Muda River education programme with Worldwide Fund for Nature Malaysia), squatters remain a major polluting source. Nonpoint sources are also extremely difficult to address, and have not been dealt with effectively. Although the general public is more educated than their forefathers of previous generations, general public apathy appears not to have been addressed: rivers continue to be treated as raw sewers. Deforestation and water catchment destruction is another serious obstacle that needs to be addressed to ensure clean rivers. Many states are still highly dependent on logging for income, and do not appear to value water resources above timber. A case in point is the Kedah state government, which is trying to log the Ulu Muda Forest Reserve that serves as a water catchment for the three states of Kedah, Perlis, and Penang (Friends of Ulu Muda II, 2009).

Uneven water distribution, pollution, over-abstraction, catchment destruction, and climate change are also reasons for river water quality deterioration. In Malaysia, as rivers are the major suppliers of fresh water for human consumption (including for industries and agriculture), water availability will be central in the country's future development and survival. Because the majority of Malaysian rivers and their basins are already badly polluted, it is projected that water supply will fall short of demand. Against this background of diminishing water resources is the ever-looming threat of population increase. Greater demands on water supply will put greater stress on rivers and on their water quality.

Floods are a major obstacle in river management and cause deterioration in river water quality. Flooding occurs seasonally as monsoon floods, monthly as tidal floods, and frequently as flash floods in urban areas (Chan et al., 2006). Malaysia is drained by 150 major river systems, of which about 100 are in Peninsular Malaysia and another 50 in East Malaysia (bin Abdullah, 2002). These systems have brought floods that have resulted in damage with significant loss of life.

During times of monsoon, especially the north-east monsoon season (November to March), many parts of the country experience floods. In recent years, severe floods have devastated the states of Johor, Kelantan, Terengganu, Pahang, and Kedah (Chan, 1996). It is estimated that more than 29,000 km^2 of Malaysia (9% of the total land area) is flood prone, as most of these areas are located in the riverine, estuary, and coastal areas (bin Abdullah, 2002). Floods affect about 1 in 10 persons, or about 3 million people in the country.

Malaysia's annual flood losses are high, including losses of life. In the 1980s, the estimated annual floods losses were about RM100 million, but this is estimated to have multiplied due to denser populations, denser properties, more infrastructures, and more intensive crops. Urban expansion and the escalation of land and property values have increased annual flood damage significantly. These losses can be tangible (e.g. housing damage) or intangible (e.g. health effects), as well as direct (e.g. in terms of working hours) or indirect (e.g. loss of business opportunities) (Chan, 2002b). The rivers' capacities for drainage have also been drastically reduced due to sedimentation, encroachment caused by construction, channelization, building of impeding structures (e.g. culverts and low bridges), and other human activities. These have not only exacerbated floods but also deteriorated river water quality (Chan, 2010).

Floods also give policy makers the wrong signal. As a result of floods, it is not uncommon for policy makers to think that Malaysia has too much water. Floods can thus be considered to be an obstacle to changing the mindset of policy makers towards implementing a water demand management approach via both mandating regulations and carrying out national water-saving campaigns, including environmental education and awareness issues.

Another serious obstacle to effective river management is the authorities' obsession with mostly structural measures, be it for river management, water abstraction, or flood control (Chan, 1999). Structural measures are essentially technical and engineering measures requiring the construction of structures such as dams, irrigation systems, physical river restorations, water treatment plants, flood alleviation canals, and retention ponds in managing rivers. Structural measures are high profile and often of mega scale. They have tremendous economic benefits in terms of generating jobs, boosting the economy, and producing huge returns. Hence, these measures are preferred by the authorities. In comparison, non-structural measures such as relocation of riverine communities, introduction of new legislation and regulations, risk mapping, land use zoning, and creating awareness and education are under-utilized. While structural measures have their benefits, their effectiveness is limited. For example, many structural river schemes have been delayed or shelved because squatters and other riverine communities refused to relocate. Structural schemes such as dams also displace large numbers of riverine inhabitants, flood heritage sites, destroy forest, and increase dam-break risk. The authorities should employ a comprehensive approach, using both measures, for more effective management of rivers.

Institutional arrangements remain yet another obstacle for the implementation of IWRM- and IRBM-related practices. Although ministries have been streamlined and government agencies revamped, there are still many ministries, departments, and agencies having overlapping functions and responsibilities relating to rivers, river corridors, and river water. Until today, there is still no single federal ministry or government agency solely entrusted with the function of managing rivers comprehensively in an integrated and holistic manner. Development plans need to be designed within a basin-wide rather than a state-wise approach. In cases of inter-state river basins, where the basin is divided amongst two or more states, there should be a joint management agency in the relevant states. Currently, there is none. For example, when Kedah decided to log the forest, there was nothing Perlis or Penang could do. Finally, it took a decision by the Federal Cabinet to stop the logging. Even so, rivers within the basin still suffer from siltation and sedimentation due to illegal logging and other developments.

Finally, there are obstacles within the existing legal framework due to outdated laws and those which do not provide adequate protection for rivers. Existing laws also do not support IWRM and IRBM adequately. Many states are also not adopting federal legislation. For example, the Land Conservation Act has only been adopted and implemented in Pahang and Penang recently. In the widest sense, the absence of a comprehensive water law or river law is considered an obstacle in effective river management. The good news is that new laws on erosion and sedimentation control are currently being drafted by the DOE. The National Water Resources Policy is also nearing completion and this would contribute towards more effective management of overall water resources, including rivers (Chin, 2012).

Conclusion

Rivers are not only our heritage, but also provide us with a lifeline of vital functions and resources. Although still work in progress, the Malaysian government at all levels is starting to do its part in river management. More importantly, the public (including the private sector and NGOs) have become proactive in protecting, conserving, and restoring our rivers so that their waters can be sustained for future use. The NGO efforts by Water Watch Penang and Global Environment Centre via a bottom-up approach complement the traditional top-down approach of the government. Increasingly, Malaysians from all walks of life, including politicians, policy makers, government officers, business people, company directors, managers of NGOs, and individuals, are getting involved in various aspects of river management. Although river conservancy and restoration remain the responsibility of the government, public support from all stakeholders is necessary for overall effectiveness of river management. The example of the Klang River Clean-up Programme should be used as a learning example and something to be built upon. This programme demonstrated that a badly degraded river such as the Klang can be restored to a good water-quality level given the right support and cooperation amongst all stakeholders. To this end, in his 2011 budget speech, the Prime Minister committed RM1.9 billion to clean up the Klang River.[1] This is good leadership and commitment, without which rivers would continue to degrade.

As an example, the Cheonggyecheon ("clear valley stream") River was paved over in the 1960s to make way for a massive boulevard and then an elevated expressway. In 2003, in an act of committed political will from the mayor of Seoul, Lee Myung-bak, a boulevard and 16 expressways were torn down to "revive" and restore the lost stream beneath. Two years later, a vibrant, wild park had replaced a traffic-choked freeway (Schabas, 2009).The revival of the Cheonggyecheon River in Seoul represents total commitment (Walsh, 2006). Can the Kelang River be our Cheonggyecheon, at least within the boundaries of Kuala Lumpur? Despite a lot of efforts at rehabilitation and restoration with a great deal of money spent, rivers in Malaysia have not improved in quality. This is because only a small section of Malaysian society has been active in river management, while the majority is apathetic and detached. Solid wastes continue to be dumped into our rivers, mainly due to apathy and poor public involvement. The government has not really reached the people effectively, with rehabilitation and restoration programmes being largely top-down or privatized, hardly involving the public. The authorities have also not tackled the squatter problem effectively, although the government's position is to be "free" from squatters when Malaysia becomes a developed nation in 2020.

Finally, more efforts and funding need to be injected to sustain and replicate programmes such as the "one state one river" programme nation-wide into "one state two rivers" and so on. Currently, this programme targets one river in each state to be funded by the federal government for overall improvement of the river ecosystem, but effectiveness is limited to only the selected river. This programme needs to be extended to all other rivers in the country, and if funds are lacking, the government should explore the option of working together with NGOs and the overall citizenry in the cleaning and restoration of rivers. Authorities can work with NGOs to increase public awareness and education in relation to rivers.

The government can continue to play its pivotal role in river management but must change its mindset to a more comprehensive and holistic approach which includes appropriate legal and institutional frameworks, governance practices, the implementation of IWRM and IRBM, and both structural and non-structural measures in managing rivers, always looking for the participation of the citizens and their many organized groups. Only then will the quality of the rivers and their waters improve, providing, in turn, a better quality of life to the population of the country.

Acknowledgements

I would like to acknowledge funding from the Long Term Research Grant Scheme (LRGS) 203/PKT/6724003 which contributed to the publication of this paper.

Note

1. Available from: http://www.bnm.gov.my/files/budget2011_en.pdf (accessed 29/3/12)

References

Ariff, M. M. (2011) Malaysians paying the cost for polluted water (Bernama News, 18 January). Available at: http://envdevmalaysia.wordpress.com/2011/01/18/malaysians-paying-the-cost-for-polluted-water/ (accessed 29 March 2012).

Asian Development Bank (2007) *Malaysia: Klang River Basin Environmental Improvement and Flood Mitigation Project*. Available at: http://www.adb.org/Documents/PCRs/MAL/26009-MAL-PCR.pdf (accessed 31 January 2012).

bin Abdullah, H. K. (2002) Integrated river basin management, in: N. W. Chan (Ed.) *Rivers: Towards Sustainable Development*, pp. 3–14 (Penang: Universiti Sains Malaysia Press).

bin Mohktar, M. (2010) Issues and framework of environmental health in Malaysia, *Journal of Environmental Health*, 72(8), pp. 24–29. Available at: http://www.faqs.org/periodicals/201004/1992261741.html (accessed 20 June 2011).

bin Mokhtar, M., Lee, Y. H. & Nawi, H. M. (2001) Water quality of discharge from a golf course and its effect on the Langat River: towards an integrated river basin management, *Malaysian Journal of Analytical Sciences*, 6, pp. 157–161.

Biswas, A. K. & Tortajada, C. (2011) Water quality management: an introductory framework, *Water Resources Development*, 27(1), pp. 5–11.

Chan, N. W. (1996) Vulnerability of urban areas to floods, *The Star [Malaysia]*, pp. 4–6, 26 January.

Chan, N. W. (1999) Employment of non-structural flood mitigation measures in alleviating flood problems in Penang, *Proceedings of the Second International Malaysian Studies Conference, 2–4 August 1999, Universiti Malaya, Kuala Lumpur* (Kuala Lumpur: Malaysian Social Science Association).

Chan, N. W. (Ed.) (2002a) *Rivers: Towards Sustainable Development* (Penang: Penerbit Universiti Sains Malaysia).

Chan, N. W. (2002b) *Pembangunan, Pembandaran dan Peningkatan Bahaya dan Bencana Air di Malaysia: Isu, Pengurusan dan Cabaran* (Penang: Penerbit Universiti Sains Malaysia).

Chan, N. W. (2005) Sustainable management of rivers in Malaysia: involving all stakeholders, *International Journal of River Basin Management*, 3(3), pp. 147–162.

Chan, N. W. (2009) Issues and challenges in water governance in Malaysia, *Iranian Journal of Environmental Health Science & Engineering*, 6(3), pp. 143–152.

Chan, N. W. (2010) Addressing flood hazards via environmental humanities in Malaysia, in: D. Efizon *et al.* (Ed.) *Proceedings of the International Seminar on Ecology, Human Habitat and Environmental Change*, September 20–21, 2010, Pekanbaru, Indonesia, pp. 46–57 (Pekanbaru: Fakultas Perikanan dan Ilmu Kelautan Universitas Riau and Institute Alam dan tamadun Melayu (ATMA) Universiti Kebangsaan Malaysia).

Chan, N. W., Koh, H. L. & Aminuddin, A. G. (2006) Developing a model of flood hazards on urban floodplains in Malaysia, in: A. A. Tajuddin & O. Lim (Eds) *Fundamental Research at USM 2002–2005, Vol. 3 (Arts)*, pp. 32–54 (Penang: Penerbit Universiti Sains Malaysia).

Chan, N. W. & Kung, H. T. (2001) Management of river pollution as a tool in water resources management: some examples from Malaysia, in: K. L. Risher (Ed.) *Proceedings of the Thirty-First Mississippi Water Resources Conference, April 10–11, 2001, Raymond, Mississippi*, pp. 108–120 (Raymond: Water Resources Research Institute and Mississippi State University).

Chi, M. (2011) Anwar: PR states getting less than the rest, *The Malaysian Insider*, 15 March. Available at: http://www.themalaysianinsider.com/malaysia/article/anwar-pr-states-getting-less-than-the-rest/ (accessed 14 February 2012).

Chin, P. F. K. (2012) Keynote Address presented at Asia Water 2012 Conference, Kuala Lumpur, 27–29 March 2012.

Chop, A. K. & Jusoh, J. (2002) The Klang River Cleanup Programme, in: N. W. Chan (Ed.) *Rivers: Towards Sustainable Development*, pp. 378–389 (Penang: Penerbit Universiti Sains Malaysia).

Department of Environment Malaysia (2008) Interim National Water Quality Standards for Malaysia. Kuala Lumpur.

Department of Environment Malaysia (2010a) *River Pollution Sources*. Available at: http://www.doe.gov.my/portal/water-marine-river-water/river-water-pollution-sources/ (accessed 31 January 2012).

Department of Environment Malaysia (2010b) *River Water Quality Monitoring*. Available at: http://www.doe.gov.my/portal/water-marine-river-water/river-water-quality-monitoring/ (accessed 31 January 2012).

Din, A. K. M. (2010) Towards sustainable sewerage development: sharing Malaysia's experiences for replication, Paper presented at *6th Ministerial Conference on Environment and Development in Asia and the Pacific (MCED-6)*, 27 September to 2 October 2010, Astana, Kazakhstan.

Economic Planning Unit (2006) *Ninth Malaysia Plan 2006–2010* (Putrajaya, Malaysia: Prime Minister's Department).

Environmental Development in Malaysia (2009) Garbage, main cause of river pollution in Penang [web log, 25 July]. Available at: http://envdevmalaysia.wordpress.com/2009/07/25/garbage-main-cause-of-river-pollution-in-penang/ (accessed 16 June 2011).

Friends of Ulu Muda II (2008) Kedah told to be alert for loggers (The Star 23 Jun 08) [web log, 26 July]. Available at: http://saveulumuda.wordpress.com/2008/07/26/kedah-told-to-be-alert-for-loggersthe-star-23-jun-08/ (accessed 16 June 2011).

Friends of Ulu Muda II (2009) Kedah tetap tebang balak (Utusan Malaysia 1 Mac 09) [web log, 10 March]. Available at: http://saveulumuda.wordpress.com/2009/03/10/kedah-tetap-tebang-balak-utusan-malaysia-1-mac-09/ (accessed 22 February 2012).

Global Environment Centre (N.d.a) Nenggiri River Rehabilitation Programme. Available at: http://www.gec.org.my/index.cfm?&menuid=20&parentid=92 (accessed 31 January 2012).

Global Environment Centre (N.d.b) One State One River community participation component. Available at: http://www.gecnet.info/index.cfm?&menuid=31 (accessed 31 January 2012).

Government of Malaysia (2001a) Rancangan Malaysia Kelapan, 2001–2005 (Kuala Lumpur: Percetakan Nasional Malaysia).

Government of Malaysia (2001b) The Third Outline Perspective Plan, 2001–2010 (Seri Kembangan: Percetakan Nasional Malaysia).

Indah Water Konsortium (N.d) http://www.doe.gov.my/portal/water-marine-river-water/river-water-pollution-sources/ (accessed 31 January 2012).

Kaur, M. (2011) Programme to improve Sungai Kinta, *The Star*, 28 May. Available at: http://thestar.com.my/news/story.asp?file=/2011/5/28/metroperak/8567570&sec=metroperak (accessed 29 March 2012).

Kuala Lumpur City Hall (N.d) Available at: http://www.dbkl.gov.my/portalv7/index.php?option=com_content&view=article&id=1372%3Aunited-and-moving-forward-with-la21&catid=8%3Acurrent-news&Itemid=15&lang=bm (accessed 29 March 2012).

Majlis Bandaraya Melaka Bersejarah (N.d) Sungai Melaka: Melaka River Cruise. Available at: http://www.mb mb.gov.my/sungai (accessed 31 January 2012).

Majlis Perbandaran Seberang Perai (N.d) Local Action 21. Available at: http://www.mpsp.gov.my/La21/ (accessed 21 June 2011).

Ministry of Health Malaysia (2002) National Drinking Water Quality Standards (Kuala Lumpur: Ministry of Health Malaysia).

Mongabay.com (2011) *Malaysia Forest Information and Data*. Available at: http://rainforests.mongabay.com/ deforestation/2000/Malaysia.htm (Accessed 31 January 2012).

Naiman, R. J. & Bilby, R. E. (1998) River ecology and management in the Pacific coastal ecoregion, in: R. J. Naiman & R. E. Bilby (Eds) *River Ecology and Management: Lessons from the Pacific Coastal Ecoregion*, pp. 1–10 (New York: Springer).

Netto, A. (2006) Death to Malaysian water contaminators? *IPS News*, 8 May. Available at: http://www.ipsnews. net/news.asp?idnews=33160 (accessed 16 June 2011).

The Nut Graph 15 August. Available at: http://www.thenutgraph.com/penang-state-govt-not-cooperating/ (accessed 31 January 2012) (2008).

Rahman, Z. A. (N.d) *Water Quality Monitoring and Modelling: Opportunity and Challenges*. Available at: http://www.iges.or.jp/en/ltp/pdf/Rhaman_ppt.pdf (accessed 31 January 2012).

Schabas, J. (2009) World Wide Wednesday: lessons from Seoul's river expressway, *Spacing Toronto*, 10 June. Available at: http://spacingtoronto.ca/2009/06/10/world-wide-wednesday-lessons-from-seouls-river-expr essway/ (accessed 31 January 2012).

Ujang, Z. (2010) Water mismanagement? The politics of polluted urban rivers, Paper presented at the Merdeka Lecture Series, 22 October 2010, Universiti Sains Malaysia, Penang.

Walsh, B. (2006) Saving Seoul, *Time*, May 15. Available at: http://www.skyscrapercity.com/showthread. php?t=348193 (accessed 29 March 2012).

Water Watch Penang (N.d) Available at: http://www.waterwatchpenang.org (accessed 31 January 2012).

Improving Groundwater Quality Management for the Sustainable Utilization of the Bangkok Aquifer System

MUKAND S. BABEL*, ALDRIN A. RIVAS*, ASHIM DAS GUPTA* & YATSUKA KATAOKA**

*Water Engineering and Management, School of Engineering and Technology, Asian Institute of Technology, Pathumthani, Thailand; **Freshwater Group, Institute for Global Environmental Strategies, Kanagawa, Japan

ABSTRACT *Several measures have been implemented to address the negative environmental consequences brought about by the overexploitation of groundwater resources in the Bangkok Aquifer System. However, such measures were mainly directed to quantity issues such as resource depletion and land subsidence, whereas quality aspects seem to have been given less attention. Given that quality deterioration, mainly chloride contamination, has affected groundwater users, this article evaluates current groundwater quality management practices in the Bangkok Metropolitan Region, points out the challenges, and provides some specific recommendations for the sustainable utilization of the valuable resource.*

Introduction

Groundwater has been relied upon as an important source of stable and safe water supply in many urban areas of the world (Foster *et al.*, 1998; UNEP, 2003). This is particularly true in Bangkok, where groundwater has comprised a huge proportion of water supply for domestic consumption as well as industrial use for several decades (Das Gupta & Babel, 2005). While groundwater is important to meeting the demands for water especially in areas where surface water is limited, unplanned and excessive extraction of the resource could result in undesirable environmental consequences (UNEP, 2003).

Bangkok has been prominently cited as one of the examples showcasing the undesirable impacts of groundwater overexploitation (e.g. UNEP, 2003; Zaporozec & Miller, 2000). Indeed, several studies have examined and emphasized the impacts of groundwater overexploitation on piezometric level and land subsidence in Bangkok and adjacent areas (e.g. Babel *et al.*, 2006a; Piancharoen & Chuamthaisong, 1976; Phien-wej *et al.*, 2006). Some also investigated quality deterioration due to overextraction, particularly chloride contamination (Babel *et al.*, 2006b; Das Gupta & Sabanathan, 1988), and studies assessing groundwater management approaches in Bangkok have made some recommendations for improvement (Babel *et al.*, 2006b; Das Gupta & Babel, 2005). However, these studies and the measures implemented by responsible agencies generally seem to focus on groundwater quantity and the literature lacks records on the investigation of governance and management policies and practices with respect to groundwater quality problems. This article tries to address this gap by assessing governance issues related to groundwater quality in the Bangkok Metropolitan Region and providing some recommendations for improving the situation and eventually for the sustainable use of the essential resource.

The Bangkok Aquifer System

Collectively known as the Bangkok Metropolitan Region (BMR), the city of Bangkok and its five surrounding provinces Nonthaburi, Pathumthani, Samut Prakan, Samut Sakhon and Nakhon Pathom, manage to meet water demand from surface water and groundwater sources. The Chao Phraya River, the largest river in the country, is the main source of surface water in these provinces, which are parts of the Lower Central Plain of Thailand and located in the deltaic plain of the Chao Phraya River. Groundwater, on the other hand, is extracted from the multilayer aquifers, known as the Bangkok Aquifer System (BAS), beneath the Lower Central Plain.

The Lower Central Plain was formed on a fault/flexure depression that was filled with clastic sediments from the Tertiary to the Quaternary ages. Aeromagnetic data indicate that the depression is underlain by various types of bedrock at depths of 400–3,500 m (Babel et al., 2006a). This plain stretches 150 km from east to west and 200 km from north to south, and the flat plain elevation ranges from 0 to 20 m above mean sea level (JICA, 1995). It is bounded to the west by the western mountain ranges and to the east by the Petchabun mountain ranges and part of the western edge of the Korat Plateau (Sinsakul, 2000). It is bounded to the south by the Gulf of Thailand and divided by monadnocks from the Upper Central Plain to the north (Yamanaka et al., 2011a). The basin floor generally slopes towards the central axis, which is located more or less along the course of the Chao Phraya River and declines southward to the Gulf of Thailand (Achalabhuti, 1974).

Overlying the basement complex are unconsolidated and semi-consolidated sediments from the Tertiary and Quaternary periods, which are believed to have been deposited under fluviatile and deltaic environments (Babel et al., 2006a), that is from the Recent to the Oligocene epochs (Das Gupta & Babel, 2005). The total thickness of the formation is found to range from about 400 to more than 1,800 m (Babel & Rivas, 2008), on top of which is the Bangkok clay consisting of about 12 m of soft marine clay stratum overlaying 8 m of desiccated stiff clay stratum (Das Gupta & Babel, 2005). As shown in Figure 1, the subsurface strata in the Bangkok area, particularly the upper 600m, are conventionally subdivided into eight aquifers (Sinsakul, 2000; Babel & Rivas, 2008) collectively known as the Bangkok Aquifer System. These aquifers were defined according to geological, hydrological, and geophysical studies, and the depth zone indicators refer to the average depth of the aquifers below the surface (Babel et al., 2006b; JICA, 1995). The aquifers are generally permeable and can yield water at 100–300 m^3/h (Das Gupta & Babel, 2005). The transmissivities for the pumped aquifers are normally in the range of 1,000–2,500 m^2/day and the storage coefficients are in the range 10^{-3} to 6×10^{-3} (JICA, 1995). The most heavily pumped aquifers are the Phra Pradaeng, Nakhon Luang, and Nonthaburi, which are the second, third, and fourth aquifers from the ground surface, respectively (AIT, 2007).

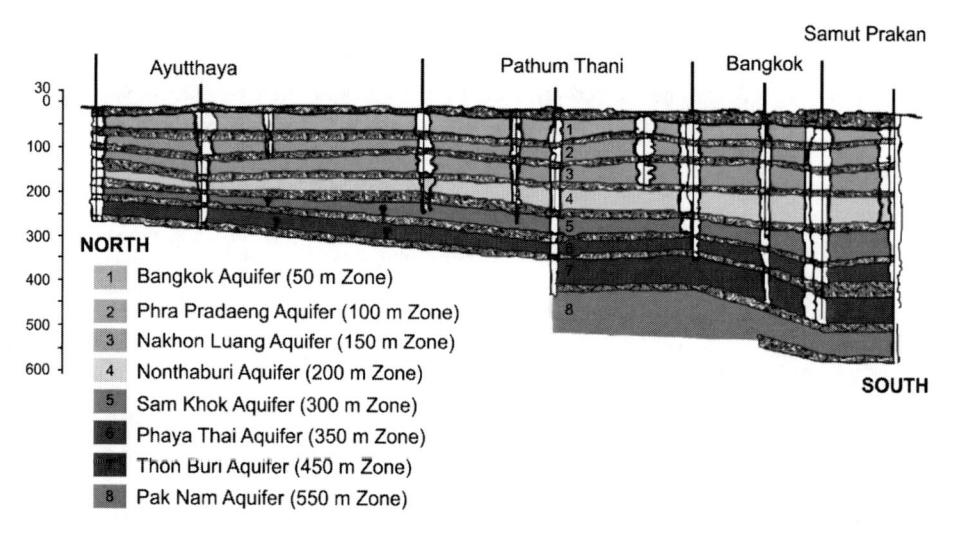

Figure 1. Schematic diagram of the Bangkok Aquifer system. *Source:* Asian Institute of Technology (2007), after Ramnarong & Buapeng (1992).

Institutional Arrangement for Groundwater Quality Management

The management of groundwater resources in Thailand is mainly under the responsibility of the Department of Groundwater Resources (DGR) in the Ministry of Natural Resources and Environment (MoNRE), which was created in 2002 under a major public sector reform of the Royal Thai Government. The establishment of the MoNRE was an attempt to draw together all government agencies that are responsible for the management and conservation of natural resources and environment. Before the establishment of the DGR, the agency responsible for groundwater resources was the Groundwater Division of the Department of Mineral Resources (DMR). Its main task was to explore, develop and supply groundwater to support the country's socio-economic development (Das Gupta & Babel, 2005).

While the public sector reform included aspects of sustainable development of water resources in the mandate of the DGR, groundwater resources management in Thailand as indicated in the Master Plan developed in 2006 (KKU, 2006) generally follows the National Economic and Social Development Plan with the long-term policy of supporting important policies for the promotion and development of agriculture, industry, tourism, and so on (Babel & Rivas, 2008). The DGR recognized the need to reorient its role and task from groundwater developer to groundwater resource evaluator and manager with its new mandate as pointed out in other assessments; however, the lack of relevant expertise on management aspects may have hindered its progress (Das Gupta & Babel, 2005).

Moreover, it should be noted that there is no official institutional body specifically responsible for overseeing the Bangkok Aquifer System. Given that groundwater management issues in the lower Chao Phraya basin are regional in nature, as the BAS covers several political administrative units or provinces, this regional aspect is important to consider in an institutional framework for the management of groundwater resources in the Bangkok Metropolitan Region (Nitivattananon, 2006). Apart from the central government, that is the DGR, there are no other specific agencies responsible for looking after the

Bangkok Aquifer System in a specific manner, and each of the provincial governments is the next administrative authority by virtue of the Decentralization Act of 1999 (Weist, 2002). Noting that local governments and state enterprises such as the Provincial Waterworks Authority (PWA) also utilize groundwater, management of the BAS, therefore, entails strong collaboration with these entities.

There are other government agencies which have a role in the management of the resource. The Office of Natural Resources and Environmental Policy and Planning (ONEP), which is also under the MoNRE, is responsible for the formulation of policy and plans for natural resources and environment conservation as well as to ensure the protection of natural resources through the appraisal of environmental impact reports on projects which tend to cause significant impacts on environmental quality (KKU, 2006). ONEP also serves as the secretariat of the National Environment Board, which is responsible for overseeing environmental issues in the country and composed of ministers from various relevant ministries (e.g. environment and natural resources, public health, industry, education, and agriculture and cooperatives) with the prime minister as the chairperson.

Other agencies that have significant roles in the management of groundwater quality are the Pollution Control Department (PCD), for the overall protection of the environment from pollution and for remediation and restoration of aquifers; the Department of Environmental Quality Promotion (DEQP), for disseminating information to the public to build participation on environmental issues and for providing environmental technology services such as research and development and transfer of technology for environmental control; and the Department of Industrial Works (DIW), for monitoring and regulating industrial wastes.

While the specific responsibility for groundwater resource quality protection falls upon the DGR, it is necessary to recognize that this function can only be carried out effectively in close collaboration with relevant agencies (Foster *et al.*, 2002b). At present, there are no known specific mechanisms for strategic coordination among the government agencies responsible for groundwater quality management. Coordination between the DGR and the PCD, for example, is on a case-by-case basis, usually when the PCD is asked by the DGR to comment on studies already nearing completion. If active collaboration and meaningful inputs are desired from the PCD, the agency should be involved in the early stage of any study related to the protection and conservation of groundwater resources, especially on the quality aspects.

A promising development concerning cooperation among government agencies has occurred in another part of the country. A massive contamination of groundwater from industrial wastes on the eastern seaboard led several government agencies (the DGR, PCD, DEQP, and DIW, among others) to form a committee in 2008 to address the issue as one government body instead of separate entities. This incident, however, has not resulted in the implementation of pre-emptive policies in other areas, because of inadequate financial and manpower resources and the assumption that such an event will not happen in other areas given the different land use and geological characteristics across the country. Nevertheless, given that some areas are inherently vulnerable, such as recharge areas, this kind of cooperation could be replicated for the Bangkok Aquifer System; it could be facilitated by identifying a specific unit or bureau within the DGR to establish and handle coordination mechanisms both within and outside the agency.

Furthermore, several studies provide indications of linkages between surface waters and the Bangkok Aquifer System. For instance, there is evidence that the *klongs* (canals) in Bangkok are hydraulically connected to shallow groundwater (Burnett *et al.*, 2009).

This is complemented by recent findings showing that recharge through vertical leakage from overlying layers, induced by groundwater pumping to the Bangkok Aquifer, the topmost aquifer, and the deeper layers, is distinctively enhanced at locations where the Bangkok clay is relatively thin (Mikita *et al.*, 2011; Yamanaka *et al.*, 2011a; Yamanaka *et al.*, 2011b). Through water balance modelling, it was found that 34% of the inflow to the aquifer system originates from the uppermost marine clay layer (Arlai, 2007). Moreover, geological information also indicates linkages between the Chao Phraya River and the aquifer system, particularly in areas where soft clay has been removed, such as the Klong Toey harbor (Rau & Nutalaya, 1981). These areas apparently coincide with distinct areas of relatively higher recharge (Yamanaka *et al.*, 2011a) and lower chloride concentration in the underlying aquifer (Babel & Rivas, 2008). The above thus implies that groundwater and surface water need to be managed in a well-coordinated manner to ensure protection and conservation of water quality (Tuinhof *et al.*, 2002). But these two resources are managed separately, with the Department of Water Resources (DWR) being responsible for surface waters. Here, the role of the National Water Resources Committee (NWRC), the country's apex body for coordinating water resources issues, plays a big part in bringing together these two agencies and laying down specific strategies and mechanisms for coordinated management of groundwater and surface waters. With respect to protecting the quality of these resources, such coordination may commence with coordinated water quality monitoring and analysis so that appropriate measures may be determined and specific joint actions may be implemented.

Regulating Extraction for Groundwater Conservation

Groundwater Use and Environmental Consequences

Extensive use of groundwater resources in the Bangkok aquifer system reportedly started in the mid-1950s, primarily to supplement surface water for public water supply as surface waters were fast becoming insufficient to satisfy increasing demand for water in the Bangkok Metropolitan Region (BMR) (Babel *et al.*, 2006b; Das Gupta & Babel, 2005). As shown in Figure 2, groundwater extraction for private uses such as factories, hotels, hospitals, and housing estates followed suit in the early 1960s, continued to increase, and exceeded extraction for public water supply in 1975. Since then, the continued increase and trend of groundwater extraction has mainly been dictated by the large number of private users.

While the Bangkok Aquifer System has a huge groundwater storage capacity, roughly estimated at 1,700 km^3 (Yamanaka, 2011a), there is a threshold (safe yield) in the amount of groundwater that may be pumped annually, beyond which negative environmental consequences can be expected (Todd, 1959). Several studies have estimated the safe yield of the Bangkok aquifer system, at values ranging from approximately 500,000 m^3/day to 1,500,000 m^3/day (JICA, 1995; KU, 2004; Piyasena, 1982). The discrepancies can be mainly attributed to the method adopted, apart from slight differences in the areal coverage. The DGR currently adopts the amount of 1.25 million m^3/day as the total safe yield for the three aquifers in the region, based on a study by Chulalongkorn University conducted in 2000 (Babel & Rivas, 2008; ONEP, 2004).

A quick comparison between pumpage (approximately 1.4 million m^3/day in 1981—see Figure 2) and estimated safe yield (1.25 million m^3/day) clearly suggests that extraction has

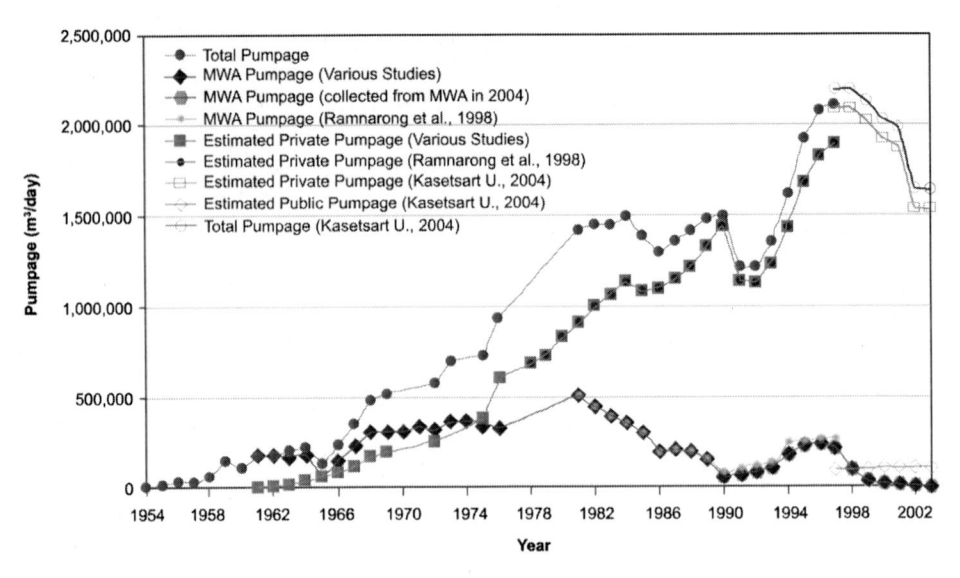

Figure 2. Groundwater pumpage in the Bangkok Metropolitan Region. *Source:* adapted from Asian Institute of Technology (2007).

gone above the threshold. Interestingly enough, depletion of groundwater resources as indicated by the significant lowering of piezometric levels of the most-pumped aquifers (Phra Pradaeng, Nakhon Luang, and Nonthaburi) occurred at around the same time, that is the late 1970s, dropping a total of more than 40 m in some areas in the mid-1990s (Babel *et al.*, 2006b). As a consequence, land subsidence at a rate of 5 to 10 cm/y occurred and has been recorded since 1978 (Babel *et al.*, 2006a), although indications of subsidence had been observed almost a decade earlier (AIT, 1982). Another major environmental consequence of groundwater overexploitation is the increase of chloride contamination of aquifers (Babel *et al.*, 2006b; Babel & Rivas, 2008), which is given specific attention in the next section of this article.

Several measures had been implemented to regulate groundwater extraction from the Bangkok Aquifer System and these are detailed elsewhere (Babel *et al.*, 2006b; Das Gupta & Babel, 2005). The most important of these measures are depicted in Figure 3 to infer their influence on groundwater extraction. In terms of legislation or policy, the most notable are the passage of the Groundwater Act of 1977 (DGR, 1977) (already amended in 1992 and 2003) and the 1983 Cabinet resolution, "Mitigation of Groundwater Crisis and Land Subsidence in Bangkok Metropolis" (DGR, 1983). While the passage of the Groundwater Act in 1977 did not seem to have an immediate influence on extraction, its later amendments, which included provisions on economic measures such as the imposition of groundwater use charges in 1992 (in addition to a nominal groundwater fee of $THB1/m^3$ enforced through a ministerial regulation in 1985) and preservation charges in 2004, had significant impacts on the amount of extraction, particularly on private users as the total cost of using groundwater ($THB17/m^3$) surpassed even the highest possible rate for piped water supply ($THB15.81/m^3$) in 2006. On the other hand, the Cabinet resolution had an immediate effect because, among other provisions, it mandated the phasing out of groundwater use in designated critical zones by all users, including government agencies and state enterprises—such as the Metropolitan Waterworks Authority, which provides public water supply in Bangkok, Nonthaburi and

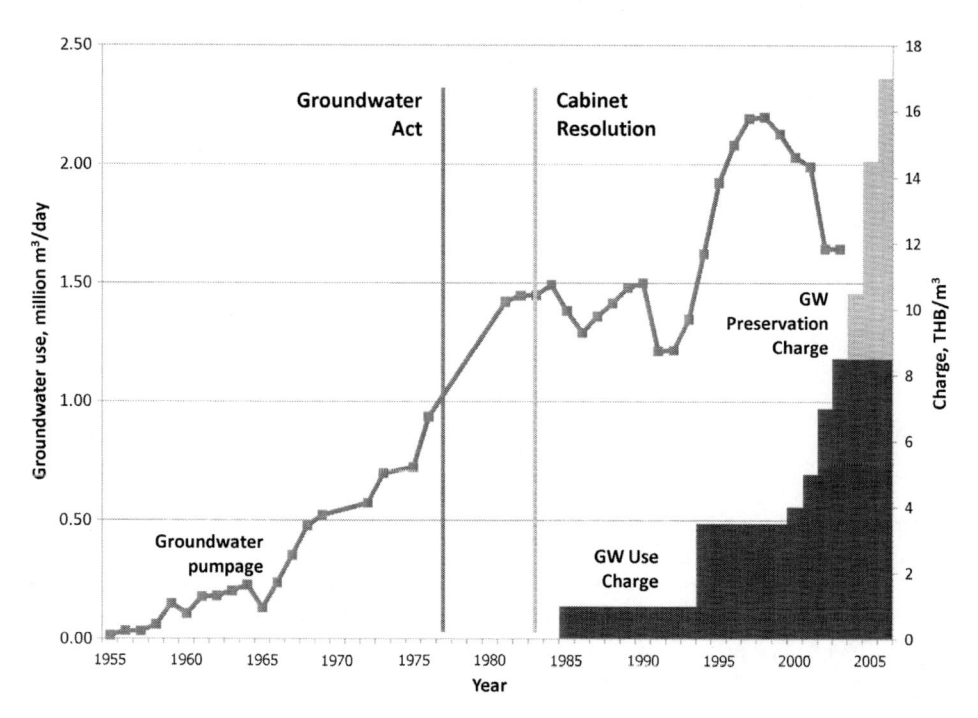

Figure 3. Groundwater use and regulation measures implemented. Data sources: Asian Institute of Technology (2007); Department of Groundwater Resources. *Note:* USD1 = THB30.

Samut Prakan. While the total water supply volume of the MWA continued to increase, its groundwater use decreased until it was completely phased out in 2004.

The effectiveness of the aforementioned measures is evident in the reduction of groundwater extraction, although the decrease after the peak usage in 1997 may indicate the effect of the Asian financial crisis on industries which were the major users of groundwater (Babel & Rivas, 2008). Nonetheless, market-based approaches such as the imposition of preservation charges have clear impacts on reducing groundwater usage; recent information shows a notable decline in use upon implementation of preservation charges in 2003, with estimated groundwater abstraction of approximately 1,100,000 m^3/day in 2007 (Mikita *et al.*, 2011).

As a result, significant improvements in groundwater piezometric levels have been observed (e.g., around 20 m of recovery from the late 1990s to the mid-2000s in the most-affected parts of the Nakon Luang and Nonthaburi aquifers—Babel & Rivas, 2008) and the rate of land subsidence in critical zones has decreased, from more than 100 mm/y in 1981 to less than 30 mm/yr in 2002 (Babel *et al.*, 2006a; Phien-wej *et al.*, 2006). However, such measures were primarily aimed at reducing extraction to address land subsidence; groundwater quality aspects seemed secondary, if they were considered at all. In particular, a specific problem concerning chloride contamination continues to affect groundwater users.

Chloride Contamination in the Bangkok Aquifer System

While it is generally accepted that the Bangkok Aquifer System is less vulnerable to contamination from pollutants introduced at the surface due to the thick Bangkok clay—though with a few exceptions in spots (Metrix Associates, 2004; Thapinta & Hudak, 2003)—intensive or uncontrolled development and abstraction of groundwater could result in deterioration of groundwater quality, such as salinity intrusion or chloride contamination (Foster *et al.*, 2002a).

Saline water intrusion in the Bangkok aquifer system has been observed since 1967 when many municipal wells in the southern parts of Bangkok yielded brackish to saline water (Ramnarong, 1999). Data from the DGR show that chloride levels ranging from 1,000 mg/L to over 11,000 mg/L were found in many locations in the Phra Pradaeng, Nakhon Luang, and Nonthaburi aquifers in the 1980s. As a result, many wells have been abandoned due to the 60-fold increase of chloride levels (Sampat, 2000).

The sources of saline water vary spatially, both horizontally and among aquifers. Seawater intrusion is believed to be a significant factor in elevated chloride concentrations in shallow aquifers (e.g. the Bangkok and Phra Pradaeng aquifers) only in some areas near the coast (Das Gupta, 1985; Dulaiova *et al.*, 2006; Rau & Nutalaya, 1981), whereas saline connate water from sediments is the main cause elsewhere, especially in the Nakhon Luang and Nonthaburi aquifers, given the flow characteristics in the aquifer system and the limited hydrogeologic connection between the deeper aquifers and the sea (Arlai, 2007; Babel & Rivas, 2008; Das Gupta & Yapa, 1982; Rau & Nutalaya, 1981; Stansfield & Garret, 1997; Yamanaka *et al.*, 2011b). The extent of chloride contamination in deeper aquifers had been exacerbated by groundwater pumping, as evident in the high levels of chloride in the late 1990s, coinciding with the peak pumping rate (AIT, 2007; KU, 2004). Such deterioration in groundwater quality is attributed to the migration of saline connate water to freshwater areas, largely through vertical leakage among aquifers due to either inherent hydraulic connectivity or improperly plugged or sealed wells (Arlai, 2007; Das Gupta, 1985; Das Gupta & Yapa, 1982).

Although significant improvements were observed in terms of recovering piezometric levels and reduction of land subsidence rate due to the implemented measures, there is no clear evidence of substantial improvement in chloride levels (Babel & Rivas, 2008). In 2008, the DGR reported to the Cabinet that corresponding significant improvements in groundwater quality remain to be seen and that restoration efforts are not enough. In fact, actions on specific measures included in the Master Plan, such as the artificial storage recovery (ASR) and defining restoration measures in high risk areas (KKU, 2006), are yet to be implemented. Indeed, it is apparent that not much has been done to specifically address chloride contamination in the Bangkok Aquifer System; this could be because there is substantial limitation in fully understanding the mechanism of chloride contamination.

It is, therefore, suggested that efforts should be intensified to increase the understanding of the mechanism of chloride contamination so that appropriate measures can be identified. This is essential because measures for groundwater quality management that are not founded on reliable scientific information are bound to fail (Ronen *et al.*, 2012). Further investigations on the role of aquitards in the leakage among aquifers, specific locations of saline connate water, and the vulnerability of individual aquifers to quality deterioration due to pumping, would be helpful, given that the potential for further deterioration of deeper aquifers is indicated in the significant recharge occurring in the Bangkok clay–covered area due to pumping (Mikita *et al.*, 2011). Though carrying out such studies has substantial cost implications, it should be accorded priority attention because contamination of the resource is almost irreversible and remediation would be even more costly. Sufficient funding could be obtained from the Groundwater

Development Fund (GDF) if rules are loosened to support projects of such nature. At present, funds from the GDF, collected mainly from groundwater use and preservation charges, are difficult to secure because clear mechanisms are not yet defined.

While funding for such studies is being sought, relevant regulations to prevent further deterioration of groundwater quality need to be vigorously enforced. For instance, comprehensive monitoring of groundwater extraction needs to be implemented, such as imposition of the use of meters and revising the manner of reporting actual consumption, which is presently dependent on the users' reports. Close coordination between the DGR, PWA, and local governments in the region in terms of monitoring groundwater abstraction is important because these local governments, especially those not covered by the MWA, and by virtue of the Decentralization Act (1999), also provide public water supply to their constituents from groundwater sources and a number of these production wells are not even registered with the DGR. Revision of the Groundwater Act may be needed to closely monitor groundwater abstraction in shallow aquifers in recharge areas, given that the Act regulates use only for aquifers deeper than 15 m.

Moreover, rules should be strictly implemented, particularly those related to prohibiting the tapping of multiple aquifers and the proper plugging and sealing of production wells to avoid transport of chloride though wells. This underscores the need for adequate technical personnel in the DGR.

Protecting Groundwater from Pollution

Although smaller in extent, instances of groundwater contamination due to introduction of pollutants from anthropogenic activities have been reported. For instance, elevated amounts of nitrate have been found in different parts of the Bangkok Aquifer System. The most common sources of nitrate are municipal and industrial wastewater, septic systems, and use of fertilizers in agricultural lands. In Pathumthani, a neighbouring province directly north of Bangkok, fertilizer application has been found to have increased five-fold the nitrate-nitrogen concentration in groundwater (Pathak *et al.*, 2004). Groundwater quality monitoring records of the DGR also revealed the presence of nitrate in the three most-utilized aquifers (Phra Pradaeng, Nakhon Luang, and Nonthaburi), with 1–6% of samples having concentrations greater than that allowed for drinking, and with much lesser contamination in deeper aquifers (Babel & Rivas, 2008). Such areas with high nitrate concentrations coincide with extensive agricultural areas in Pathumthani, Bangkok, and Nakhon Pathom, as well as orchard areas in Nonthaburi and Samut Sakhon (Umezawa *et al.*, 2009). Evidences of bacterial contamination exceeding drinking water quality standards were also found in shallow groundwater in Bangkok near the On Nuch Waste Disposal Center (Watananugulkit *et al.*, 2003). In addition, small concentrations of volatile organic compounds (VOC) were found in groundwater beneath industrial estates (Channarong *et al.*, 2004).

Safeguarding groundwater resources from pollution could be achieved in two ways: aquifer and wellhead protection. The former is an active measure because it leads to protecting high-risk areas by controlling land use or activities, while the latter is a passive measure because it leads to protecting water supply wells from contaminants (Metrix Associates, 2004). Protection of the aquifer system is important because once groundwater is contaminated, it is extremely costly and exceedingly difficult to return it to its pristine and usable condition.

Aquifer Protection

Several pieces of legislation are in place which do include provisions which could be a basis for the protection of groundwater aquifers. For instance, the Land Development Act of 2008 (ONEP, 2010), repealing the 1983 version, includes provisions on land use planning and measures for improvement and conservation of soil and water resources, and provides the legal basis for the declaration of soil and water conservation areas. The Town Planning Act of 1975 (DCP, 1975) contains provisions for the control and regulation of the use of land with prescribed rules, methods, and conditions under which the owner or occupier of the land must modify, alter, or suspend use of land. More importantly, the Enhancement and Conservation of National Environmental Quality Act (NEQA) of 1992 (repealing the 1975, 1978, and 1979 versions) (DEQP, 2010), considered the most significant environmental legislation, provides the legal basis for the protection and conservation of watershed areas or areas that are naturally composed of fragile ecosystems and are sensitive and vulnerable to destruction or impacts of human activities by declaring them conservation areas or pollution control areas.

Other relevant laws include the Factories Act of 1992 (DIW, 1992a) for the issuance of ministerial rules regarding the standards and methods of controlling discharge of waste, pollutants, or anything that affects the environment as a result of the engagement in a factory business; and the Hazardous Substances Act (1992), replacing the old Toxic Substances Act of 1967 and 1973, which, aside from controlling the production, transport, and disposal of hazardous substances, also includes provision for the designation of areas for prohibition of possession, disposal, or use of any hazardous substance. Interestingly, the Hazardous Substances Act provides exemption from compliance of its provisions for some government agencies, local administrations, state enterprises, and others as identified by the Ministry of Industry (Babel & Rivas, 2008). With such exemptions, it may be difficult to assess the effectiveness of the management of hazardous waste without proper monitoring directed at these agencies.

In accordance with the laws enumerated above, several important regulations and standards have also been promulgated or established. These include wastewater discharge criteria for factories situated in industrial estates; industrial effluent standards; effluent standards for industrial and industrial-estate sources; land effluent standards; soil quality standards; building effluent standards; effluent standards for coastal, brackish, and inland aquaculture; and effluent standards for pig farms, gas stations, and oil terminals, among others (Babel & Rivas, 2008).

The information above provides an impression that there seem to be more than sufficient laws and regulations to protect aquifers from contamination due to anthropogenic activities, such as inappropriate land use and waste disposal. There are some concerns, however, that the focus is more on surface water and groundwater is less regarded. For instance, while Cabinet resolutions released in 1979, 1988, and 1992 (NEB, 1992) identified restricted zones where activities are controlled and prohibit specific industries with toxic substances and heavy metals in wastewater for protecting the surface water sources of the BMR, specific regulations that restrict particular land uses for the purpose of protecting groundwater, especially in recharge areas, are not found (Babel & Rivas, 2008). The sector-wise implementation of the aforementioned legislations may nonetheless have positive effects on groundwater quality, but further study would be needed to determine this.

Aside from the lack of specific regulations for protecting groundwater resources from pollution, lack of enforcement seems to be a major problem. By virtue of the Decentralization Act of 1999, local officials are authorized as pollution control officials to implement the provisions of NEQA. However, local governments have not yet attained capacities and readiness for solving environmental problems (ONEP, 2007). Moreover, the different functions of individual government agencies could be a hindrance for the successful implementation of relevant measures. For instance, the Department of Industrial Works is mandated to ensure compliance of factories concerning proper treatment and disposal of wastewater. Though it conducts inspections, DIW records suggest that enforcement is inadequate. This could be because the main task of the DIW is to support and promote industrial development (Nippon Koei, 1999).

Moreover, specific local regulations seem lacking. Phien-wej et al., (2006) argued that there is a lack of land use zoning laws for managing the growth of Bangkok and the utilization of its infrastructure and facilities. This, surely, has implications for the quality of groundwater resources in the area if appropriate actions are not in place.

Efficient protection of groundwater resources from contamination requires information on priority or vulnerable areas so that limited resources can be directed appropriately. Several studies have already identified the recharge areas of the Bangkok Aquifer System (Metrix Associates, 2004; Mikita et al., 2011) and pinpointed the vulnerable and high-risk areas (Metrix Associates, 2004). As an illustration, DGR data from one monitoring well in Nakhon Pathom showed nitrate concentrations of more than 200 mg/L (Babel & Rivas, 2008), which is much higher than the Thai drinking water quality standard (45 mg/L), and this is of particular concern as the area appears to be part of the recharge area of the aquifers and considering also that groundwater is extensively used for domestic consumption in this area. However, there seems to be lack of attention given to these areas to ensure that groundwater resources are protected. As a matter of fact, recommendations of a study conducted for the protection of groundwater quality in the Central Plain of Bangkok (Metrix Associates, 2004), such as the designation of groundwater protection zones and the implementation of the polluters-pay principle, have yet to be implemented (Babel & Rivas, 2008). An important step towards protecting such areas is to declare them conservation or pollution control areas or to revise environmental quality standards for these areas in accordance with NEQA so that appropriate mechanisms can be enforced. In relation to this, there are indications as to the need of sharing of relevant information by the DGR with other agencies, because it seems that other agencies, the PCD for example, are not aware of some relevant information, such as the locations of recharge areas so that appropriate measures may be implemented to protect them. Moreover, potential sources of pollution need to be distinguished so that appropriate monitoring and control mechanisms can be established to prevent contamination.

Wellhead Protection

Among the factors implicated in the transport of contaminants in the Bangkok aquifer system is the leakage of contaminated water through unplugged or improperly plugged wells, as indicated in the distribution of chloride concentration in specific locations (Das Gupta, 1985; Das Gupta & Yapa, 1982). While regulations exist requiring a well to tap only one aquifer (Babel & Rivas, 2008), in reality groundwater production wells are reportedly tapping several aquifers, especially in areas of high consumption.

To protect aquifers from contamination at the wellhead, guidelines are provided concerning the draining or discharging of water into groundwater wells. In fact, standards of quality of water to be pumped into groundwater wells have been established (Babel & Rivas, 2008). Moreover, the Groundwater Act and several ministerial regulations and notifications explicitly require the grouting or sealing of well holes around casings so that groundwater from other aquifers will not mix with the tapped aquifer, the protection of the well against the entry of outside water, and the plugging of terminated or abandoned wells. However, previous regulations (such as Ministry of Industry notifications nos. 4, 10, and 12, as referred to in Babel & Rivas, 2008) state that the plugging of wells requires the supervision of a certified engineer or geologist only for wells with diameters larger than 100 mm. As a result, it is highly likely that many wells might have been abandoned and improperly plugged, resulting in leaks in the well. This, however, has been corrected with an MoNRE regulation released in 2008 which now requires that all plugging be in accordance with approved materials and methods and should be done under the supervision of a certified technician and with the presence of a local groundwater office staff. With this revision, the authorities hope that no more terminated or abandoned wells contribute to the leakage of contaminated water into other areas or aquifers.

Thus, while there have been some positive developments concerning regulations for the drilling and plugging of wells to protect groundwater resources, what remains to be seen is the determination of authorities to enforce such important regulations. Efficient enforcement needs significant resources and it is important to consider the availability of sufficient numbers of specialized or trained personnel. Earnest measures also need to be implemented to protect wells from flooding, which frequently occurs in the region, and this entails strict enforcement of regulations or standards related to proper location and drainage around wells.

Moreover, although laws and regulations impose penalties for violations, there have been very few environmental criminal prosecutions pursued or penalties levied. Current penal laws were found to have had minimal deterrent effect. With the increasing awareness of environmental problems and increasing attention to environmental laws, it is reasonable to expect more attention to enforcement and heavier punishment for violators in the future (Tilleke and Gibbins, 2007).

Groundwater Quality Monitoring

Information on groundwater quantity and quality in Bangkok has been collected as early as 1965. However, it was only in 1978 that the groundwater monitoring network was established with 60 observation wells. The distribution and density of the monitoring wells was based on the importance of areas for supply, the rates of decline of the piezometric levels, and land subsidence in each area (Ramnarong, 1999). With a network of monitoring stations across the region, information on water levels, ground surface elevations, and concentrations of several water quality parameters have been continuously being recorded, first by the Groundwater Division of the Department of Mineral Resources and now by the DGR. As of 2008, there were 144 stations with a total of 462 monitoring wells under operation, with most stations having at least 3 monitoring wells to cover the Phra Pradaeng, Nakhon Luang, and Nonthaburi aquifers (Figure 4). The DGR plans to increase the number of stations and wells to cover areas where data are desired.

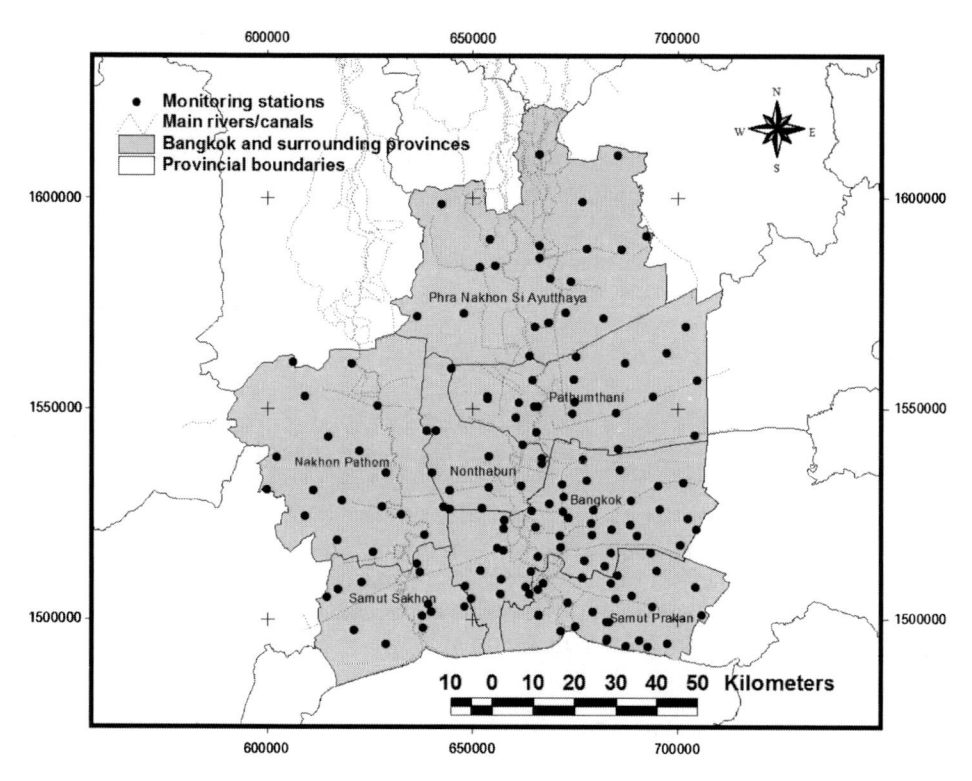

Figure 4. Distribution of monitoring stations in the Bangkok Metropolitan Region. Data source: DGR records as of 2008.

With the general understanding that the quality of groundwater does not change abruptly, collection of groundwater samples from the monitoring wells is usually done once a year, in contrast to groundwater level measurements, which are conducted monthly. While the DGR has specific procedures for collecting groundwater samples, their implementation remains suspect, particularly with respect to the amount of purging required and the proper scheduling to obtain reliable data. This should not be taken for granted, because the quality of data is paramount in groundwater quality management (Ronen *et al.*, 2012; Tuinhof *et al.*, 2002). Moreover, the DGR prepares and publishes annual reports on groundwater levels and quality, but water quality data are not actually synchronized with piezometric level data. Though such annual reports include isochlor maps, the degree of chloride contamination is oversimplified in that the range used does not reflect variations in concentrations above 1,000 mg/L, which covers a large portion of the BMR. An operational database which could be accessed by other relevant agencies such as the PCD and DEQP to aid in planning is also lacking.

It is also important to note that fewer groundwater quality parameters (18) are being regularly monitored, compared to the number in groundwater quality standards for drinking (23) or for conservation (38). Parameters being monitored at present include calcium, chloride, carbonate, calcium carbonate, fluoride, iron, bicarbonate, potassium, magnesium, manganese, sodium, nitrite, nitrate, hardness, pH, sulfate, electrical conductivity, and TDS. Only recently (2008) has the DGR planned to collect and analyze samples for heavy metals and VOC; whether this will be part of the overall monitoring system is unclear. There is thus an immediate need to re-evaluate the objectives of monitoring, and, given the financial constraints, to identify the most important parameters to be monitored based on recent information available, especially considering the presence of micropollutants such as pesticides, nitrate, and bacteriological contaminants in several areas, in some of which groundwater is widely used for drinking (Kruawal *et al.*, 2005).

Given that groundwater within major productive aquifers in the central BMA is mainly replenished by downward leakage across confining layers (Onodera *et al.*, 2009; Yamanaka *et al.*, 2011b), the importance of monitoring the quality of groundwater in upper aquifers cannot be overemphasized. The potential for contamination of the deeper aquifers may be sufficiently known if the uppermost (Bangkok) aquifer, which has extensive high chloride contamination, is sufficiently monitored, considering that the shallow aquifers are hydraulically connected with the *klongs* in Bangkok (Burnett *et al.*, 2009) which are exposed to pollution, and this aquifer is hydraulically connected with underlying aquifers (Arlai, 2007; Das Gupta & Sabanathan, 1988; Rau & Nutalaya, 1981).

Furthermore, there has been no known regulation for the monitoring and reporting of groundwater quality data from groundwater production wells by private well owners or other government agencies. At present, groundwater quality data are only required during groundwater drilling and well development or test pumping. Although well owners may be collecting information on the quality of the groundwater they are using, regular monitoring and reporting of groundwater quality data from selected abstraction or production wells would provide a more complete picture of groundwater quality changes and trends.

Concluding Remarks

The limited attention given to the protection of groundwater resources in the Bangkok Aquifer System from pollution and prevention of further quality deterioration may be attributed to the reliance on the natural protection provided by the thick clay layer, the availability of good-quality groundwater in deeper aquifers, and the availability of surface water for public water supply. However, the importance of conserving and improving the quality of groundwater should not be set aside, given that the potential of contamination from anthropogenic activities exists. Active collaboration among relevant agencies is essential to protect the resources from further deterioration and this underscores the need for adequate technical staffing and accurate and extensive monitoring and timely sharing of groundwater quality data.

Considering that groundwater is intended to be used at the optimal level to support economic development without compromising the society and the environment, a total or extensive ban of groundwater use over a large area like the Bangkok Metropolitan Region is not a preferred measure because it will neglect the benefits that can be obtained from the use of the resource. Moreover, the importance of the resource is expected to be recognized more given the increasing demand for water and that the abundance of surface water is threatened by the changing climate in which Thailand is expected to receive less precipitation in the future (Bates *et al.*, 2008). Yet, if groundwater extractions are not properly regulated on the basis of reliable information on mechanisms of groundwater flow and salinity intrusion, groundwater quality could deteriorate further, given the trend of increasing extraction from deeper aquifers. Sufficient funding should be allocated for studies that improve the understanding of the role of aquitards in chloride contamination, delineation of saline connate water areas, and the vulnerability of individual aquifers with respect to groundwater pumping. These measures, targeted to addressing groundwater quality issues, need to be implemented alongside quantity-related measures for comprehensive sustainable management and use of the resource.

References

Achalabhuti, C. (1974) Petroleum geology of the Gulf of Thailand, Paper presented at the *Conference on Circum-Pacific Energy and Mineral Resources,* Honolulu, Hawaii, 26–30 August (Tulsa, OK: American Association of Petroleum Geologists).

Arlai, P. (2007) *Numerical modeling of possible saltwater intrusion mechanism in the multiple-layer coastal aquifer system of the Gulf of Thailand,* Ph.D. dissertation, University of Kassel, Germany. Available at: http://www.upress.uni-kassel.de/online/frei/978-3-89958-293-2.volltext.frei.pdf (accessed 28 August 2008).

Asian Institute of Technology [AIT] (1982) *Groundwater Resources in Bangkok Area: Development and Management Study: Comprehensive Report 1978–1982,* Research report no. 137, submitted to the Office of National Environment Board and Department of Mineral Resources (Pathumthani, Thailand: Asian Institute of Technology).

Asian Institute of Technology [AIT] (2007) *Sustainable Water Management Policy (SWMP) Study on Groundwater Management, Bangkok, Thailand,* Case study report submitted to the Institute for Global Environmental Strategies (IGES), Japan (Pathumthani, Thailand: Asian Institute of Technology).

Babel, M. S., Das Gupta, A. & Sto. Domingo, N. D. (2006a) Land subsidence: a consequence of groundwater exploitation in Bangkok, Thailand, *International Review for Environmental Strategies,* 6(2), pp. 307–328.

Babel, M. S., Das Gupta, A. & Sto. Domingo, N. D. (2006b) Policy measures and options for improved groundwater resources management in Bangkok, Thailand, *Regional Development Dialogue,* 27(1), pp. 108–129.

Babel, M. S. & Rivas, A. A. (2008) *Groundwater quality management policy research in Bangkok and vicinity,* Final research report submitted to the Institute for Global Environmental Strategies (IGES), Japan (Pathumthani, Thailand: Asian Institute of Technology).

Bates, B. C., Kundzewicz, Z. W., Wu, S. & Palutikof, J. P. (Eds) (2008) *Climate Change and Water,* Technical paper (Geneva: Intergovernmental Panel on Climate Change).

Burnett, W., Chanyotha, S., Wattayakorn, G., Taniguchi, M., Umezawa, Y. & Ishitobi, T. (2009) Underground sources of nutrient contamination to surface waters in Bangkok, Thailand, *Science of the Total Environment,* 407(9), pp. 3198–3207.

Channarong, S., Milintawisamai, M., Soonthornteja, P. & Boonsongpairaj, S. (2004) Development of technique on investigation of groundwater contamination by volatile organic compounds (VOC) from industry, in: *Research Report of Environmental Research and Training Center of DEQP: 2001–2003* (Bangkok: Department of Environmental Quality Promotion).

Das Gupta, A. (1985) Simulated salt-water movement in the Nakhon Luang aquifer, Bangkok, Thailand, *Ground Water,* 23(4), pp. 512–522.

Das Gupta, A. & Babel, M. S. (2005) Challenges for sustainable management of groundwater use in Bangkok, *Water Resources Development,* 21(3), pp. 453–464.

Das Gupta, A. & Sabanathan, S. (1988) Saltwater transport in a heterogeneous formation: a case study, *Transport in Porous Media,* 3, pp. 217–256.

Das Gupta, A. & Yapa, P. (1982) Saltwater encroachment in an aquifer: a case study, *Water Resources Research,* 18(3), pp. 546–556.

Department of City Planning (DCP) (1975) Town Planning Act 1975. Available at: http://cpd.bangkok.go.th/eng-map.html (accessed 29 March 2012) .

Department of Environmental Quality Promotion (DEQP) (2010) The Enhancement and Conservation of National Environment Quality Act 1992. Available at: http://www.deqp.go.th/website/52/index.php?option=com_content&view=article&id=3988&Itemid=92&lang=en (accessed 27 March 2012).

Department of Groundwater Resources (DGR) (1977) Groundwater Act 1977 (in Thai). Available at: http://www.ratchakitcha.soc.go.th/DATA/PDF/2520/A/069/8.PDF (accessed 28 March 2012) .

Department of Groundwater and Resources (DGR) (1983) Cabinet Resolution 1983 (in Thai). Available at: http://gcl.dgr.go.th/pdf/groundwater_Act.pdf (accessed 29 March 2012).

Department of Industrial Works (DIW) (1992a) Factories Act 1992 (in Thai). Available at: http://hawk.diw.go.th/content.php?mode=laws&tabid=1 (accessed 27 March 2012).

Department of Industrial Works (DIW) (1992b) Hazardous Substance Act 1992 (in Thai). Available at: http://haw
k.diw.go.th/content.php?mode=laws&tabid=3 (Accessed 27 March 2012) .

Dulaiova, H., Burnett, W., Wattayakorn, G. & Sojisuporn, P. (2006) Are groundwater inputs into river-dominated
areas important? The Chao Phraya River – Gulf of Thailand, *Limnology and Oceanography*, 51(5),
pp. 2232–2247.

Foster, S., Lawrence, A. & Morris, B. (1998) *Groundwater in urban development: assessing management needs
and formulating policy strategies* Technical Paper 390 (Washington, DC: World Bank).

Foster, S., Garduño, H., Kemper, K., Tuinhof, A., Nanni, M. & Dumars, C. (2002a) *Groundwater Quality
Protection: Defining Strategy and Setting Priorities*, GW-MATE Briefing Note No. 8 (Washington, DC:
World Bank).

Foster, S., Tuinhof, A., Kemper, K., Garduño, H. & Nanni, M. (2002b) *Characterization of Groundwater
Systems: Key Concepts and Frequent Misconceptions*, GW-MATE Briefing Note No. 2 (Washington, DC:
World Bank).

Japan International Cooperation Agency (JICA) (1995) *The Study on Management of Groundwater and Land
Subsidence in the Bangkok Metropolitan Area and Its Vicinity, Final Report* (Tokyo: Japan International
Cooperation Agency).

Kasetsart University (KU) (2004) *Effect of Groundwater Over-Pumping Mitigation: Mathematical Model Study.*
Final project report submitted to the Department of Groundwater Resources, Bangkok, Thailand (Bangkok:
Kasetsart University).

Khon Kaen University (KKU) (2006) *Master Plan of Groundwater Management and Development*, Final report
submitted to the Department of Groundwater Resources, Bangkok, Thailand (Khon Kaen, Thailand: Khon
Kaen University).

Kruawal, K., Sacher, F., Werner, A., Müller, J. & Knepper, T. (2005) Chemical water quality in Thailand and its
impacts on the drinking water production in Thailand, *Science of the Total Environment*, 340, pp. 57–70.

Metrix Associates Co., Ltd (2004) *The Study of Groundwater Quality Protection in the Central Plain*, Final
project report submitted to the Department of Groundwater Resources, Bangkok, Thailand (Bangkok: Metrix
Associates).

Mikita, M., Yamanaka, T. & Lorphensri, O. (2011) Anthropogenic changes in a confined groundwater flow sytem
in the Bangkok basin, Thailand. Part I: Was groundwater-recharge enhanced? *Hydrological Processes*,
25(17), pp. 2726–2733.

National Environmental Board (NEB) (1992) Cabinet resolutions released in 1979, 1988 and 1992. Available at:
http://www.wepa-db.net/policies/law/thailand/restricted_zone.htm (accessed 27 March 2012) .

Nippon Koei Co., Ltd (1999) *The Study for the Master Plan on Sewage Sludge Treatment/Disposal and
Reclaimed Wastewater Reuse in Bangkok in the Kingdom of Thailand*, Final report (main report) (Tokyo:
Japan International Cooperation Agency and Bangkok Metropolitan Administration).

Nitivattananon, V. (2006) Comments on the article Babel *et al.*, (2006), "Policy Measures and Options for
Improved groundwater Resources Management in Bangkok, Thailand", *Regional Development Dialogue*,
27(1), pp. 132–134.

Office of Natural Resources and Environmental Policy and Planning (ONEP) (2004) *State of Environment Report
2004* (Bangkok: Office of Natural Resources and Environmental Policy and Planning, Ministry of Natural
Resources and Environment).

Office of Natural Resources and Environmental Policy and Planning (ONEP) (2007) *Preparation of the
Environmental Management Plan B.E. 2550–2554 (2007–2011) Project: Executive Summary* (Bangkok: Office
of Natural Resources and Environmental Policy and Planning, Ministry of Natural Resources and Environment).
Available at: http://www.onep.go.th/oneb/appimages/download/26.pdf (in Thai) (accessed 10 March 2008).

Office of Natural Resources and Environmental Policy and Planning (ONEP) (2010) *Thailand's National
Capacity Self-Assessment: United Nations Convention to Combat Desertification*, p. 96, (Bangkok: Office of
Natural Resources and Environmental Policy and Planning, Ministry of Natural Resources and
Environment). Available at: http://chm-thai.onep.go.th/chm/Doc/NCSA/TH_NCSA_UNCCD_final_report.
pdf (accessed 29 March 2012).

Onodera, S., Saito, M., Sawano, M., Hosono, T., Taniguchi, M., Shimada, J., Umezawa, Y., Lubis, R., Buapeng,
S. & Delinom, R. (2009) Erratum to "Effects of intensive urbanization on the intrusion of shallow
groundwater into deep groundwater: examples from Bangkok and Jakarta", *Science of the Total
Environment*, 407(9), pp. 3209–3217.

Pathak, B. K., Kazama, F. & Iida, T. (2004) Monitoring of nitrogen leaching from a tropical paddy field in Thailand, *Agricultural Engineering International: the CIGR Journal of Scientific Research and Development*, 6(4), pp. 2–9.

Phien-wej, N., Giao, P. & Nutalaya, P. (2006) Land subsidence in Bangkok, Thailand, *Engineering Geology*, 82, pp. 187–201.

Piancharoen, C. & Chuamthaisong, C. (1976) Groundwater of Bangkok Metropolis, Thailand, in: *Proceedings of the International Hydrogeological Conference,* 31 May to 5 June, 1976, Budapest .

Piyasena, N. (1982) *Rehabilitation of a depleted aquifer system through artificial recharge—an application to Bangkok*, Doctoral dissertation No. GT-82-1, Asian Institute of Technology, Bangkok, Thailand.

Ramnarong, V. (1999) Evaluation of groundwater management in Bangkok: positive and negative, in: J. Chilton (Ed.) *Groundwater in the Urban Environment: Proceedings of the 27th IAH Congress*, pp. 51–62 (Rotterdam: Balkema).

Ramnarong, V. & Buapeng, S. (1992) Groundwater resources of Bangkok and its vicinity impact and management, in: *Proceedings, Geological Resources of Thailand: Potential for Future Development, Bangkok, Thailand,*17–24 November, pp. 172–184.

Ramnarong, V., Buapeng, S., Chootnatut, S. & Loupensri, A. (1998) *Groundwater and land subsidence crisis in Bangkok metropolitan and vicinity*, Technical Report, Vol. 3/1998 (Bangkok, Thailand: Department of Mineral Resources) .

Rau, J. & Nutalaya, P. (1981) Chloride contamination in aquifers of the Central Plain, Thailand, *Geotechnical Engineering*, 12, pp. 123–151.

Ronen, D., Sorek, S. & Gilron, J. (2012) Rationales behind irrationality of decision making in groundwater quality management, *Ground Water*, 50(1), pp. 27–36.

Sampat, P. (2000) *Deep Trouble: The Hidden Threat of Groundwater Pollution*, Worldwatch Paper 154 (Washington, DC: Worldwatch Institute). Available at: http://www.worldwatch.org/system/files/EWP154.pdf (accessed 15 April 2007).

Sinsakul, S. (2000) Late Quaternary geology of the Lower Central Plain, Thailand, *Journal of Asian Earth Sciences*, 18, pp. 415–426.

Stansfield, K. & Garrett, C. (1997) Implications of the salt and heat budgets of the Gulf of Thailand, *Journal of Marine Research*, 55, pp. 935–963.

Thapinta, A. & Hudak, P. (2003) Use of geographic information systems for assessing groundwater pollution by pesticides in Central Thailand, *Environment International*, 29, pp. 87–93.

Tilleke & Gibbins International (2011) *Thailand Legal Basics, updated December 14, 2011.* Available at: http://www.tilleke.com/resources/thailand-legal-basics (accessed 27 March 2012).

Todd, D. (1959) *Ground Water Hydrology* (New York: Wiley).

Tuinhof, A., Foster, S., Kemper, K., Garduño, H. & Nanni, M. (2002) *Groundwater Monitoring Requirements for Managing Aquifer Response and Quality Threats*, GW-MATE Briefing Note No. 9 (Washington, DC: World Bank).

Umezawa, Y., Hosono, T., Onodera, S., Siringan, F., Buapeng, S., Delinom, R., Yoshimizu, C., Tayasu, I., Nagata, T. & Taniguchi, M. (2009) Erratum to "Sources of nitrate and ammonium contamination in groundwater under developing Asian megacities", *Science of the Total Environment*, 407(9), pp. 3219–3231.

United Nations Environment Programme (UNEP) (2003) *Groundwater and Its Susceptibility to Degradation: A Global Assessment of the Problem and Options for Management* (Nairobi: UNEP Division of Early Warning and Assessment).

Watananugulkit, R., Intim, C., Patnukao, P. & Tansathit, P. (2003) Assessment of impact on water quality of leachate at On-nuch Disposal Site Center in Bangkok, *Journal of Scientific Research Chulalongkorn University*, 28, pp. 97–110, (Special Issue 1, NRC-EHWM).

Weist, D. (2002) *Thailand's decentralization: Progress and prospects*, Decentralization and Local Government in Thailand, The KPI Congress III, pp. 425–456 (Nonthaburi, Thailand: King Phapokkao Institute).

Yamanaka, T., Mikita, M., Lorphensri, O., Shimada, J., Kagabu, M., Ikawa, R., Nakamura, T. & Tsujimura, M. (2011a) Anthropogenic changes in a confined groundwater flow system in the Bangkok Basin, Thailand. Part II: How much water has been renewed? *Hydrological Processes*, 25(17), pp. 2734–2741.

Yamanaka, T., Shimada, J., Tsujimura, M., Lorphensri, O., Mikita, M., Hagihara, A. & Onodera, S. (2011b) Tracing a confined groundwater flow system under the pressure of excessive groundwater use in the lower central plain, Thailand, *Hydrological Processes*, 25(17), pp. 2654–2664.

Zaporozec, A. & Miller, J. (2000) *Ground-Water Pollution* (Paris: UNESCO).

Nutrient Balance Assessment in the Mekong Basin: Nitrogen and Phosphorus Dynamics in a Catchment Scale

INA LILJESTRÖM, MATTI KUMMU & OLLI VARIS

Water & Development Research Group, Aalto University, Finland

ABSTRACT *Tropical regions are typically rather poorly covered by nutrient enrichment information, despite th eir soaring population, urbanization, industrialization, and intensifying agriculture. We provide an overview of nutrient fluxes and their temporal and spatial patterns in the Mekong River for 1985–2005. Total inorganic nitrogen fluxes increased significantly, while phosphorus fluxes increased less steeply. The majority of fluxes originated from agricultural and from forest and shrubland areas. Although the Mekong is not yet facing severe water quality problems, the concurrent rapid development can be expected to accelerate nutrient enrichment. There is thus an urgent need to improve water quality monitoring and pollution control measures, and to give water quality issues more weight at the policy level.*

Introduction

Global riverine nitrogen and phosphorus inputs into the oceans have tripled during the second half of the 20th century due to human impact (Jennerjahn *et al.*, 2004). Numerous studies exist on catchment-level changes that influence nutrient cycling and lead to nutrient enrichment, changes in algal and fish ecology, deterioration of water for drinking and recreational purposes, and other consequences (e.g. Meybeck & Helmer, 1992; IOC, 1994; Kristensen & Hansen, 1994; Bootsma & Hecky, 1999; Smith *et al.*, 2003; Jennerjahn *et al.*, 2004; LWA, 2005). The critical nutrient levels at which eutrophication occurs, however, vary from one aquatic environment to another (see e.g. Di & Cameron, 2002). Regarding, among others, algal growth, there are significant differences between tropical and temperate regions (WHO, 1999).

Tropical aquatic environments are known to support a broad variety of ecosystems and biodiversity (Dudgeon, 2000). Nevertheless, there is generally little quantitative information on various processes, structures, and functions of tropical river systems (LWA, 2005; Sidle *et al.*, 2006). Meybeck (1982), already over a quarter of century ago, concluded that nutrient mass balances of watersheds in the tropics are much less studied than those in the temperate regions. This bias is still today more than obvious.

The Mekong is Southeast Asia's largest international river and one of the planet's greatest river systems. It has a drainage area of 795,000 km^2 and a length of 4,800 km (MRC, 2005) (Figure 1). Regarding water quality, the Mekong is not as well studied as other large tropical rivers, yet its nutrient concentrations are reported to be relatively low compared to some other tropical rivers (Voss *et al.*, 2006). Water quality and nutrient balances in general are generally reported to indicate only small or modest human influence (e.g. Booty, 2001; White, 2002; Snidvongs & Teng, 2006; Campbell, 2007; MRC, 2007, 2010).

In the Mekong, problems (e.g. algal blooms related to eutrophication) are most often considered to be local, seasonal, and moderate in impact (Booty, 2001; Snidvongs & Teng, 2006). However, during the past two decades, increasing amounts of wastewater and agricultural high-nutrient-content leaching water have entered the river through its tributaries (Snidvongs & Teng, 2006). Booty (2001) found that the nutrients generated from urban centres such as Vientiane and Phnom Penh have a potential to cause concern in the future. Fedra *et al.* (1991) found that tributaries in north-east Thailand showed signs of eutrophication, and such signs continue to exist (Snidvongs & Teng, 2006). Kummu *et al.* (2006), Lamberts (2006), and Lamberts & Koponen (2008) pointed out that scientific information on eutrophication and related production biology of Tonle Sap Lake remains elusive, and Varis & Keskinen (2006) emphasized the high uncertainties and risks in drawing any conclusions on the threats to its eutrophication. Campbell (2007, p. 12), after analyzing the Mekong River Commission's (MRC's) water quality monitoring results, concluded, however, that water quality is not a "serious issue in the lower Mekong either now or in the immediate future". MRC (2010) represents a sharply contrasting view, reporting significantly growing trends in concentrations of total phosphorus and ammonium in the Mekong mainstream, and a decreasing trend in dissolved oxygen. An alert was given for certain nutrient enrichment hotspots located at the delta and around major urban centres, plus on the possible negative water quality impact of the intensive dam construction in the basin (MRC, 2010, pp. 60–68).

The most challenging water quality issue in the Mekong River is probably in the delta in Vietnam. According to Fedra *et al.* (1991), the mainstreams of the delta were already too contaminated to be used as drinking water in the early 1990s. The MRC (2003, 2010) has reported phosphorus levels in the delta that approach those typical for eutrophic waters and excessive algal blooms. Eutrophication occurs annually (Snidvongs & Teng, 2006), and nutrient concentrations are increasing (Campbell, 2007). White (2002) suggested an increasing trend in nutrient levels in the Mekong and Bassac Rivers in the lower parts of the basin. Campbell (2007) maintained that the water quality in the delta is poor, the phosphorus concentrations corresponding to those of a eutrophic temperate stream according to the classification by Dodds *et al.* (1998).

Altogether, Booty (2001, p. 24) concluded, "there appears to be little research data on the key nutrient processes taking place in the Mekong River system". According to Hawkins & Suthep (2005), there is a lack of information on nutrient limitations and their magnitude in the Lower Mekong Basin (LMB; see division between LMB and Upper Mekong Basin in Figure 1). Hart *et al.* concluded (2001, p. 30) that sufficient water quality data exist to conduct only a "preliminary assessment of the potential for eutrophic conditions to exist", underlining that important chlorophyll *a* concentration data are lacking for the entire LMB. The nutrient data availability has been improving considerably ever since, as manifested by MRC (2010), yet biological data as well as chlorophyll *a* trends await improvement.

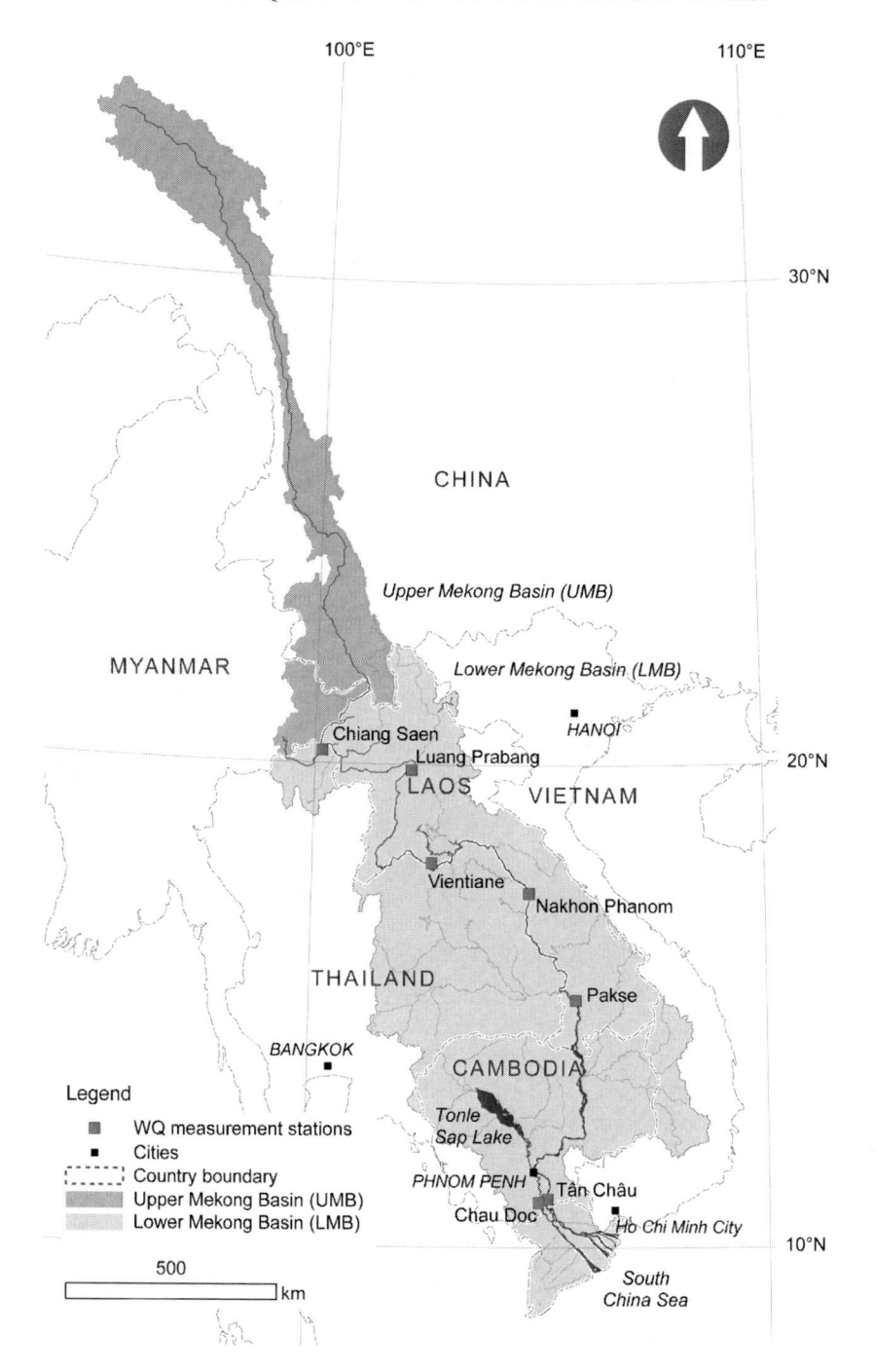

Figure 1. Map of the Mekong basin and water quality (WQ) measurement stations used in this study (modified from Johnston & Kummu, 2012).

Economic activities and land use changes have, however, increased rapidly within the Mekong River Basin (MRB) during the past decades (see e.g. White, 2002; MRC, 2003, 2005, 2010; Iida et al., 2004; Lu & Siew, 2006; Hart & Pollino, 2007; Keskinen et al., Forthcoming). Further, the Mekong is at the moment under extremely rapid economic development, which includes various water-resources-related projects, such as hydro-power projects and irrigation schemes (see e.g. Keskinen, 2006, 2008; Sokhem & Sunada, 2006, 2008; King et al., 2007; Varis et al., 2008). In terms of population growth, it is estimated that the population of the Mekong River basin will increase from 72 million (the estimate for the year 2000) to over 100 million by 2050 (Varis et al., 2012). Increasing human population densities have usually been found to cause increased stream nutrient amounts within a catchment (Peierls et al., 1991). According to Bootsma & Hecky (1999), land use within a catchment area is connected to water characteristics and quality. Yoshimura et al. (2009) indeed predict an increase of 13–25% in nutrient levels in the Mekong mainstream by the 2020s.

This paper has two goals. The first is to assess the status of nitrogen and phosphorus dynamics in the Mekong on the basis of available data. Different features of the nutrient dynamics, such as fluxes, seasonal variations, and trends, are calculated and analyzed. This information provides a needed overview on the current levels of nutrients in the Mekong mainstream, as most existing studies only tackle local water quality (e.g. Iida et al., 2011; Irvine et al., 2011) or future predictions (Campbell, 2007; Yoshimura et al., 2009), and thus information on the overall picture, observed trends as well as connecting nutrient fluxes to land use, is limited. The second goal is to find a method that could be used to estimate and describe the nutrient dynamics in terms of leaching and fluxes of the LMB, for which geoinformatic system data exists. Such a method could describe how the nutrient fluxes are distributed geographically and by land cover type over the LMB.

Data and Methods

Water Quality Data and Analysis

Water quality data was analyzed to obtain information on the Mekong's nutrient fluxes. The entire basin's export rates of nitrogen and phosphorus (kg/ha/y) were estimated. Monitoring data series from 1985 to 2005 were provided by the MRC. The MRC has monitored the water quality of the LMB since 1985 at a total of 98 water quality sampling stations (MRC, 2003). The analyzed elements include nitrate plus nitrite (NO_{32}), ammonium (NH_4), total nitrogen (TIN), orthophosphate (PO_4), and total phosphorus (TOTP) at five mainstream sites and two delta sites. For the two delta sites we had data only for limited number of years; thus, those stations were not used in the trend analysis.

Four different analyses were carried out:

- The average monthly flux and concentration of nutrients were calculated for the monitoring sites with data records of 15–20 years in order to find out which months carry the largest nutrient amounts.
- The correlation between flooding and riverine nutrient transportation was analyzed to see whether larger water amounts always transport larger nutrient amounts or if the process is more complex.
- Trend analyses were conducted for nutrient delivery peak months (July–September) for the years 1985–2005 by using a Mann-Kendal test (Mann, 1945;

Kendall, 1975) and Sen's (1968) slope estimate. The analyses were done with the MAKESENS spreadsheet template (Salmi *et al.*, 2002).

- The average annual TIN and TOTP fluxes transported by the Mekong River at five mainstream sites and at two delta sites were calculated (see station locations in Figure 1). The results give an indication of the river's average annual nutrient load into the ocean as well as average nutrient export rates (nutrient · kg/ha/y) at the included sites.

Methods: Catchment Scale Nutrient Flux Modelling

The modelling part includes an experimental assessment of the LMB's nutrient fluxes. We aimed to identify an appropriate catchment-scale model in order to estimate nutrient fluxes of the LMB on the catchment scale. Nutrient assessment methods provide information on where nutrients enter the river and can thus be used to assess nutrient policies and their effectiveness (EEA, 2005). TIN and TOTP were included. Due to limited data availability, the modelling of nutrient fluxes was only applied to the LMB, and not to the entire Mekong River basin.

Booty (2001) recommended that the nutrient loadings into the Mekong River system be determined for later mass balance modelling of the river. Current data and knowledge do not enable more than one-dimensional nutrient studies; a simple empirical model is suggested to be used first (Booty, 2001). Sidle *et al.* (2006) underlined that it is important to develop an appropriate approach for modelling catchment processes in tropical Asia, where data are scarce. For basin-wide assessments, simple methods are more suitable, according to Vassiljev & Stålnacke (2005).

After a review of 40 different models (Liljeström, 2007), the WinCMSS approach (Atech Group, 2000) was chosen to model the nutrient fluxes of the LMB. The method was found straightforward, robust, and relatively flexible, not requiring large amounts of detailed data. WinCMSS estimates the diffuse nutrient emissions, which is suitable for the LMB, where industry and population are scarce. The model uses a consistent technique for the whole basin and relatively quickly gives indicative estimations for the basin's nutrient dynamics. The method is linear and allows calculations to be conducted in spreadsheets (e.g. Microsoft Excel). WinCMSS does not generate new water quality or other data, but only manipulates existing information. The disadvantages include that the method is not able to estimate nutrient retention, that is the movement or transformation of nutrients across the landscape or through the river system (e.g. sedimentation, assimilation, and denitrification).

The WinCMSS method estimates annual diffuse nutrient exports on the basis of nutrient export coefficients and on spatial land-cover data. In this study, the method's estimations were further improved by adding a modifying factor that considers the different LMB sub-areas' annual runoff rates. The results are given in tonnes per year (t/y) and as average generation rates (kg/ha/y). We used land cover data prepared from MRC (2001) and runoff data from MRC (2005). Table 1 shows the land cover types and their respective areas within the LMB.

A nutrient export coefficient expresses the nutrient amount that is generated from a land cover type per unit area and unit time (Novotny, 2003). According to the Atech Group (2000), studies have shown that nutrient leaching from different land cover types are often similar to each other, even when located in different geographical regions. A literature review did not identify estimates or empirical research results on LMB nutrient export rates.

Table 1. The areas of the land cover categories and their percentages of the total area of the LMB (MRC, 2001), presented together with the corresponding N and P export coefficients used in the assessment.

Land cover category	Area (1,000 ha)	Area (% of total)	N export (kg/ha/y)	P export (kg/ha/y)
Agricultural area	25,241	40.41	3.5–24.7	0.4–3.1
Forest	23,264	37.24	1.0–7.3	0.04–0.29
Woods and shrubland	11,006	17.62	1.5–10.8	0.09–0.62
Water	1,013	1.62	*	*
Other/clouds	997	1.60	6.36	0.42
Inundated forest	383	0.61	1.0–7.3	0.04–0.29
Rocks/barren land	236	0.38	*	*
Wetland	217	0.35	*	*
Urban	68	0.11	6.9	2.4
Mangrove	34	0.06	0	0
Total	**62,465**	**100.00**		

* The nutrient export from water surfaces, rocks/barren land and wetlands is estimated on the basis of rainfall nutrient content. The N and P rainfall contents that are used are 0.77 mg/L and 0.04 mg/L, respectively.

Export coefficients developed in other regions, tropical and temperate, were therefore used. For the largest land cover type (agricultural land) a new local export coefficient was developed based on monitoring data of the Korat Plateau, which is a vast agricultural area (for details, see Liljeström, 2007, pp. 53–57). The nutrient export coefficients used in this study are presented in Table 1. The export rates of the agricultural, woods and shrubland, and forest areas varied according to runoff depth. The nutrient export from the areas marked as "other/clouds" was estimated as a weighted average of the export coefficients describing the nutrient export rates of the three largest land cover types, that is agricultural area, forest, and woods and shrubland (for details see Liljeström, 2007, pp. 69–72).

Results

Water Quality Analysis

The monthly pattern of the annual nutrient flux was rather similar at all five mainstream sites and followed the same pattern as the distribution at Chiang Saen and Nakhon Phanom (Figure 2). The three peak months were July, August and September, followed by October and then June, for both TIN and TOTP. The three peak months accounted for 52–63% of the annual TIN flux and for 59–68% of the annual TOTP flux, depending on the site.

The comparison of the nutrient flux history with the flood history of the selected five mainstream sites was done for the years 1985–2004. The results at the Nakhon Phanom site are presented in Table 2. High flood years only roughly coincided with the high nutrient flux years. At Nakhon Phanom the greatest flooding of the studied period occurred in 1994, which corresponds to the 8th largest annual TIN load and the 5th largest annual TOTP load. Nutrient loads at Nakhon Phanom were greater than the loads of 1994 even in years when the total flow volume was reported as below the average level. This indicates that the largest water quantities do not always transport the largest nutrient fluxes and that large amounts of nutrients are occasionally transported by relatively small water quantities.

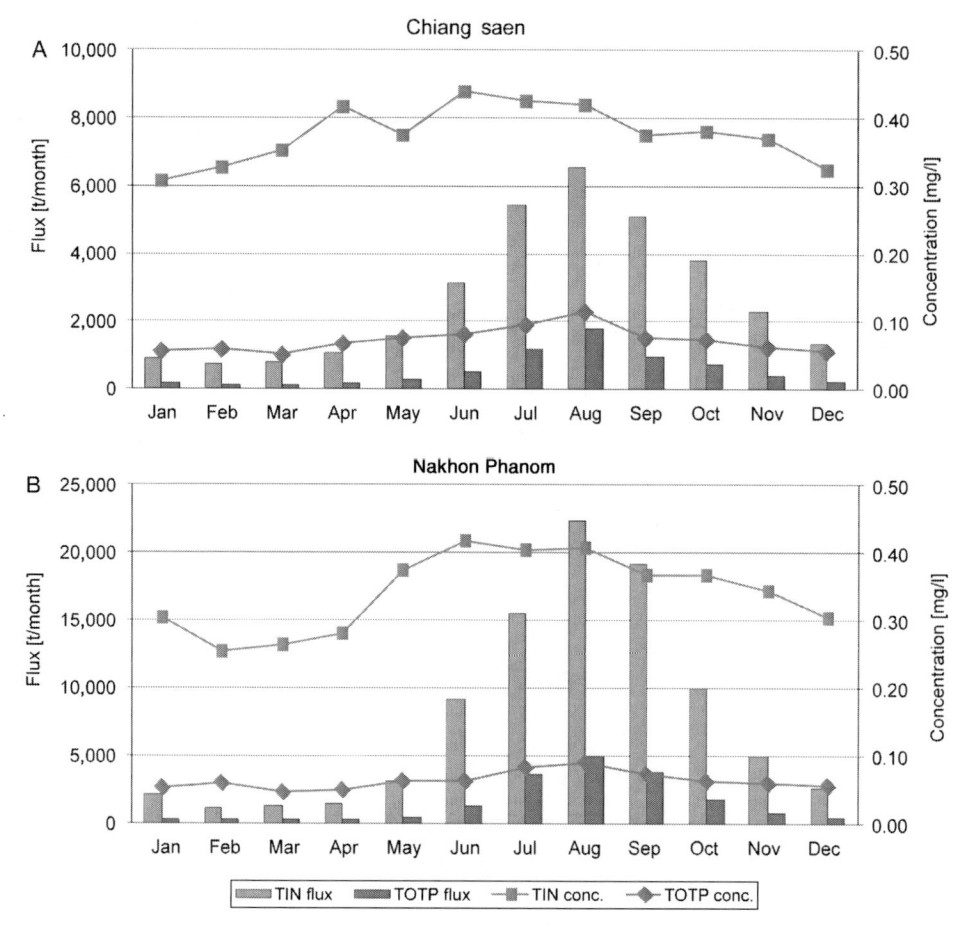

Figure 2. Average monthly nutrient fluxes and nutrient concentrations during 1985–2005 at (a) Chiang Saen and (b) Nakhon Phanom (see station locations in Figure 1).

Trend analysis of peak-month (July–September) nutrient fluxes was conducted for five mainstream sites. The results for Chiang Saen and Nakhon Phanom are illustrated in Figure 3, while results of trend and slope analyses are summarized in Table 3. For all sites, the trend of the TIN flux was positive and showed an increase towards the end of the study period. The coefficient of determination (R^2) values of the regression lines vary between 0.09 and 0.53. The trend was statistically very significant ($p < 0.01$) for all sites except Chiang Saen ($p < 0.1$) (Table 3). The TOTP flux trends were also positive and the R^2 values ranged from 0.01 to 0.48 (Table 3). The trend was significant, however, only at two sites (Chiang Saen and Nakhon Phanom). The TOTP flux series were thus not as uniform or as steep as the TIN flux series.

Part of these increased nutrient loads can be explained by a growing trend in discharges: in all stations but Chiang Saen the discharge had an increasing trend (appendix, Table A3). The discharge trends were not, however, statistically significant, except in Nakhon Phanom (appendix, Table A3). The average annual nutrient concentration trends were, nevertheless, alone statistically significant at the same stations as the flood season fluxes (appendix,

Table 2. June–November TIN (total inorganic nitrogen) and TOTP (total phosphorus) flux at Nakhon Phanom, in descending order and with corresponding flood recurrence intervals. A blank cell means that the flood condition of the year was below normal level, according to MRC (2005, p. 38).

Year	TIN flux [t]	Flood recurrence interval	Year	TOTP flux [t]	Flood recurrence interval
2001	144,851	5–10	2002	55,527	5–10
2000	144,678	5–10	2004	41,207	
2004	110,247		1995	22,153	10–20
1999	106,214	2–5	2000	19,278	5–10
1995	103,107	10–20	1994	18,908	>20
1996	90,179	2–5	2001	15,051	5–10
1990	89,044		1990	14,680	
1994	78,844	>20	1993	14,474	
1985	69,235		1999	14,051	2–5
1993	66,218		1989	13,972	
1986	54,365		1991	12,457	
1991	53,373		1997	11,068	2–5
1998	51,311		1988	8,578	
1988	44,759		1998	8,137	
1989	39,618		1992	6,888	
1987	33,390		1986	5,330	
1992	31,156		1985	5,275	
1997	data incomplete	2–5	1987	4,537	
2002	data incomplete	5–10	1996	data incomplete	2–5
2003	data incomplete		2003	data incomplete	

Tables A1 and A2). Interestingly, for the TIN values, the maximum concentrations had a stronger positive trend than the average concentrations in most of the stations (appendix, Table A1), while for the TOTP this was not the case (appendix, Table A2).

The calculated average annual nutrient fluxes at five mainstream sites and two delta sites can be seen in Table 4. The nutrient fluxes increased in the downstream direction, except after Chiang Saen and Nakhon Phanom. The sum of the fluxes at the two delta sites, My Thuan and Can Tho, indicates the total annual nutrient export from the Mekong River basin. The My Thuan site is located in the Mekong mainstream and the Can Tho site in the Bassac River. The estimated total annual nitrogen flux was 288,231 t/y and the total annual phosphorus flux 55,475 t/y. Table 4 also shows the average annual nutrient yield (kg/ha/y) delivered from the watersheds of the mainstream sites, and the nutrient export rate of the entire Mekong River basin into the South China Sea.

Catchment Scale Nutrient Model

The results of the modelling of generated diffuse nutrient export within the LMB in WinCMSS are presented in Figure 4. The TIN emissions (Figure 4a) were largest in sub-basins that lie close to the mainstream and where annual runoff is largest, as well as in the delta. The average nitrogen emissions are very large (> 12 kg/ha/y) only in a few sub-basins, with most sub-basins belonging to the lowest emission ranges. The majority of the sub-basins (74 of 104) belong to the two lowest nitrogen emission ranges (0–4 and 4–8 kg/ha/y).

The estimated annual TOTP emissions (Figure 4b) were large (> 2 kg/ha/y) or medium-sized (1–2 kg/ha/y) only in a few sub-basins. The largest phosphorus emissions were

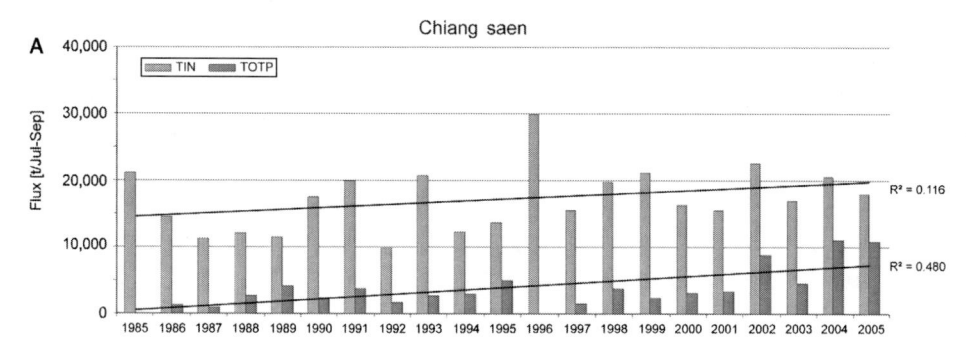
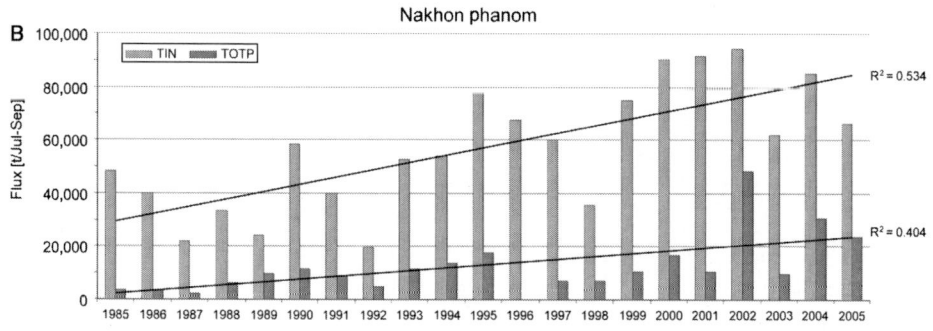

Figure 3. TIN (total inorganic nitrogen) and TOTP (total phosphorus) fluxes during peak months (July–September) during the years 1985–2005, at A: Chiang Saen, and B: Nakhon, displayed with regression lines and R^2 values. See station locations in Figure 1 and trend analysis results in Table 3.

generated from small or medium-sized sub-basins downstream of Vientiane, downstream of Pakse, and from the large delta sub-basin. Around half of the sub-basins (56 of 104) belonged to the lowest phosphorus emission range (0–0.5 kg/ha/y) (Figure 4b).

The results obtained with the WinCMSS model were mainly larger than the results based on monitored data (Table 5). All obtained TIN fluxes were larger than the monitored

Table 3. Regression analysis, Mann-Kendall trend test and Sen's slope analysis results for peak months (July–September) TIN (total inorganic nitrogen) and TOTP (total phosphorus) fluxes.

Monitoring site	TIN				TOTP			
	R^2	Z	Signif.	Q	R^2	Z	Signif.	Q
Chiang Saen	0.116	1.72	+	318	0.480	3.08	**	223
Luang Prabang	0.439	3.08	**	1011	0.010	0.55		27
Vientiane	0.462	2.89	**	1116	0.070	0.81		55
Nakhon Phanom	0.534	3.41	***	2705	0.404	3.28	**	854
Pakse	0.310	2.82	**	1617	0.046	0.68		118

Notes: Coefficient of determination R^2 represents the goodness of fit of a linear regression to the trend. Z indicates the direction of the trend: positive Z upward, negative Z downward. *Signif.* is the statistical significance of the trend, while Q indicates the slope estimate based on Sen's slope analysis. See also Tables A1, A2, and A3 in the appendix.
*** trend at $\alpha = 0.001$ level of significance; ** trend at $\alpha = 0.01$ level of significance; + trend at $\alpha = 0.1$ level of significance

Table 4. Average annual TIN (total inorganic nitrogen) and TOTP (total phosphorus) fluxes at selected monitoring sites and an estimate of the Mekong River's average annual nutrient delivery from catchment to ocean.

Monitoring site	Catchment area (km^2)	TIN (t/yr)	TIN yield (kg/ha/yr)	TOTP (t/yr)	TOTP yield (kg/ha/yr)
Chiang Saen	189,000	59,170	3.13	7,496	0.40
Luang Prabang	268,000	50,436	1.88	6,086	0.23
Vientiane	299,000	64,090	2.14	9,673	0.32
Nakhon Phanom	373,000	169,829	4.55	21,157	0.57
Pakse	545,000	109,084	2.00	17,329	0.32
My Thuan	–	151,489	–	26,604	–
Can Tho	–	136,742	–	28,870	–
Mekong River[1]	760,000	288,231	3.63	55,475	0.70

[1] Sum of fluxes at My Thuan (Mekong River) and Can Tho (Bassac River).
Note: For My Thuan and Can Tho, only data for 2003–2005 was used.

ones (Table 5). The modelled TOTP flux output was larger than the results based on monitored data except for at Nakhon Phanom and in the delta. However, the obtained TOTP fluxes were of a reasonable order of magnitude, except in the delta, where the assessed flux was lower than the monitored average flux (Table 5).

The distribution of the nutrient fluxes over the different land cover categories is presented in Figure 5. For both nitrogen and phosphorus, the agricultural areas of the LMB accounted for the majority of the nutrient flux from catchment into river system. Forest and

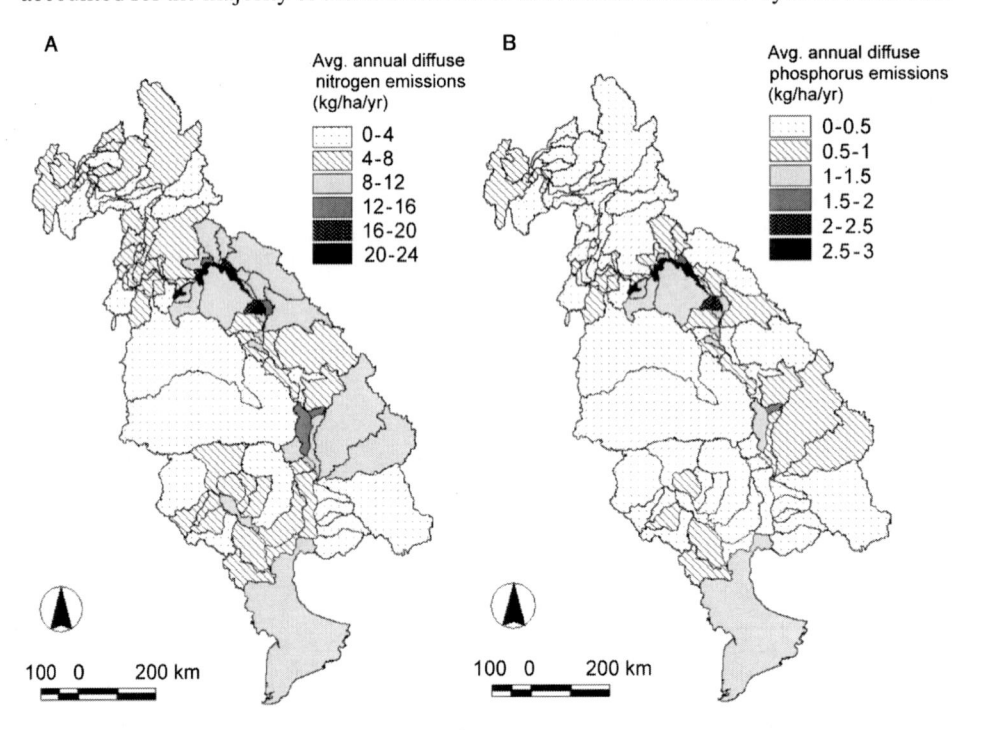

Figure 4. Average annual diffuse emissions from the Lower Mekong Basin. A: Average annual total nitrogen diffuse emissions. B: Average annual total phosphorus diffuse emissions.

Table 5. Average annual TIN (total inorganic nitrogen) and TOTP (total phosphorus) fluxes at five mainstream sites and in the delta, as estimated by the catchment-scale modelling and observed in monitoring data.

Monitoring site	TIN (t/year)		TOTP (t/year)	
	Modelled	Observed[1]	Modelled	Observed[1]
Chiang Saen	[59,170][2]	59,170	[7,496][2]	7,496
Luang Prabang	93,105	50,436	10,256	6,086
Vientiane	107,143	64,090	11,475	9,673
Nakhon Phanom	171,339	169,829	17,111	21,157
Pakse	243,207	109,084	24,534	17,329
Mekong	**404,685**	**288,231**	**38,392**	**55,475**

[1] Sum of fluxes at My Thuan (Mekong River) and Can Tho (Bassac River).
[2] Only monitored data available because site is located in the uppermost part of the LMB.

woods-and-shrubland were the second and third most important generators of nutrient flux. The fourth most important contribution to the total nutrient flux was the rainfall nutrient content that enters the system directly through the water surfaces. All other land cover categories accounted for less then 1% of the total nutrient flux, except that the undefined "other/clouds" areas contributed 1.8% (N) and 1.3% (P) of the total flux. The three most important nutrient contributor land cover categories accounted for 92.8% of the TIN flux, and for 95.1% of the TOTP flux.

Discussion

We assessed the nutrient dynamics in the LMB. Although several reports exist on water quality and nutrients in the Mekong, they dominantly represent the general level only, without connecting nutrient concentration analyses analytically to land cover, nutrient leaching, nutrient retention, or runoff data (e.g. Booty, 2001; White, 2002; MRC, 2003, 2010; Campbell, 2007). Further, the existing analyses are mostly based on nutrient concentration data only and the effects of land use changes on nutrient balances have not

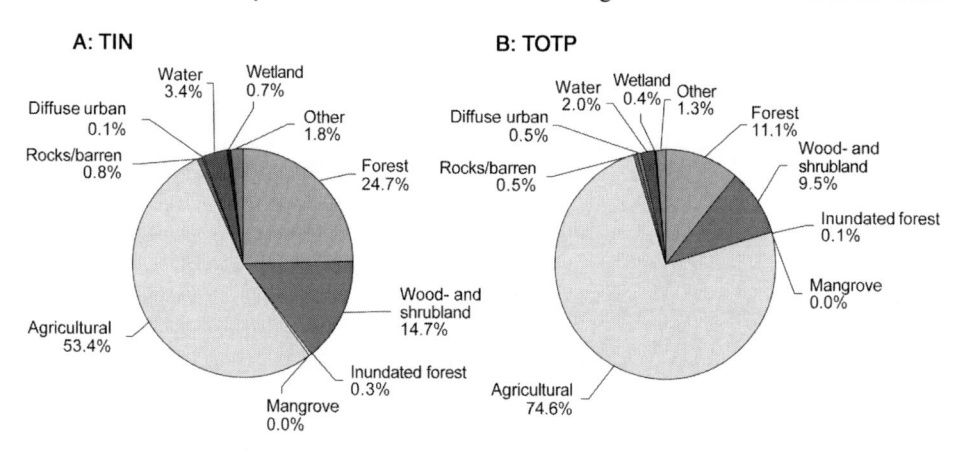

Figure 5. Nutrient fluxes from LMB catchments into the river network, percentage breakdown per land cover category. A: Total nitrogen (TIN) flux; B: Total phosphorus (TOTP) flux. *Note:* point pollution is not included in the estimation.

been analyzed systematically in any of the found reports. Our comprehensive analysis on nutrients in the LMB thus provides valuable baseline information on the nutrient flux trends over the past two decades and analysis on land use impact on these fluxes.

Generally, nutrient balances are reported to indicate a fairly good status for the Mekong's water quality. There are, however, many reports on increasing nutrient leaching (e.g. Snidvongs & Teng, 2006), and the delta especially has been seen as an area of concern because of increased nutrient concentrations (e.g. Campbell, 2007). Many classify the eutrophication problems as local and seasonal. Some reports on water quality and nutrient dynamics (e.g. Campbell, 2007) do not express concern about LMB nutrient levels, or directly suggest that nutrient issues are not of concern. However, MRC (2010) reports statistically significant growing trends in total phosphorus and ammonium concentrations, in line with our findings. They also report a decreasing trend in dissolved oxygen concentration. MRC (2010) expresses clear worries about this development.

Some specific consequences of eutrophication, such as fish deaths, algal blooms, and increased water hyacinth growth, could be especially serious for people in the LMB because many of the basin's inhabitants have a very close relationship to surrounding waters. Literature indicates (Wilson *et al.*, 2005) that if, for example, nitrogen concentrations increase to levels of 1 mg/L, there is a risk that water hyacinth growth in the LMB would reach maximum capacity during the hottest months of the year (when temperatures are around 30°C). Based on the observed data, the maximum nitrogen concentrations during our study periods were 0.5–0.8 mg/L in the Mekong mainstream, while in the delta area the concentration has already at various times exceeded the critical level of 1 mg/L. Water hyacinth growth risk zones should thus be identified and nutrient pollution prevention actions started in these possible risk zones. We equally support the concerns expressed by Snidvongs & Teng (2006) on the mounting risk for algal blooms in the Mekong River.

There seems to be consensus on the region's increasing land cover changes and accelerating economic activities (e.g. White, 2002; MRC, 2003; Keskinen, 2006, 2008; Sokhem & Sunada, 2006, 2008; Hart & Pollino, 2007; King *et al.*, 2007; Varis *et al.*, 2008). Little concern, however, exists in the Mekong regarding the possibility of future negative changes in the river's nutrient balances, although much literature clearly states that population growth and catchment level changes influence a river system's water quality (e.g. Meybeck & Helmer, 1992; IOC, 1994; Kristensen & Hansen, 1994; Bootsma & Hecky, 1999; Smith *et al.*, 2003; Jennerjahn *et al.*, 2004; LWA, 2005). This concern is, however, increasing (MRC, 2010).

Yoshimura *et al.* (2009) predict an increase of 13–25% in nutrient levels in the Mekong mainstream by the 2020s. If this kind of trend continues with a warmer future climate, as predicted by climate change studies (e.g. Västilä *et al.*, 2010), measures to better manage the nutrients in the river system should be developed in the near future to prevent eutrophication. On the other hand, the plans to build various large reservoirs to the Mekong mainstream and tributaries might actually trap a large part of the nutrients, particularly those bounded to suspended sediments (Kummu & Varis, 2007; Kummu *et al.*, 2010). Yet, the MRC (2010) maintains that the dams may critically change the nutrient flushing conditions, and thus lead to increasing eutrophication.

Data and Research on Eutrophication

Experimental research on nutrient leaching does exist to some extent, for example at local universities and local research institutes. Research material or results are, however, hardly publicly available. Data on plot-scale nutrient leaching have not been published or are not easily available. Only one literature estimate of nutrient delivery rates of the Mekong River on the catchment scale was found: White (2002). Data availability in the region is not large enough for a more detailed study.

Despite years of continuous improvements, the MRC's monitoring programme still has room for improvement. Nutrient concentration monitoring is too scarce and should be more frequent, especially during the transition from wet season to dry season and vice versa, when discharge varies highly in time and quantity. Nutrient monitoring on and around Tonle Sap Lake is scarce. Monitoring should be increased to start identifying the lake's nutrient dynamics, which are believed to be complex and variable. Further, most parts of the Mekong River basin, for example most tributaries, seem to fall outside the scope of nutrient concentration analyses and investigations, as indicated by a sparse monitoring network. We welcome MRC's recent (2010) activity in this regard, and the agreement of LMB countries that they will "make every effort to maintain acceptable/good water quality", as a part of the MRC's *Procedures for Water Quality* (MRC, 2011). Besides increasing temporal and spatial coverage of the conventional monitoring parameters, we wait particularly for the availability of biomonitoring data and studies in production biology (MRC, 2010) in order to better understand the current level and threats of eutrophication in the Mekong River and its tributaries. Apart from eutrophication-related aspects, other aspects of water quality such as heavy metals and micropollutants call for further studies and improved data collection.

Water Quality Analysis

Our water quality analyses provided information on nutrient dynamics of the LMB. The nutrient fluxes of the mainstream were highest between July and September. The nutrient flux peak months of tributaries are June–October (Liljeström, 2007). It is suggested that mainstream nutrient dynamics differ from tributary nutrient dynamics. Further, the latter might vary significantly from one tributary to another. Nutrient research should thus be carried out both in the mainstream and tributaries. The results further indicate that nitrogen and phosphorus movements across the basin differ, as phosphorus movement is slightly more seasonal compared to nitrogen movement. All in all, information on nutrient movement seasonality can allow degradation prevention measurements to be more effectively focused.

We found that water quantity movement across the basin and river nutrient flux did not always correlate. The flood history analyses show that relatively large water quantities often, but not always, transport relatively large amounts of nutrients. Our analysis also revealed that flood conditions below normal level occasionally do transport very large nutrient quantities. Rain intensity, rain duration and frequency, and the arrival time of the monsoon are suggested to be factors that, in addition to water quantity, influence the movements of nutrients across the basin.

The trend analysis revealed an augmentation in the TIN fluxes during the last two decades. Changes in TOTP fluxes were less readable. This is somewhat in contrast with the results reported by MRC (2010), in which the total phosphorus and ammonium concentrations had grown significantly whereas total nitrogen concentration had not shown a significant growing trend. This may be due to the different study period in the analyses; MRC's study was for 2000–2008 whereas ours was for mainly 1985–2005. In fact, MRC

(2010, p. 62) indicates sharply growing total phosphorus concentrations since 2005, suggesting that our time window might not have captured the most recent developments sufficiently. When comparing with temperate rivers, the Mekong River nitrogen levels do not indicate eutrophication at the sampling sites analyzed in this study, but phosphorus levels do, locally and during some times of the year. On the basis of the water quality analysis of this study, it can be concluded that seasonality exists in the LMB river system's tropic state. Nitrogen is suggested to be the limiting nutrient in much of the LMB river system. This gives an alert for the sensitivity of the river to cyanobacteria blooms. However, it is likely that large seasonal and temporal variations exist in the basin's limiting nutrient.

Catchment Scale Nutrient Model

Our catchment-scale assessment resulted in estimates of the diffuse nutrient emissions generated in the LMB. The WinCMSS assessment model was chosen after a review of approximately 40 methods, and turned out to be a straightforward, rough, and relatively suitable model for a large catchment, where data are sparse. The model was successful in delivering basic nutrient dynamics information, according to the study's aims. Our assessment thus showed that enough basic land cover and nutrient leaching data exist to perform rough catchment-scale analyses on nutrient fluxes of the LMB.

Our model results revealed that the agricultural areas account for the largest part of both nitrogen (53%) and phosphorus (75%) fluxes. The forest and woods-and-shrubland areas are the next most important nutrient contributors (Figure 5). The MRC, however, maintains (2010) that 40% of the nutrient load comes from agriculture—far less than our estimate (Figure 5).

Subsistence farming is still more common than commercial farming in large parts of the LMB (MRC, 2003, 2010). Although farming practices are mostly of traditional type, agricultural areas already account for the largest nutrient fluxes in the basin. Commercial farming and growing fertilizer use have recently become more common, and this trend will continue (MRC, 2003, 2010). As agricultural land is the largest land cover type of the basin, it is possible that intensification of farming practices, followed by increased nutrient leaching, could also increase the nutrient fluxes in the LMB. It is recommended to identify more precisely which agricultural practices, crop types, and fields generate the largest amounts of nutrients into the LMB water body.

The model resulted in considerably higher nitrogen and lower phosphorus fluxes than those calculated on the basis of observations (Table 5). Our model results (Table 5) can also be compared with those published by the MRC (2010) for the Mekong basin: 225,000 t of nitrogen and 37,000 t of phosphorus annually. Our modelled nitrogen estimation is high in comparison, while the MRC (2010) result for phosphorus matches well with our modelled result.

The modelled and observed nutrient fluxes are presented in Table 6 separately for the upper and middle LMB region (north of Nakhon Phanom) and the lower LMB region (south of Nakhon Phanom, i.e. the area from which the floodplains start along the mainstreams). The WinCMSS assessment succeeded much better in modelling the areas north of Nakhon Phanom than for the areas south of it (Table 6). This indicates that, understandably, the used method is unable to describe important floodplain nutrient processes and dynamics. The LMB floodplain nutrient dynamics should thus be studied separately with more-detailed models and approaches.

Table 6. Annual TIN (total inorganic nitrogen) and TOTP (total phosphorus) flux estimation results of the WinCMSS approach and the water quality analysis. The results are shown separately for the watersheds north and south of Nakhon Phanom (see location in Figure 1).

Area	TIN (t/year)		TOTP (t/year)	
	Modelled	Observed[1]	Modelled	Observed[1]
North of Nakhon Phanom	171,339	169,829	17,111	21,157
South of Nakhon Phanom	233,346	118,402	21,281	34,318
Mekong	**404,685**	**288,231**	**38,392**	**55,475**

[1] Sum of fluxes at My Thuan (Mekong River) and Can Tho (Bassac River).

Conclusions

Tropical riverine nutrient dynamics is a relatively little-studied subject, especially when compared with investigations done in the temperate zones. Our aim in this article was to assess the nutrient dynamics in the Mekong River and model the main sources of nutrients within the Lower Mekong basin. We found that the nutrient fluxes coincided approximately with the flood peak and are thus highest between July and September. The concentrations, however, peak at most of the stations at the beginning of the flood season (April–June). The analyses revealed that water flow quantities and riverine nutrient transportation do not always correlate. Relatively small water quantities do occasionally transport very large amounts of nutrients. The trend analysis indicated that total inorganic nitrogen (TIN) fluxes increased statistically significantly during the analyzed two decades (1985–2005) while total phosphorus (TOTP) fluxes also increased, but not as steeply as TIN fluxes.

The catchment-scale modelling generated information on the Lower Mekong Basin's nutrient export distribution by sub-basin and by land cover category. The assessment succeeded rather well in describing the TIN and TOTP fluxes along the entire mainstream north of Nakhon Phanom while results were less accurate for the stations downstream from there. The exceptional hydrology and water quality dynamics of the lower Mekong floodplains might partly explain the failure of the nutrient estimates. According to the modelling results, the majority of the LMB nitrogen flux originates from agricultural areas (53%) and forest and woods-and-shrubland areas (39%). For the phosphorus flux the figures are 75% and 21%, respectively.

The growing and urbanizing population, the accelerating land use changes and the increasing economic activities will most probably increasingly influence the aquatic ecosystems of the Mekong River. It is expected that fertilizer use will grow within the basin countries in the near future; commercial farming is already becoming more frequent. Thus, systematic basin-wide research on nutrients should be one of the top priorities in the basin. Particular attention should be paid to key tributaries and the Tonle Sap system, as well as to the relative and absolute contributions of point sources and diffuse sources. Protecting the basin from future negative consequences would require that information be developed and research expanded. There is a need to start to focus attention on why and when deterioration of the basin's water quality will occur and how it could be minimized. The opportunity to start nutrient investigations in time is good and thus too valuable to be missed. Enhanced public and scientific discussion about the level and sufficiency of knowledge is necessary.

Acknowledgements

The authors are grateful to colleagues at the Water & Development Research Group at our home institution for their thoughtful comments and inspiration. This work received funding from the Maa- ja vesitekniikan tuki ry (Soil and Water Technology Foundation) and from the Academy of Finland (Project 133748). Matti Kummu also received funding from the postdoctoral funds of Aalto University.

References

Atech Group (2000) *Aggregated Nutrient Emissions to the Murray-Darling Basin* (Canberra: National Pollutant Inventory, Environment Australia).

Bootsma, H. A. & Hecky, R. E. (1999) Nutrient cycling in Lake Malawi/Nyasa, in: H. A. Bootsma & R. E. Hecky (Eds) *Water Quality Report, Lake Malawi/Nyasa Biodiversity Conservation Project*, pp. 215–241 (Salima: Malawi Inland Fisheries Research Centre SADC/GEF project).

Booty, W. (2001) *Options for Modelling of Transboundary Water Quality, Final Report* (Vientiane: Mekong River Commission Secretariat, Environment Programme ME and WUP WG-1).

Campbell, I. (2007) Perceptions, data, and river management: lessons from the Mekong River, *Water Resources Research*, Vol. 43, W02407, DOI: 10.1029/2006WR005130.

Di, H. J. & Cameron, K. C. (2002) Nitrate leaching in temperate agroecosystems: sources, factors and mitigating strategies, *Nutrient Cycling in Agroecosystems*, 64(3), pp. 237–256.

Dodds, W. K., Jones, J. R. & Welch, E. B. (1998) Suggested classification of stream trophic state: distributions of temperate stream types by chlorophyll, total nitrogen, and phosphorus, *Water Research*, 32(5), pp. 1455–1462.

Dudgeon, D. (2000) The ecology of tropical Asian rivers and streams in relation to biodiversity conservation, *Annual Review of Ecology, Evolution and Systematics*, 31, pp. 239–263.

EEA (2005) *Source Apportionment of Nitrogen and Phosphorus Inputs into the Aquatic Environment*, Report No. 7/2005 (Copenhagen: European Environment Agency).

Fedra, K., Winkelbauer, L. & Pantulu, V. R. (1991) *Expert Systems for Environmental Screening: an Application in the Lower Mekong Basin*, RR-91-19 (Laxenburg, Austria: International Institute for Applied Systems Analysis).

Hart, B. & Pollino, C. (2007) *Environmental Risk Assessment Training, Final Report* (Vientiane: Mekong River Commission).

Hart, B. T., Jones, M. J. & Pistone, G. (2001) *Transboundary Water Quality Issues in the Mekong River Basin*, Water Studies Centre, Monash University, Australia, in association with NSR Environmental Consultants, Australia (Vientiane: Mekong River Commission).

Hawkins, P. & Suthep, S. (2005) *Integrated Basin Flow Management Specialist Report, Water Quality* (Vientiane: Mekong River Commission, Water Utilisation Programme/Environment Programme).

Iida, T., Inkhamseng, S., Yoshida, K. & Tanji, H. (2011) Characterization of water quality variation in the Mekong River at Vientiane by frequent observations, *Hydrological Processes*, 25(23), pp. 3590–3601.

Iida, T. et al. (2004) Seasonal variations in nutrient loads in the Mekong River at Vientiane, Lao PDR, in: *Proceedings of the International Conference on Advances in Integrated Mekong River Management*, 25–27 October 2004, Vientiane, Lao PDR, pp. 195–200 (Japan: Research Group, MRC, JST).

IOC (1994) *IOC-SAREC Field Study Exercise on Nutrients in Tropical Marine Waters, 5–15 April 1994, Mombasa, Kenya*, Workshop Report No. 99 (Intergovernmental Oceanographic Commission, UNESCO).

Irvine, K. N., Richey, J. E., Holtgrieve, G. W., Sarkkula, J. & Sampson, M. (2011) Spatial and temporal variability of turbidity, dissolved oxygen, conductivity, temperature, and fluorescence in the lower Mekong River–Tonle Sap system identified using continuous monitoring, *International Journal of River Basin Management*, 9(2), pp. 151–168.

Jennerjahn, T. C., Ittekkot, V., Klöpper, S., Adi, S., Nugroho, S. P., Sudiana, N., Yusmal, A., Prihartanto & Gaye-Haake, B. (2004) Biogeochemistry of a tropical river affected by human activities in its catchment: Brantas River estuary and coastal waters of Madura Strait, Java, Indonesia, *Estuarine, Costal and Shelf Science*, 60(3), pp. 503–514.

Johnston, R. M. & Kummu, M. (2012) Water resource models in the Mekong basin: a review, *Water Resources Management*, 26(2), pp. 429–455.

Kendall, M. G. (1975) *Rank Correlation Methods*, 4th ed. (London: Charles Griffin).

Keskinen, M. (2006) The lake with the floating villages: socioeconomic analysis of the Tonle Sap Lake, *International Journal of Water Resources Development*, 22(3), pp. 463–480.

Keskinen, M. (2008) Water resources development and impact assessment in the Mekong basin: which way to go? *Ambio*, 37(3), pp. 193–198.

Keskinen, M., Kummu, M., Käkönen, M. & Varis, O. (Forthcoming) Mekong at the crossroads: next steps for impact assessment of large dams, *Ambio*.

King, P., Bird, J. & Haas, L. (2007) *The Current Status of Environmental Criteria for Hydropower Development in the Mekong Region: A Literature Compilation*, Consultants Report to ADB, MRCS and WWF (Vientiane, Lao PDR: Joint Initiative on Environmental Criteria for Hydropower in the Mekong Region).

Kristensen, P. & Hansen, H. O. (Eds) (1994) *European Rivers and Lakes: Assessment of their Environmental State*, EEA Environmental Monographs 1 (Copenhagen: European Environment Agency).

Kummu, M., Lu, X. X., Wang, J. J. & Varis, O. (2010) Basin-wide sediment trapping efficiency of emerging reservoirs along the Mekong, *Geomorphology*, 119(3–4), pp. 181–197.

Kummu, M., Sarkkula, J., Koponen, J. & Nikula, J. (2006) Ecosystem management of the Tonle Sap Lake: an integrated modelling approach, *International Journal of Water Resources Development*, 22(3), pp. 497–519.

Kummu, M. & Varis, O. (2007) Sediment-related impacts due to upstream reservoir trapping, the Lower Mekong River, *Geomorphology*, 85(2–3), pp. 275–293.

Lamberts, D. (2006) The Tonle Sap Lake as a productive ecosystem, *International Journal of Water Resources Development*, 22(3), pp. 481–496.

Lamberts, D. & Koponen, J. (2008) Flood pulse alterations and productivity of the Tonle Sap ecosystem: a model for impact assessment, *Ambio*, 37(3), pp. 178–184.

Liljeström, I. (2007) *Nitrogen and Phosphorus Dynamics in the Mekong Basin: Nutrient balance Assessment in a Catchment Scale*, Master's thesis, Water Resources Laboratory, Department of Civil and Environmental Engineering, Helsinki University of Technology, Finland.

Lu, X. X. & Siew, R. Y. (2006) Water discharge and sediment flux changes over the past decades in the Lower Mekong River: possible impacts of the Chinese dams, *Hydrology and Earth System Sciences*, 10(2), pp. 181–195.

LWA (2005) *Australia's Tropical Rivers: Program Plan and Prospectus 2005–2010* (Canberra: Australian Government, Land & Water Australia).

Mann, H. B. (1945) Nonparametric test against trend, *Econometrica*, 13(3), pp. 245–259.

Meybeck, M. (1982) Carbon, nitrogen and phosphorus transported by world rivers, *American Journal of Science*, 282(4), pp. 401–450.

Meybeck, M. & Helmer, R. (1992) An introduction to water quality, in: D. Chapman (Ed.) *Water Quality Assessments: A Guide to Use of Biota, Sediments and Water in Environmental Monitoring*, 2nd Ed, Chapter 1 UNESCO/WHO/UNEP).

MRC (2001) *Metadata for MRC Secretariat GIS Core Datasets* (Phnom Penh: Mekong River Commission).

MRC (2003) *State of the Basin Report: 2003* (Phnom Penh: Mekong River Commission).

MRC (2005) *Overview of the Hydrology of the Mekong Basin* (Vientiane: Mekong River Commission).

MRC (2007) *Diagnostic Study of Water Quality in the Lower Mekong Basin*, MRC Technical Paper No. 15 (Vientiane: Mekong River Commission).

MRC (2010) *State of the Basin Report 2010* (Vientiane: Mekong River Commission).

MRC (2011) *Procedures for Water Quality* (Phnom Penh and Vientiane: Mekong River Commission).

Novotny, V. (2003) *Water Quality, Diffuse Pollution and Watershed Management*, 2nd ed (New Jersey: Wiley).

Peierls, B. L., Caraco, N. F., Pace, M. L. & Cole, J. J. (1991) Human influence on river nitrogen, *Nature*, 350(6317), pp. 386–387.

Salmi, T., Määttä, A., Ruoho-Airola, T. & Amnell, T. (2002) *Detecting Trends of Annual Values of Atmospheric Pollutants by the Mann-Kendall Test and Sen's Slope Estimates – the Excel Template Application MAKESENS*, Publications on Air Quality No. 31 (Helsinki: Finnish Meteorological Institute).

Sen, P. K. (1968) Estimates of the regression coefficient based on Kendall's tau, *Journal of the American Statistical Association*, 63(324), pp. 1379–1389.

Sidle, R. C., Tani, M. & Ziegler, A. D. (2006) Catchment processes in Southeast Asia: atmospheric, hydrologic, erosion, nutrient cycling, and management effects, *Forest Ecology and Management*, 224(1–2), pp. 1–4.

Smith, S. V., Swaney, D. P., Talaue-McManus, L., Bartley, J. D., Sandhei, P. T., McLaughlin, C. J., Dupra, V. C., Crossland, C. J., Buddemeier, R. W., Maxwell, B. A. & Wulff, F. (2003) Humans, hydrology, and the distribution of inorganic nutrient loading to the ocean, *BioScience*, 53(3), pp. 235–245.

Snidvongs, A. & Teng, S. (2006) *Global International Waters Assessment: Mekong River*, GIWA Regional Assessment 55 (University of Kalmar, Sweden, on behalf of United Nations Environment Programme).

Sokhem, P. & Sunada, K. (2006) The governance of the Tonle Sap Lake, Cambodia: integration of local, national and international levels, *International Journal of Water Resources Development*, 22(3), pp. 399–416.

Sokhem, P. & Sunada, K. (2008) Population growth and natural-resources pressures in the Lower Mekong Basin, *Ambio*, 37(3), pp. 219–224.

Varis, O. & Keskinen, M. (2006) Policy analysis for the Tonle Sap Lake, Cambodia: a Bayesian network model approach, *International Journal of Water Resources Development*, 22(3), pp. 417–432.

Varis, O., Keskinen, M. & Kummu, M. (2008) Mekong at the crossroads, *Ambio*, 37(3), pp. 146–149.

Varis, O., Kummu, M. & Salmivaara, A. (2012) Ten major river basins in monsoon Asia-Pacific: an assessment of vulnerability, *Applied Geography*, 32(2), pp. 441–454.

Vassiljev, A. & Stålnacke, P. (2005) Statistical modelling of riverine nutrient sources and retention in the Lake Peipsi drainage basin, *Water Science & Technology*, 51(3–4), pp. 309–317.

Västilä, K., Kummu, M., Sangmanee, C. & Chinvanno, S. (2010) Modelling climate change impacts on the flood pulse in the Lower Mekong floodplains, *Journal of Water and Climate Change*, 1(1), pp. 67–86.

Voss, M., Dombar, D., Loick, N. & Dippner, J. W. (2006) Riverine influence on nitrogen fixation in the upwelling region off Vietnam, South China Sea, *Geophysical Research Letters*, 33(7), L07604.

White, I. (2002) *Water Management in the Mekong Delta: Changes, Conflicts and Opportunities*, IHP-VI, Technical Documents in Hydrology, No. 61, International Hydrological Programme (Paris: UNESCO).

Wilson, J. R., Holst, N. & Rees, M. (2005) Determinants and patterns of population growth in water hyacinth, *Aquatic Botany*, 81(1), pp. 51–67.

WHO (1999) *Toxic Cyanobacteria in Water: A Guide to their Public Health Consequences, Monitoring and Management* (London: E & FN Spon, on behalf of WHO).

Yoshimura, C., Zhou, M. C., Kiem, A. S., Fukuami, K., Hapuarachchi, H. A. P., Ishidaira, H. & Takeuchi, K. (2009) 2020s scenario analysis of nutrient load in the Mekong River Basin using a distributed hydrological model, *Science of the total Environment*, 407(20), pp. 5356–5366.

Appendix

Table A1. Mann-Kendall trend test and Sen's slope analysis results for annual average, maximum, and minimum total inorganic nitrogen (TIN) concentrations. Z indicates the direction of the trend: positive Z upward, negative Z downward. *Signif.* is the statistical significance of the trend, while Q indicates the slope estimate based on Sen's slope analysis.

Monitoring site	TIN (avg)			TIN (max)			TIN (min)		
	Z	*Signif.*	Q	Z	*Signif.*	Q	Z	*Signif.*	Q
Chiang Saen	1.06		0.002	2.20	*	0.008	−1.99	*	−0.003
Luang Prabang	2.51	*	0.006	2.42	*	0.009	1.81	+	0.004
Vientiane	2.26	*	0.009	2.45	*	0.016	1.78	+	0.005
Nakhon Phanom	2.02	*	0.006	1.66	+	0.008	1.60		0.005
Pakse	2.02	*	0.005	2.45	*	0.008	0.91		0.001

* trend at $\alpha = 0.05$ level of significance
+ trend at $\alpha = 0.1$ level of significance

Table A2. Mann-Kendall trend test and Sen's slope analysis results for the annual average, maximum and minimum total phosphorus (TOTP) concentrations. Z indicates the direction of the trend: positive Z upward, negative Z downward. *Signif.* is the statistical significance of the trend, while Q indicates the slope estimate based on Sen's slope analysis.

Monitoring site	TOTP (avg)			TOTP (max)			TOTP (min)		
	Z	*Signif.*	Q	Z	*Signif.*	Q	Z	*Signif.*	Q
Chiang Saen	2.75	**	0.003	3.11	**	0.010	1.79	+	0.001
Luang Prabang	−0.69		0.000	0.06		0.000	−1.61		−0.001
Vientiane	−0.57		0.000	−0.33		−0.001	0.00		0.000
Nakhon Phanom	2.08	*	0.002	1.33		0.003	−0.39		0.000
Pakse	−0.57		0.000	0.18		0.000	−1.25		0.000

** trend at $\alpha = 0.01$ level of significance
* trend at $\alpha = 0.05$ level of significance
+ trend at $\alpha = 0.1$ level of significance

Table A3. Mann-Kendall trend test and Sen's slope analysis results for the annual average discharge. Z indicates the direction of the trend: positive Z upward, negative Z downward. *Signif.* is the statistical significance of the trend, while Q indicates the slope estimate based on Sen's slope analysis.

Monitoring site	Discharge		
	Z	*Signif.*	Q
Chiang Saen	0.00		−0.08
Luang Prabang	0.27		18.3
Vientiane	1.36		40.1
Nakhon Phanom	2.63	**	217.6
Pakse	0.75		90.0

** trend at $\alpha = 0.01$ level of significance

Index